Enabling Occupation
An Occupational Therapy Perspective

Revised Edition

Canadian Association of Occupational Therapists

First Edition, 1997
Revised Edition, 2002

Enabling Occupation: An Occupational Therapy Perspective was
researched and written for the Canadian Association of Occupational
Therapists by:
   Elizabeth Townsend (Editor)
   Sue Stanton
   Mary Law
   Helene Polatajko
   Sue Baptiste
   Tracey Thompson-Franson
   Christine Kramer
   Fern Swedlove
   Sharon Brintnell
   Loredana Campanile

Published by
  CAOT Publications ACE
  Ottawa, Ontario

Copies may be purchased from:

Canadian Association of Occupational Therapists
CTTC Building, Suite 3400
1125 Colonel By Drive
Ottawa, ON K1S 5R1
Tel: (613) 523-2268 or 800-434-2268
Fax: (613) 523-2552

CAOT PUBLICATIONS ACE   www.caot.ca

Des exemplaires sont également disponibles en français sous le titre :
   Promouvoir l'occupation : une perspective de l'ergothérapie

© Canadian Association of Occupational Therapists, 2002

ISBN 978-1-895437-58-X

Enabling Occupation
An Occupational Therapy Perspective

Revised Edition

Researched and written for

Canadian Association of Occupational Therapists

By

Elizabeth Townsend (Editor)
Sue Stanton
Mary Law
Helene Polatajko
Sue Baptiste
Tracey Thompson-Franson
Christine Kramer
Fern Swedlove
Sharon Brintnell
Loredana Campanile

Dedicated to:

MURIEL DRIVER

**OCCUPATIONAL THERAPY SERVICE PROVIDER,
EDUCATOR, AND RESEARCHER**

January 14, 1920 - January 23, 1972

**Her vision of occupational therapy continues to propel
occupational therapists
to realize the potential of their profession**

MURIEL DRIVER

$\mathcal{A}$ tribute to Muriel Driver was published in the Canadian Journal of Occupational Therapy in 1972 shortly after her death (Marjoribanks, 1972). Today, most occupational therapists know Muriel Driver because the prestigious Muriel Driver Memorial Lecture is presented at the Annual Conference of the Canadian Association of Occupational Therapists. The privilege of delivering this Lecture is awarded to an occupational therapist in Canada whose enthusiasm and creativity have inspired others and advanced occupational therapy. The 18 Muriel Driver Memorial Lectures presented since 1975 have explored the scope of practice, management, professionalization, leadership and core concepts in occupational therapy. Of the 10 Collaborators on this project, five have been Muriel Driver Memorial Lecturers.

Muriel Driver graduated from the University of Toronto in 1941 and practised as an occupational therapist for 31 of her 52 years. From 1943 to 1945, she served in Canada and overseas in the Canadian Army Medical Corps. She organized the first occupational therapy department at Runnymede Hospital for the Chronically Ill in Toronto in 1946. After completing a post-graduate certificate in Neuromuscular Disorders at Warm Springs, Georgia, she returned to Canada but was soon invited to became Director of Occupational Therapy and Instructor in the Warm Springs Post-Graduate School. Driver returned to Canada in 1959 at the request of the Canadian Association of Occupational Therapists to organize the Special Course on Occupational Therapy at Kingston, Ontario. When Queen's University established a programme in occupational therapy in 1967, she became a Senior Lecturer.

Muriel Driver's most cited article is her 1967 Keynote Address to the Canadian Association of Occupational Therapists' Annual Conference in Halifax, Nova Scotia on *A Philosophic View of the History of Occupational Therapy in Canada* (Driver, 1968). She traced occupational therapy's history through three eras. In Era I, she highlighted the humanitarian, holistic origins of "occupational work" by "occupational workers" in 19th century "moral treatment" programmes. Growth and innovation were seen in Era II as occupational therapists opened curative workshops and training programmes for World War I veterans, and formed the Canadian Association of Occupational Therapists in 1926. She warned occupational therapists that Era III, following World War II, was a time to "reason carefully, scrutinizing our body of professional knowledge for its thin, its flimsy, its fuzzy claims...both good and bad must be viewed critically, not necessarily negatively...Let us borrow the courage and ingenuity from Era I, the enthusiasm and determination from Era II combining this with the educational and financial resources of Era III. Our next era, from 1967 must be the era of research" (p.60). Developments from 1967 to the early 1990s can be described as Era IV, with Era V devoted to Enabling Occupation.

TABLE OF CONTENTS

TABLES and FIGURES

FIGURES

TABLES

$\mathcal{I}$n May 1995, Bonnie Sherr Klein delivered the Keynote Address at the Annual Conference of the Canadian Association of Occupational Therapists. Speaking to the conference theme, *Partners in Practice*, she invited occupational therapists to become allies in partnership with clients. She spoke from her perspective as a woman with physical limitations resulting from strokes caused by a brain stem malformation that ruptured in 1987. Her address was insightful, honest, and humorous.

Throughout her address, she spoke about the importance of doing what has meaning for her. Without using the term, she emphasized the importance of occupation in her life, and encouraged occupational therapists to consider a client's definition of client-centred practice. She urged occupational therapists to become allies with individuals with disabilities and with advocacy groups. When invited to write a foreword for this document, Sherr Klein asked that this address be presented in edited form. With her permission, verbatim excerpts of Sherr Klein's address are offered for reflection.

"...Congratulations for choosing to go forward with your commitment to client-centred practice. I was probably invited because I am now the ultimate client - from several months in a hospital intensive care unit; through half a year in hospital and a rehabilitation institute; another year and a half of formal rehabilitation as an out-patient; and more than five years now of self-directed, informal rehabilitation...my definition of rehabilitation includes my professional work and my political activism for disability rights."

A few vignettes illustrate what Sherr Klein then told the audience about her experience with occupational therapists.

An occupational therapist helped her to solve a severe problem arising from Carpal Tunnel Syndrome by "building up the diameter of the grips [of my scooter Gladys] to change the functional angle of my wrists with a cushioning material to absorb shocks. We used sponge and a roll of hockey tape. It was simple and cheap and it has changed my life. I think that's a good occupational therapy story. What's good about it is that she really looked at how I lived. No one else had ever looked at Gladys."

In addition, "an occupational therapist was helpful in very specific, functional ways. She taught me how to brush and even floss my teeth. How to put on a bra by snapping it in front and then sliding it around. I admired how the occupational therapists had thought through and dissected the tasks. Most important she gave me a lapboard and started me writing. She wrote my name in kindergarten block letters for me to copy. She urged me to write a sentence every day."

Sherr Klein reminded occupational therapists about the danger of taking away hope by insisting that people be realistic. During her first assessment with an occupational therapist, she felt "...very respected. I came to like her a lot. She was doing the right thing in asking me what my goals and objectives were. I answered with a straight face - that my goal was to play tennis doubles by the summer. She knew much more than I knew, that it was probably terribly unrealistic. She laughed in my face....As an experienced occupational therapist, she knew that not being able to walk or to play tennis was NOT the end of the world. She knew that there is life after disability, that you can make great adaptation. But I didn't know that as a person who had just become disabled. She could have tried to bridge that gap - if we were partners, or allies."

We were reminded by Sherr Klein that occupational therapists tend to lose focus on occupations that have meaning for people. "The occupational therapists worked with humiliating seriousness. We played shuffleboard and ping-pong, but no one explained that they were to practice our balance, and I was too out of it to understand. Everything seemed random and irrelevant. We did pre-kindergarten puzzles with large wooden pieces, carnival games with clown face targets, and uninspired, paint-by-number crafts. My partner devoted herself to a pre-fabricated wooden nativity scene for Christmas, while I made potholders... as it happens I was in the middle of making a film (not potholders) when I had the stroke."

"I would work during my weekend off and return exhausted. I was often scolded for wearing myself out on the film. I felt as if I was cheating on my rehabilitation work...when I was doing my real work of film-making. It was not until after the film was finished and released nearly one and a half years after the stroke that I realized myself that this was my occupational therapy (as occupational therapy was probably meant to be). It required all my previous skills and experience, plus many new adaptations; it was going to be useful; it reconnected me to the wide world outside my body; it forced me to 'come out' and be seen in public; and it brought me validation as a productive person. I regained a sense of my self."

Sherr Klein then talked about independent living, disability rights, and language and threw a challenge to occupational therapists.

"...occupational therapy is good at addressing [an individual's] disability - optimizing our function and adapting surroundings - but not so good about addressing those handicaps imposed by society: attitudes, especially bigotry, like that we should not be parents, or that we don't belong on public transportation. You don't help us learn how to adapt society to us, i.e., how to remove those barriers. You haven't seen it as your role..."

"I am inviting you to be allies in an exciting endeavour. What might this mean - professionally and personally? Professionally - to realize your own stated objectives, you need to
- actively recruit and hire qualified people with every kind of disability into the profession, not just as tokens
- ensure accommodation and access in your places of training and employment
- include us (not just as tokens) on all boards, decision-making bodies, curriculum policy, etc. so we can speak for ourselves
- pay us for our expertise as consultants and role models; people with disabilities are severely under-employed
- re-think rehabilitation completely, in partnership with recipients and ex-recipients; think creatively, not just the HOW but the WHY of everything you do; remember the relationship between healing and creativity

Why isn't all this happening if we share common objectives? It is important to discuss barriers or obstacles to partnership because they are real."

Referring to a list that she had elicited from the audience about what makes occupational therapy GREAT and HARD:

"You are an occupational therapist because you enjoy helping others. You have the best of intentions, but the helping role is problematic. The politics of helping requires you to have a 'helpee', someone dependent, a patient, or client, or consumer. This means that there is a have and have not, a hierarchical relationship. The relationship is paternalistic or maternalistic. It is hard to let go.

Some of your other obstacles are that there is pressure for you to be professional, to have an identity as medical providers. Your identity does not lie in being allies with consumers. The pressure is to be scientific. To be cost effective. There are institutional demands. Politics.

How can you overcome these barriers, the imbalances between us? Make coalitions with us, and advocate for our issues, as individuals and as professional organizations. Use your experience and credentials to support our needs for dignity and inclusion.

Learn our issues, read our literature and our journals. Make sure you know what is being said in periodicals such as those published by the Canadian Coalition on Disability, various disability organizations, the coalition of provincial organizations, DAWN (DisAbled Women's Network), and Disabled People's International. Learn the laws and local services in your area to see what our lives are really like. Above all, ASK US QUESTIONS.

AS CITIZENS, you don't have to get heavily involved, but consciousness-raise in little, everyday ways. Bring up *access* at every opportunity in your life. Question our absence at venues that have anything to do with us, or ones that don't, for example your clubs, schools, places of worship. We should be everywhere because we are everywhere. What would happen if you started to notice the times that you are in a homogeneous ability group, and you began to question it?

PERSONALLY, get to know us, not just as clients but as fellow human beings. This may feel awkward, but take risks, including the risk of being rebuffed. Probably this won't happen, but if it does, you will be able to work it out. Most of us appreciate allies. When I can speak for myself, I want to, but a lot of the time, I'm tired or I'm frustrated and I can't speak well. Acknowledge your vulnerability as persons with abilities who will likely be persons with disabilities if you live long enough.

Finally, take good care of yourselves. Allies need support too. We're all in it for the long haul. The work isn't easy but it is real and rewarding. The process of learning to be an ally will bring you back to the reasons each of you chose to become occupational therapists. I hope you will become even better ones."

Bonnie Sherr Klein
Vancouver, British Columbia

ACKNOWLEDGEMENTS

A Process of National Collaboration

Enabling Occupation: An Occupational Therapy Perspective is a landmark document for occupational therapists in Canada and possibly the world. Authorship is attributed collectively to the Canadian Association of Occupational Therapists (CAOT) which provided four years of financial and organizational support for the process of national collaboration which has produced a Canadian occupational therapy perspective. The men and women who volunteered their time and expertise in this collaborative process represent administrative, clinical, consulting, educational and research perspectives from across Canada. They either offered or were invited to participate on the recommendation of CAOT's Board of Directors.

After two meetings to outline the contents and organization of the new document, the nine Collaborating Authors and Editor took responsibility for researching and writing chapters using teleconferences, telephone, fax and a group list on electronic mail to communicate ideas. Sixteen Contributors provided submitted written material on particular topics and reviewed drafts; thirty-three occupational therapy reviewers commented, individually or in groups, on at least one draft other than the final copy. A Canadian sociologist, Dr. Jenny Blain, provided an outsider's eye at each major stage and made sure that recommendations from the 1992 CAOT Guidelines Impact Study were followed. Ongoing contact with the full membership of CAOT was maintained by extending invitations to comment on evolving ideas summarized frequently in the CAOT National Newsletter, or presented at CAOT Annual Conferences in 1995 and 1996. Discussions were infused with a growing sense of direction, as the profession is rapidly evolving after almost 100 years since its inception.

Chapter 1, *Introduction* was developed by the Editor in consultation with others. With contributions from Collaborators and Contributors,

Sharon Brintnell and I developed Chapter 2, *Context of Occupational Therapy*. Mary Law wrote Chapter 3, *Core Concepts of Occupational Therapy*, coordinating contributions from Helene Polatajko, Sue Baptiste and myself. With contributions from Christine Kramer, Tracey Thompson-Franson, and Loredana Campanile, where possible at a distance, Sue Stanton wrote Chapter 4, *Linking Concepts to a Process for Working with Clients,* and Chapter 5, *Linking Concepts to a Process for Organizing Occupational Therapy Services.* Cary Brown (Contributor) and Fern Swedlove were the primary authors for Chapter 6, *Using New Guidelines.* Chapter 7, *Vignettes* was written, with editorial suggestions from others, by Sharon Brintnell, Christine Kramer, and Tracey Thompson-Franson (Collaborators), and Jo Clark (Contributor); Sue Stanton coordinated the final draft of this chapter.

Names and bibliographic sketches of Collaborating Authors, and names of Contributing Authors, Reviewers and Members of the CAOT Client-Centred Practice Committee are listed so that readers are introduced to the people whose diverse perspectives have shaped this process of national consultation.

I am extremely grateful for the opportunity to coordinate and participate in this important process.

Elizabeth (Liz) Townsend
Halifax, 1997

EDITOR
Elizabeth Townsend, Ph.D., O.T.(C)

... is a founding member and an Associate Professor in the School of Occupational Therapy at Dalhousie University in Halifax, Nova Scotia. She has been a member of all national Task Forces that developed five volumes of guidelines for client-centred practice in occupational therapy, and that consulted with researchers who developed the Canadian Occupational Performance Measure. She proposed and monitored the Impact Study that examined the uses and usefulness of the three original Guidelines. Over her career, Liz has promoted a broad view of occupational therapy and its potential influence on world problems. She was the 1993 recipient of the Muriel Driver Memorial Lectureship. Her special concern is in enabling occupation with people who have long-term mental health problems. Liz is the founding and continuing Chairperson of the CAOT Client-Centred Practice Committee which has monitored the development of these new guidelines. Her contributions to the new guidelines were both as a collaborating writer and editor.

COLLABORATING AUTHORS (listed alphabetically)

Sue Baptiste, M.H.Sc., O.T.(C)

... is an Associate Professor in the School of Rehabilitation Science, Faculty of Health Sciences, McMaster University, Hamilton, Ontario. She is involved in the development of problem-based, learner-centred educational environments within medical and rehabilitation educational programmes world-wide and is the current Director for Faculty Development. Sue received the 1988 Muriel Driver Memorial Lectureship. Her areas of interest span chronic pain and work, innovative organizational models, roles for the emerging health care system, challenges to occupational therapy inherent in the new era of health care, development of the Canadian Occupational Performance Measure, and visioning a different future.

Sharon Brintnell, M.Sc., O.T.(C)

... is Professor and past Chair of the Department of Occupational Therapy at the University of Alberta. She is a past president of CAOT, and the 1986 recipient of the Muriel Driver Memorial Lectureship. She is the Director of the Occupational Performance Analysis Unit at the University of Alberta. Sharon initiated the guidelines process during her CAOT Presidency, and served on all previous Guidelines Task Forces as well as chairing the Working Group that developed *Occupational Therapy Guidelines for Client-Centred Mental Health Practice*. Her major areas of interest are the functional profiles of individuals with disabling mental disorders and those whose occupational performance has been altered by trauma. She also studies values in persons who have had major changes in role functions.

Loredana Campanile, M.Sc., O.T.(C)

... is presently the Academic Coordinator of Clinical Education at the School of Physical and Occupational Therapy at McGill University. She became a Collaborator when she was Assistant Professor and Associate Director of the undergraduate programme in Occupational Therapy at McGill University, and continued to provide input while teaching at the University of Zimbabwe, Africa. Her major areas of interest are fieldwork instruction and vocational rehabilitation.

Christine Kramer, M.Ed., O.T.(C)

... formerly the Regional Supervisor of Occupational Therapy for Para Med Health Services in southwestern Ontario, is working as a community occupational therapist with Thera Care and Community Rehabilitation in southern Ontario. Her major area of interest is in the development and evaluation of services in the community and other settings which are non-traditional in occupational therapy. She is also interested in case management from an occupational therapy perspective, and in strengthening service coordination between health institutions and the community.

Mary Law, Ph.D., O.T.(C)

... is an Associate Professor in the School of Rehabilitation Science and the Department of Clinical Epidemiology and Biostatistics at McMaster University. She is also Director of the Neurodevelopmental Clinical Research Unit, a partnership between researchers at McMaster University and 20 children's treatment centres in Ontario. Mary was the 1991 recipient of the Muriel Driver Memorial Lectureship, and one of the primary researchers and authors of the *Canadian Occupational Performance Measure*. She is a member of the American

Occupational Therapy Foundation Academy of Research. Her current research includes evaluation of the effectiveness of a client-centred, functional approach to therapy with young children with cerebral palsy. She has a major interest in examining environmental constraints that affect the daily occupations of children with disabilities.

Helene Polatajko, Ph.D., O.T.(C)

... is Professor and Chair in the Department of Occupational Therapy and was the founding Director of the graduate programme in Occupational Therapy at The University of Western Ontario. She was the 1992 recipient of the Muriel Driver Memorial Lectureship and is a member of the American Occupational Therapy Foundation Academy of Research. She has numerous publications in a number of areas. Her major areas of interest are the investigation of human occupation, and the enablement of occupational performance and occupational competence. She has a particular interest in studying the enablement of occupational competence in children with Development Coordination Disorder (children with mild motor problems). She is an author of the *Canadian Occupational Performance Measure*.

Susan Stanton, M.A., O.T.(C)

... is a faculty member in the Division of Occupational Therapy in the School of Rehabilitation Sciences at the University of British Columbia. Her primary areas of research are adaptation post-stroke by people who experience a stroke and their partners; and organizational change in health care.

Fern Swedlove, B.Sc.(O.T.), O.T.(C)

... is a senior occupational therapist at Saint Boniface General Hospital in Winnipeg, Manitoba. Her areas of interest are varied; she has worked in the community, long-term care and rehabilitation units and presently practices in a seniors' day hospital. In the past few years, she has been particularly interested in facilitating the application of the client-centred practice model in her facility.

Tracey Thompson-Franson, B.Sc.(O.T.), O.T.(C)

... practices in Victoria, British Columbia. She has been both the occupational therapy clinical resource specialist for Geriatric Services and Residential Care programmes at the Greater Victoria Hospital Society (GVHS), and the Director of Care at the Rose Manor Society's residence for seniors. She has recently returned to GVHS and is the occupational therapist on the Transitional Care team. One of her interests is promoting interpretation and application of occupational therapy theory in the context of interdisciplinary service environments.

CONTRIBUTING AUTHORS

Elizabeth Bell, M.Sc., O.T.(C)
Assistant Professor
School Fieldwork Coordinator
School of Occupational Therapy
Dalhousie University
Halifax, Nova Scotia

Monica Bettazzoni, M.Ed., O.T.(C)
Clarke Institute of Psychiatry, and
Lecturer,
Department of Occupational Therapy
University of Toronto
Toronto, Ontario

Margaret Brockett, M.Ed, O.T.(C)
Consultant in professional ethics and
health care ethics education, and
Clinical Lecturer
School of Rehabilitation Science
McMaster University
Hamilton, Ontario

Cary Brown, M.A., O.T.(C),
Physical Therapy Department
Security Forces Hospital,
Riyadh, Saudi Arabia

Jo Clark, B.Sc.O.T., O.T.(C)
Section Head
Occupational Therapy in Mental Health,
Vancouver Hospital & Health Sciences
    Centre
University of British Columbia Pavilions
Vancouver, British Columbia

Jude Driscoll, O.T.M., O.T.(C)
Occupational Rehabilitation Manager
Prince Edward Island Workers
    Compensation Board
Charlottetown, Prince Edward Island

Mary Egan, M.Sc., O.T.(C)
Programme in Occupational Therapy
University of Ottawa
Ottawa, Ontario

Marcia Finlayson, M.Sc., O.T.(C)
Community Health Sciences
University of Manitoba
Winnipeg, Manitoba

Virginia Fearing, B.Sc.(O.T.), O.T.(C)
Head of Occupational Therapy Services
Vancouver Hospital & Health Sciences
    Centre
University of British Columbia Pavilions
Vancouver, British Columbia

Marie Gage, M.Sc., O.T.(C)
Consultant
Collective Wisdom Management
Haliburton, Ontario

Jacqueline McGarry, Dip.O.T.,
    B.Sc.(O.T.), Dip.A.T., O.T.(C)
Private Practitioner
Ilderton, Ontario

Laura MacGregor, M.Sc., O.T.(C)
Coordinator, Occupational Therapy and
    Physical Therapy Assisant Programme
Conestoga College
Kitchener, Ontario

Leann Merla, B.Sc.(O.T.), O.T.(C)
University Hospital
London, Ontario

Bill Miller, M.Sc., O.T.(C)
University of Western Ontario
London, Ontario

Barbara O'Shea, M.Sc., O.T.(C)
Director and Professor
School of Occupational Therapy
Dalhousie University
Halifax, Nova Scotia

Elizabeth Scott, M.Sc., O.T.(C)
Vice-President of Professional Services
Head, Occupational Therapy Department
Clarke Institute of Psychiatry, and
Lecturer, Department of Psychiatry
University of Toronto
Toronto, Ontario

MEMBERS OF THE CAOT CLIENT-CENTRED PRACTICE COMMITTEE, 1992-1996

Sheila Banks, M.A., O.T.(C)
Jennifer Bennett, B.Sc.(O.T.), O.T.(C)
John Dicks, B.Sc.(O.T.), O.T.(C)
Scott Irwin, B.Sc.(O.T.), O.T.(C)

Randi Norve Monroe, B.Sc.(O.T.), O.T.(C)
Angela Naugle, B.Sc.(O.T.), O.T.(C)
Angela Stairs, B.Sc.(O.T.), O.T.(C)

OCCUPATIONAL THERAPY REVIEWERS

Adrienne Amato, Ontario
Kim Benincasa, Ontario
Carol Bowlby, Nova Scotia
Carrie Clark, Ontario
Denise DeLaat, Ontario
Ann Dixie, Ontario
Isabel Dyck, British Columbia
Jan Gauthier, British Columbia
Jacqueline Gilbert, Quebec
Sandra Hale, British Columbia
Jane Jones, Ontario
Alice Kusznir, Ontario
Micheline Marazzini, Quebec
Carol Mirkopoulos, Ontario
Nonie Medcalf, British Columbia
Aruna Mitra, Ontario
Ann Moore, Nova Scotia

Susan Nagle, Ontario
Wendy Parkinson, Ontario
Barbara Rackow, British Columbia
Heather Richardson, Alberta
Line Robichaud, Quebec
Jan Robinson, Ontario
Marci Rose, Ontario
Hardeep Sadra, Ontario
Teri Shackleton, Ontario
Carol Stephenson, Ontario
Sylvie Tétreault, Quebec
Guylaine Vandal, Quebec
Constance Vanier, Quebec
Anne Wilcox, Ontario
Martha Wilke, Ontario
Marcia Wilson, British Columbia

EXTERNAL REVIEWER

Jenny Blain, Ph.D.
Department of Sociology and Anthropology
Mount Saint Vincent University, Halifax, Nova Scotia

ORGANIZATIONAL AND FUNDING SUPPORT

The Canadian Association of Occupational Therapists funded all expenses required to facilitate the volunteer labour acknowledged above, as well as for the publication of the document.

Gratitude for organizing support and funding are extended particularly to the following people:

Heather Gillespie, Coordinator of the CAOT Professional Promotion Division
Roma Maconachie, Former Coordinator of the Professional Promotion Division
Anne Strickland, CAOT Executive Director

PUBLICATION ASSISTANCE

Geraldine Moore, Editor, CAOT Publications ACE

PROJECT ASSISTANCE

Secretarial and technical assistance.
Karen Arseneault
Yvonne Ling
David Ripley

Text layout
Hans Posthuma

Graphics
Barbara Cooper, Ph.D., McMaster University, Hamilton
Mary Clark Green, Westprint Communications, Vancouver
Doug Porter, Virtual Image Productions, Halifax

PREFACE 2002

AUTHOR:
Elizabeth Townsend

Introduction

Preface 2002 is a tribute to the Canadian Association of Occupational Therapists (CAOT) and to the 80 Canadian occupational therapists who contributed to national guidelines development from 1980 to 1997. *Enabling Occupation: An Occupational Therapy Perspective*, first published by CAOT in 1997, includes *Preface 2002* based on two decisions. First, as a long-time contributor to Canadian guidelines, I would present my own perspective, rather than call another Task Force. Second, the 1997 publication of *Enabling Occupation* would remain unchanged and would be honoured intact as a period document.

Hilary Jarvis, 1979-1980 President of CAOT, telephoned me at my farm home in Prince Edward Island in November 1979 with an invitation to participate in a guidelines project. *Preface 2002* was drafted in that same farm home in December 2001 as I reflected on 35 years of clinical, managerial, educational and research experience in Uganda, Newfoundland, Alberta, Ontario, Prince Edward Island and Nova Scotia, where my work is currently located. To my own surprise, my enthusiasm for enabling occupation is continually re-generated by the enthusiasm I have encountered for these guidelines in Canada and around the world.

Offered in *Preface 2002* are reflections on the evolution of the concepts and practice of enabling occupation since 1997. Comments begin with brief notes on Canadian occupational therapy guidelines and on research for the preface. A short client perspective sets the stage for three sections: a focus on occupations, enabling approaches, and outcomes related to occupational quality of life, empowerment and justice.

Background

Since 1983 Canada has published six national, consensus guidelines (Canadian Association of Occupational Therapists [CAOT], 1991, 1993, 1997; Department of National Health and Welfare, 1983, 1986, 1987), and one outcome measure, the *Canadian Occupational Performance Measure* (Law, Baptiste, McColl, Opzoomer, Polatajko, & Pollock, 1990), for the client-centred practice of occupational therapy. With growing clarity over the years, these guidelines described the focus or domain of occupational therapy, the client-centred process of practice, and occupational therapists' targeted outcomes with clients (Clark Green, 2000; Townsend, 1998a). They also adopted the emerging language of occupation, enablement and justice, used most explicitly in the 1997 guidelines, *Enabling Occupation*. Stated in language that is still topical in 2002, occupational therapists were challenged through guidelines to address three hallmarks of best practice: a focus on occupations, enabling approaches in client-centred practice, and outcomes related to occupational quality of life, empowerment and justice.

Occupational therapists' best practice is difficult to implement in systems that, as yet, are not organized or accountable for enabling occupation. Notwithstanding implementation difficulties, the concepts and approaches described in *Enabling Occupation* are being embraced by a growing number of occupational therapists worldwide. Since June 1997, as Table A summarizes, sales of the textbook alone have exceeded 8,000 copies (English and French) in 38 countries, including Canada (S. Baal, personal communication, November 21, 2001).

A brief summary of the methods used to gather information for the preface is as follows. A Preface Survey requesting feedback on what holds true and what needs updating was distributed in October 2001 by e-mail to 58 occupational therapists who were Canadian authors of or contributors to *Enabling Occupation*, or who are international users of the book. The Preface Survey was also posted on the CAOT web page in October and November 2001. Five client spokespersons were invited to write a client perspective. An occupational therapist responded to my invitation to keep a one-week diary of reflections on enabling occupation in personal and professional circumstances. I also reviewed Canadian and international occupational therapy journals, plus the international *Journal of Occupational Science*, from June 1997 to December 2001. Additional information on the research theory and methodology of this project is available from this author.

A Client Perspective

Occupational therapists' best practice starts in the practical, everyday world by listening to client perspectives (Campbell, Copeland, & Tate, 1998; Peloquin, 1997; Rudman, Cook, & Polatajko, 1997). In her Foreword to the 1997 publication of *Enabling Occupation*, Bonnie

---

Conceptual Foundations of Occupational Therapy:

Hallmarks of best practice

- Focus on occupations

- Enabling approaches

- Outcomes related to occupational quality of life, empowerment and justice

Table A: World Distribution

Enabling Occupation: An Occupational Therapy Perspective
June 1997 to November 2001

	English	French	Total
Textbook	7,287	957	8,244
Workbook (*Enabling Occupation*)	698	17	715
Workbook (*Spirituality in Enabling Occupation*)	536	15	551

Sold in 38 countries:

Australia	Austria	Belgium	Brazil
Canada	Denmark	Finland	France
Germany	Hong Kong	Iceland	India
Ireland	Israel	Italy	Japan
Korea	Luxembourg	Malawi	Malaysia
New Zealand	Norway	Philippines	Portugal
Qatar	Saudi Arabia	Scotland	Singapore
South Africa	Spain	Sweden	Switzerland
Taiwan	The Netherlands	Uganda	United Arab Emirates
United Kingdom	United States of America		

Sherr-Klein[1], a former occupational therapy client, extended an invitation for us "to be allies in an exciting adventure" (p. ix). Her invitation was to actively recruit and hire persons with every kind of disability into the profession, and to ensure accommodation and access for persons with a disability in education and employment. She invited us to include persons with a disability in all decision-making and policy-making bodies and to pay for the expertise of persons with a disability. When I contacted her in October, 2001 with an invitation to update her comments, she replied:

> I'm interested in your description of 'occupation' as the making of meaning, as that is also one definition of art….Art and rehabilitation have a great deal in common: both involve risk-taking and living with uncertainty; they ask us to be open-minded, to look for new pathways around obstacles, to paint outside the lines. And yet to learn discipline, to persevere, to problem-solve and synthesize. Art is not a frill, as it is sometimes regarded (especially by bottom-liners) but is the very essence of life… In my experience, service providers are excited and challenged by the work we are creating and can collaborate with us to create these opportunities and push the boundaries of possibilities (e.g., our Board and volunteers have included service providers). I encourage you to be on the lookout for the artists in your community.

Sherr-Klein tells us that her own focus on occupations is on art making,

[1]Bonnie Sherr-Klein, Artist & Author: *Slow Dance: A Story of Stroke, Love, and Disability* (1997, Vintage Canada).

and that she wants to collaborate with service providers such as occupational therapists. Her concerns are in enabling the empowerment of persons with a disability to "create these opportunities" and to "push the boundaries of possibilities." While advocating for the inclusion of persons with a disability in decision-making and policy-making bodies, volunteer agencies are not just waiting patiently to be asked, rather they "have included service providers" in their own organizations. Sherr-Klein implies that the outcomes that matter for persons with a disability are occupational. Her comments speak to quality of life and empowerment as persons with a disability "look for new pathways around obstacles, to paint outside the lines."

Focus on Occupations

Occupations and Occupational Performance: Sherr-Klein's and many others' invitations to focus on meaningful occupations have stimulated a renaissance of writing about occupation as the domain of concern of occupational therapy and the emerging interdisciplinary, academic field of occupational science (Whiteford, Townsend, & Hocking, 2000). *Enabling Occupation* offers summaries of 11 Key Features of Occupation (Table 4, p. 34), and new features are continually emerging. For example, Emerson (1998) introduced another feature, that of "flow and occupation" which starts from "subjective occupational experience" (p. 38). "Occupational engagement" was introduced by looking at the "meaning of occupational engagement in life-threatening illness" (Vrkljan & Polgar, 2001, p. 237), and by describing and reflecting on the experience of occupational engagement by persons with a severe or persistent mental illness (Rebeiro & Cook, 1999).

Also explored since 1997 have been experiences and features of particular occupations. For example, experiences in the occupation of pet ownership were presented by Allen, Kelligrew and Jaffe (2000). Segal (1998) looked at family occupations when children have attention deficit/hyperactivity disorder. Leisure was explored by Suto (1998) as an occupation and as an interest in occupational therapy. Smith explored relationships between developmental technology and occupation (2000). Rebeiro's research with persons with a mental illness concluded that "a broader conceptualization of occupation-as-means and as-end most clearly reflects what Adolf Meyer (1922) told us about occupation and most clearly looks like occupational therapy" (1998, p. 18). Meyer, a psychiatrist and founder of the American Occupational Therapy Association, wrote that "a new step was to arise from a freer conception of work, from a concept of free and pleasant and profitable *occupation – including recreation and any form of helpful enjoyment as the leading principle"* (Meyer, 1922, p. 2).

Strongly related to the increasing focus on occupations is occupational therapists' interest in occupational performance. More comments were offered in the Preface Survey and more are available in the literature on the Canadian Model of Occupational Performance (CMOP) than on any other part of *Enabling Occupation*. The CMOP graphically illustrates the relationship between occupation and three forces that shape and are shaped by occupations: the environment, persons and spirituality. A central question is whether the CMOP truly focuses on occupations. As one Preface Survey respondent said:

> I really think that, having gone to some lengths in the profession to define occupation-based concepts and language, that the core of a national model should be built around an occupation concept. As constructed, the model seems to be a general model that could perhaps be used by many professions. (Preface Survey, Respondent #10)

Also with reference to occupations as depicted in the CMOP, another respondent stated that: "one area within the CMOP that needs much more work, I think, is the taxonomy used for occupation" (Preface Survey, Respondent #14). Some who question the categorization and classification of occupations argue that:

> it is impossible to give an individual's occupation any meaning other than the subjective meaning that they, themselves, choose to give it. In the postmodern worldview, occupations have no categories or boundaries, therefore it is necessary to further emphasize the subjective meaning (which is itself a postmodern term) of an individual's occupation in relation to their narrative, as well as emphasizing the occupation's multiplicity and multi-dimensionality. (Weinblatt & Avrech-Bar, 2001, p. 169)

Although contentious as a classification, the CMOP categories of self-care, productivity and leisure provided a research framework for examining the limitations of people with multiple sclerosis (Finlayson, Winkler Impey, Nicolle, & Edwards, 1998).

Occupations Shaped by and Shaping Environments, Persons and Spirituality: Survey respondents and the literature have called for more exploration to understand the impact of the environment on persons and of persons on their environment (Dyck & Jongbloed, 2000; Forwell, Whiteford, & Dyck, 2001). There have also been passionate debates about spirituality, notably in the 1997 special editions on spirituality published by *The Canadian Journal of Occupational Therapy* and *The American Journal of Occupational Therapy*. Whalley Hammell (2001) has proposed a shift away from this contentious concept to consider intrinsicality, while Christiansen (1999) and Unruh, Versnel and Kerr (2002) have proposed that we consider as an alternative the concept of occupational identity.

To me, a focus on occupations both explains the profession's name and signals the important, practical occupational contributions of this profession to society. A critical point in explaining this focus is that occupations are broadly defined to include and extend beyond the job-related occupations that have typically been included in national occupational classifications used for census-taking, research and economic planning.

The CMOP is not a model of client-centred practice since there is no illustration of the relationship between clients and professionals. Rather, the 1997 Model was designed to illustrate the profession's focus on occupations in relation to the environment, persons and spirituality, although I agree that the focus on occupations could be more clearly highlighted. I celebrate our inclusion of the environment both as a location of practice and as an important reference to the context of occupations in real, everyday life. My preference is to retain the broad concept of spirituality rather than to adopt other concepts that will also be contentious. Our inclusion of spirituality is generating important world debates in and outside occupational therapy about meaning, identity, community, connectedness, inclusion, intrinsicality, self, other and the universe.

Critical analyses of occupation and of the CMOP are needed to refine occupational therapy thinking. We need to strategize the implementation of a greater focus on occupations in the clinical, managerial, consulting, educational and research practices of occupational therapy. To move forward as a profession, we need to explore the advantages and/or limits of placing occupational performance at the core of the CMOP and other occupational therapy models worldwide (e.g., Chapparo & Ranka, 1998; Hagedorn, 1997; Kielhofner, 1995; Reed & Sanderson, 1999). To locate our broad view of occupation in the public realm – in other words to become more publicly visible and known – we need to examine more fully the economic, social and political as well as the personal dimensions of occupation.

Enabling Approaches: Client-Centred Processes and Principles

Occupational therapists are still asking, 20 years after the notion was first introduced, what does client-centred practice mean (Corring & Cook, 1999)? Are we truly client-centred (Rebeiro, 2000)? Why is it so difficult to do (Wilkins, Pollock, Rochon, & Law, 2001)? Sherr-Klein's invitation for occupational therapists to be allies with clients is still problematic for many occupational therapists, although enablement and client-centred practice are more frequent topics in the literature since rather than before 1997. From the early 1980s to the mid-1990s, Canadian occupational therapists used the language of client-centred practice to depict individualized, group and organizational level approaches that enable clients to participate as decision-making partners in their therapy. With the publication of the 1997 guidelines, *Enabling Occupation*, the language shifted. Enabling approaches employ the processes and principles for being client-centred.

Examples of literature on enabling or client-centred practice include texts by Law (1998) and Sumsion (1999) with descriptions and case studies to illustrate client-centred approaches. In *Individuals in Context*, Fearing and Clark (2000) described client-centred enabling approaches within the framework of an Occupational Performance Process Model. Gage (1997) analyzed the collaborative approach of enablement as a synergistic relationship in which there is a sharing of knowledge and expertise between the occupational therapist and the client. Dubouloz, Chevrier and Savoie-Zajc (2001) described the meaning transformation that clients and therapists experience as they journey together toward:

> a process of adaptation that allows for profound personal change in occupational therapy clients. ...the results highlight the primary role of critical reflection amongst occupational therapy clients and underline the importance of deconstructing common values and beliefs which could slow down the process of change. Moreover the development of new values and beliefs is a vehicle for change in occupational therapy. (p. 171)

A tool for quality evaluation of community based occupational therapy services was considered with reference to the values of client-centred practice. Hong, Pearce and Withers (2000) asked, how client-centred can occupational therapy assessments be? Hebert, Thibeault, Landry, Boisvenu, and Laporte (2000) compared a quality evaluation tool for use in community based services against four features of client-centred practice: client experience and knowledge about occupations must be valued; clients are active partners in the occupational therapy process; it is necessary to take risks to facilitate positive change; and client-centred practice in occupational therapy is based on the promotion of occupation. They concluded that a quality improvement tool can be useful in "the emergence of a practice profile highlighting strengths and weaknesses" (p. 153). Stern, Restall and Ripat (2000) developed methods to assess the client-centredness of practice. McColl (1998) asked, "What do we need to know to practice occupational therapy in the community?" (p. 11). She considered three models for community practice: client-centred, community-based rehabilitation and independent living, and she challenged occupational therapists to examine their use of theory to meet the requirements for practice in the community.

Sachs and Linn (1997) looked at client advocacy to uncover professional and environmental factors in "protecting clients from other professionals or family members, representing clients to others, taking care of their needs...[with] a focus on personal rather than social injustice" (p. 213). Rebeiro (2000) offered client perspectives on occupational therapy practice. The clients with severe and persistent mental illness who participated in her study affirmed occupational therapists' philosophical assumptions and beliefs in client-centred practice. However, they pointed with concern at the non-client-centredness of:

> prescriptive activity...[and] the lack of sufficient involvement in decision-making and advocacy, as well as the lack of recognition of their expertise and knowledge in mental health services. Occupational therapists' beliefs in client-centred enabling were not perceived to be an integral aspect of the occupational therapy care they received ...[and] client visions might potentially lead practice into uncharted horizons. (p. 13)

The occupational therapist who kept a diary for a week wrote:

> Attended my son's Individual Educational Plan…I wondered, how do I *enable* the teacher to understand his disengagement from learning, in which she was 'hoping for an opening of the situation to new possibilities…' *Enabling* includes the therapist as a part of the process and [as someone] who is also changed through the process. As I went through my week, I *enabled* others, was *enabled* by situations, *enabled* myself, and became a part of the changes which occurred. Then I realized that is how daily life works and that *enabling* occupation is an important part of how we live.

My perspective on enabling approaches and client-centred practice is that there is progress in our understanding although there is still much to learn. Basic values, beliefs, concepts, processes and principles of enabling or enablement are still being defined. Power needs the greatest attention since this is the central feature in transforming hierarchical, professional practice into enabling, client-centred practice focused on occupational outcomes, as described below.

Outcomes Related to Occupational Quality of Life, Empowerment and Justice

How will occupational therapists actually implement enabling approaches with targeted outcomes related to occupational quality of life, empowerment and justice? Why are client-centred enabling approaches that focus on occupational outcomes so difficult to implement in everyday practice?

To answer these questions, occupational therapists can learn from the sociology of professions. Professions have historically worked in a hierarchy in which their expertise is valued and privileged above the experiential knowledge of those who seek professional services (Coburn, 2000; Friedson, 1986). The implication is that client-centred enabling approaches face an uphill challenge to transform professional and managerial dominance into collaborative power sharing. In 2002, health services are being managed to decrease the length of stay and to streamline the health workforce by employing fewer professionals and more non-professionals. Private insurers and the public sector increasingly use standard protocols to manage and control occupational therapy and other services. Accountability tends to prize economic factors and individualistic, medicalized outcomes above holistic outcomes, such as quality of life, or community-oriented outcomes, such as empowerment and justice.

Yet occupational therapists' practical, occupational outcomes that enable empowerment and justice are congruent with powerful democratizing forces worldwide. Weinblatt and Avrech-Bar (2001) recognize this in their analysis of postmodernism that:

focuses on what is on the margins, what has been forgotten and pushed aside (citing Rosenau, 1994). This postmodern principle actually makes space for the diversity and uniqueness of the occupational therapy patient population and supports the "empowerment" approach... According to the client-centred approach, it is important that clients understand why an occupational therapy clinician has been included in their program, and they must be allowed access to sources of information relevant to their treatment and assured that they will receive the most appropriate treatment for their specific case (citing Baum & Law, 1997). (p. 168)

From a population perspective, our focus on occupational quality of life and empowerment is to enhance opportunities for living (Law, Steinwender, & Leclair, 1998). Moreover, addressing occupational challenges with at-risk or disadvantaged populations is a democratizing, justice-oriented practice (Wilcock, 1998a, 1998b).

One way to look at the journey toward truly enabling occupational outcomes is to identify and analyze barriers experienced in everyday practice. Recently, Wilkins et al. (2001) analyzed barriers at the systems level (e.g., funding, teams), at the level of the occupational therapist (e.g., time, knowledge of client-centred practice), and at the level of client perceptions (e.g., expecting an "expert," not a collaborator). Another way to look at the journey toward enabling occupational out-comes is to map the context of practice as a blueprint for change (Townsend, 1996). Sumsion and Smyth (2000) cite as one of the "barriers to client-centredness and their resolution," that "the therapist has difficulty taking risks in order to support client goals" (p. 19). With this important insight into the need for risk taking, occupational therapists can map what structural and organizational features discourage risk taking, beyond the personality traits of the occupational therapist or the clients (Westmoreland, 1999). A map of barriers can guide systems-level action toward enabling occupational outcomes in alliances with client organizations, as advocated by Sherr-Klein and others.

After many years of struggle to articulate and demonstrate what occupational therapists do, I am convinced that occupational therapists need to engage in systems-level critiques and action planning. With more critical occupational therapy perspectives, we might re-orient front-line practice, the management of services, the education of occupational therapists, and research. Our profession's ability to implement our best practice requires us to change the ways in which the management and professional regulation of practice invisibly and unconsciously "overrule" occupational therapists' good intentions (Townsend, 1998b, 1999).

Let us be open to questions as a stimulus for growth (Bossers, Dernaghan, Hodgins, Merla, O'Connor, & Kessel, 1999). For instance, what do clients say about early discharge hospital-at-home policies (Lane, 2000)? What involvement should children have in their own goal setting (Missiuna, & Pollock, 2000)? How can legislation enable consumer empowerment (Redick, McClain, & Brown, 2000)? How can we be client-centred in the tools used to measure our professional competence (Salvatori, Baptiste, & Ward, 2000)? What educational approaches will enable students to integrate our visionary focus on enablement and occupation into the hard realities of everyday practice (Banks, Bell, & Smits, 2000; Smits & Ferguson, 2000; Wood, Nielson, Humphry, Coppola, Baranek, & Rourk, 2000; Yerxa, 1998)? What organizational and funding structures do we need to advance the evidence-based practice of enabling occupation (von Zweck, 1999), and to grow our fledgling but promising research required to advance the theory and practice of enabling occupation (Egan, 2001)? Where are we in developing economic evaluations of occupational therapy (Landry & Matthews, 1998)? What is empowerment and occupational justice and what can occupational therapists do about these community-oriented outcomes (Wilcock & Townsend, 2000; Townsend & Wilcock, in press)? Occupational therapists stand with other health professionals at what Corbett and Corbett (1999) described as the "nexus of healthcare trends" (p. 111). As we work at such a strategic nexus, how can we make occupation visible as an important determinant of health, quality of life, empowerment and justice? How can we work *with* clients and stop making plans and speaking *for* them?

Conclusion

CAOT sponsored Visioning Together for Leadership: The Vancouver Leadership Forum, October 1, 1999. In attendance were over 70 representatives from CAOT and the national associations of educators and regulators (Baptiste, 2000). Since 1997, Presidents of CAOT have emphasized the importance of leadership with a vision (Bressler, 1997; Reimer, 1998). Moreover, as Picard (2000) noted, "our political influence is dependent on our numbers and our ability to work cohesively at all levels of government" (p. 215). It seems that the 1997 publication of *Enabling Occupation* offers a benchmark for occupational therapists to raise questions and examine opportunities for change (Fearing, 2001). One can meet the challenges of enabling occupation by dismissing this ideal as impossible to implement. Alternately, one can raise awareness and take risks in alliances with others who support democratizing forces in the world (Westmorcland, 1999). Reflecting on ways of knowing, contexts of practice, and assumptions, Kinsella (2001) reminds occupational therapists that:

> By acknowledging contradictions between what we say and what we do, we can work to change our behaviours to bring them into line with what we say we believe. Sometimes we come to recognize the need to change our espoused theory of practice, whereas sometimes we recognize the need to change our behaviours. At other times this exercise raises awareness of systemic barriers to our practices, which compel us to take action in a larger realm, perhaps to change work environments, to become more political, or to advocate for broader changes in the systems in which we work. (p. 197)

I believe strongly that our progress towards enabling occupation depends on empowering ourselves as occupational therapists to seek change with our clients as partners. Together, we can target outcomes that enhance their quality of life, empowerment and just opportunities. In the end, occupational therapists are the agents of this profession's destiny.

Author

Elizabeth Townsend, Ph.D., O.T. (C), Reg. (N.S.)

Editor, *Enabling Occupation: An Occupational Therapy Perspective*, and Former Chair, Client-Centred Practice Committee, Canadian Association of Occupational Therapists. Elizabeth Townsend is also Professor and Director of the School of Occupational Therapy, Faculty of Health Professions, Dalhousie University, Halifax, Nova Scotia.

Acknowledgements

Collaborators on Preface 2002 have been Jennifer Smart, Dalhousie University M.Sc.(O.T.) student and Research Assistant; Tammy Coles, student occupational therapist/Research Assistant; Gina Meacoe, who coordinated the distribution and collection of the Preface Survey through CAOT; Preface Survey Respondents; and those who provided client perspectives. Three anonymous reviewers helped greatly in attending to details and in prompting clarity, while Mary Egan's gentle, clear-thinking editorial work made it a pleasure to finalize revisions. Jacinthe Savard was a very insightful editor for the French version. Katie Moore, daughter of the 1997 *Enabling Occupation* Editor Geraldine Moore, provided family continuity in this project by completing the copy editing in a timely and capable fashion. All of these contributions were invaluable to the project.

References for Preface 2002

Allen, J.M., Kelligrew, D.H., & Jaffe, D. (2000). The experience of pet ownership as a meaningful occupation. *Canadian Journal of Occupational Therapy, 67*, 271-278.

Banks, S., Bell, E., & Smits, E. (2000). Integration tutorials and seminars: Examining the integration of academic and fieldwork learning by student occupational therapists. *Canadian Journal of Occupational Therapy, 67*, 93-100.

Baptiste, S. (2000). Visioning together for leadership. *Canadian Journal of Occupational Therapy, 67*, 81-85.

Baum, C., & Law, M. (1997). Occupational therapy practice: Focusing on occupational performance. A*merican Journal of Occupational Therapy, 51*, 277-288.

Bossers, A.M., Dernaghan, J., Hodgins, L., Merla, L., O'Connor, C., & Kessel, M.V. (1999). Defining and developing professionalism. *Canadian Journal of Occupational Therapy, 66*, 116-121.

Bressler, S. (1997). CAOT: Guiding you through the right channels. *Canadian Journal of Occupational Therapy, 64*, 167-173.

Campbell, M., Copeland, B., & Tate, B. (1998). Taking the standpoint of people with disabilities in research: Experiences with participation. *Canadian Journal of Rehabilitation, 12*, 95-104.

Canadian Association of Occupational Therapists. (1991). *Occupational therapy guidelines for client-centred practice.* Toronto, ON: CAOT Publications.

Canadian Association of Occupational Therapists. (1993). *Occupational therapy guidelines for client-centred mental health practice.* Toronto, ON: CAOT Publications ACE.

Canadian Association of Occupational Therapists. (1997). *Enabling occupation: An occupational therapy perspective.* Ottawa, ON: CAOT Publications ACE.

Chapparo, C., & Ranka, J. (1998). *Occupational performance model: Australia.* Sydney, NSW: School of Occupation and Leisure Studies, University of Sydney.

Christiansen, C.H. (1999). Defining lives: Occupation as identity: An essay on competence, coherence and the creation of meaning. *American Journal of Occupational Therapy, 53*, 547-558.

Clark Green, M. (2000). The Canadian way. *Occupational Therapy Now, 2(3)*, 3.

Coburn, D. (Ed.). (2000). Medicine, nursing and the state. Toronto, ON: Garamond Press.

Corbett, K., & Corbett, J.C. (1999). The new professional: The nexus of healthcare trends. *Canadian Journal of Occupational Therapy, 66*, 111-115.

Corring, D.J., & Cook, J.V. (1999). Client-centred care means that I am a valued human being. *Canadian Journal of Occupational Therapy, 66*, 71-82.

Department of National Health and Welfare. (1983). *Guidelines for the client-centred practice of occupational therapy* (H39-33/1983E). Ottawa, ON: Author.

Department of National Health and Welfare. (1986). *Intervention guidelines for the client-centred practice of occupational therapy* (H39-100/1986E). Ottawa, ON: Author.

Department of National Health and Welfare. (1987). *Toward outcome measures in occupational therapy* (H39-114/1987E). Ottawa, ON: Author.

Dubouloz, C.J., Chevrier, J., & Savoie-Zajc, L. (2001). Processus de transformation chez un groupe de personnes cardiaques suivies en ergothérapie pour une modification de leur equilibre du fonctionnement occupationnel. *Canadian Journal of Occupational Therapy, 68*, 171-185.

Dyck, I., & Jongbloed, L. (2000). Women with multiple sclerosis and employment issues: A focus on social and institutional environments. *Canadian Journal of Occupational Therapy, 67*, 337-346.

Egan, M. (2001). Canadian occupational therapy research: The little profession that could. *Canadian Journal of Occupational Therapy, 68*, 143-148.

Emerson, H. (1998). Flow and occupation: A review of the literature. *Canadian Journal of Occupational Therapy, 65*, 37-44.

Fearing, V.G. (2001). Muriel Driver Lecture. Change: Creating our own reality. *Canadian Journal of Occupational Therapy, 68*, 208-216.

Fearing, V.G. & Clark, J. (2000). *Individuals in context: A practical guide to client-centred practice*. Thorofare, NJ: Slack Incorporated.

Finlayson, M., Winkler Impey, M., Nicolle, C., & Edwards, J. (1998). Self-care, productivity and leisure limitations of people with multiple sclerosis in Manitoba. *Canadian Journal of Occupational Therapy, 65*, 299-308.

Forwell, S.J., Whiteford, G., & Dyck, I. (2001). Cultural competence in New Zealand and Canada: Occupational therapy students' reflections on class and fieldwork curriculum. *Canadian Journal of Occupational Therapy, 68*, 90-103.

Freidson, E. (1986). *Professional powers: A study of the institutionalizaton of formal knowledge*. Chicago: University of Chicago Press.

Gage, M. (1997). From independence to interdependence: Creating synergistic health care teams. *Canadian Journal of Occupational Therapy, 64*, 174-184.

Hagedorn, R. (1997). *Foundations for practice in occupational therapy*. London: Churchill-Livingston.

Hebert, M., Thibeault, R., Landry, A., Boisvenu, M., & Laporte, D. (2000). Introducing an evaluation of community based occupational therapy services: A client-centred practice. *Canadian Journal of Occupational Therapy, 67*, 146-154.

Hong, C.S., Pearce, S., & Withers, R.A. (2000). Occupational therapy assessments: How client-centred can they be? *British Journal of Occupational Therapy, 63*, 316-318.

Kielhofner, G. (1995). *A model of human occupation: Theory and application*. Baltimore: Williams & Wilkins.

Kinsella, E.A. (2001). Reflections on reflective practice. *Canadian Journal of Occupational Therapy, 68*, 195-198.

Landry, D.W., & Matthews, M. (1998). Economic evaluation of occupational therapy: Where are we at? *Canadian Journal of Occupational Therapy, 65*, 160-167.

Lane, L. (2000). Client-centred practice: Is it compatible with early discharge hospital-at-home policies? *British Journal of Occupational Therapy, 63*, 310-315.

Law, M. (Ed.). (1998). *Client-centred occupational therapy*. Thorofare, NJ: Slack Incorporated.

Law, M., Baptiste, S., McColl, M., Opzoomer, A., Polatajko, H., & Pollock, N. (1990). The Canadian occupational performance measure: An outcome measure for occupational therapy. *Canadian Journal of Occupational Therapy, 57*, 82-87.

Law, M., Steinwender, S., & Leclair, L. (1998). Occupation, health and well-being. *Canadian Journal of Occupational Therapy, 65*, 81-91.

McColl, M.A. (1998). What do we need to know to practice occupational therapy in the community? *American Journal of Occupational Therapy, 52*, 11-18.

Meyer, A. (1922). The philosophy of occupation therapy. Archives of Occupational Therapy, 1, 1-10, reprinted in *American Journal of Occupational Therapy, 31*, 639-642.

Missiuna, C., & Pollock, N. (2000). Perceived efficacy and goal setting in young children. Canadian *Journal of Occupational Therapy, 27*, 101-109.

Peloquin, S. (1997). Nationally speaking: The spiritual depth of occupation: Making worlds and making lives. *American Journal of Occupational Therapy, 51*, 166-168.

Picard, H. (2000). Together in action. *Canadian Journal of Occupational Therapy, 67*, 211-216.

Rebeiro, K. (1998). Occupation-as-means to mental health: A review of the literature and a call for research. *Canadian Journal of Occupational Therapy, 65*, 12-19.

Rebeiro, K. (2000). Client perspectives on occupational therapy practice: Are we truly client-centred? *Canadian Journal of Occupational Therapy, 67*, 7-14.

Rebeiro, K.L., & Cook, J.V. (1999). Opportunity not prescription: An exploratory study of the experience of occupational engagement. *Canadian Journal of Occupational Therapy, 66*, 176-187.

Redick, A.G., McClain, L., & Brown, C. (2000). Consumer empowerment through occupational therapy: The Americans With Disabilities Act, Title III. *American Journal of Occupational Therapy, 54*, 207-213.

Reed, K.L., & Sanderson, S.N. (1999). *Concepts of occupational therapy* (4th ed.). Philadelphia: Lippincott, Williams, & Wilkins.

Reimer, L. (1998). Themes to lead CAOT into the future. *Canadian Journal of Occupational Therapy, 65*, 179-182.

Rosenau, P.V. (1994). Health politics meets post-modernism: Its meaning and implications for community health organizing. *Journal of Health Politics, Policy and Law, 19*, 303-333.

Rudman, D.L., Cook, J.V., & Polatajko, H. (1997). Understanding the potential of occupation: A qualitative exploration of seniors' perspectives on activity. *American Journal of Occupational Therapy, 51*, 640-650.

Sachs, D., & Linn, R. (1997). Client advocacy in action: Professional and environmenta factors affecting Israeli occupational therapists' behaviour. *Canadian Journal of Occupational Therapy, 64*, 207-215.

Salvatori, P., Baptiste, S., & Ward, M. (2000). Development of a tool to measure clinical competence in occupational therapy: A pilot study. *Canadian Journal of Occupational Therapy, 67*, 51-60.

Segal, R. (1998). The construction of family occupations: A study of families with children who have attention deficit/hyperactivity disorder. *Canadian Journal of Occupational Therapy, 65*, 286-292.

Smith, R.O. (2000). Technology and occupation: Contemporary viewpoints: The role of occupational therapy in a developmental technology model. A*merican Journal of Occupational Therapy, 54*, 339-340.

Smits, E., & Ferguson, J. (2000). Integration tutorials and seminars: A creative learning approach for occupational therapy curricula. *Canadian Journal of Occupational Therapy, 67*, 86-92.

Stern, M., Restall, G., & Ripat, J. (2000). The use of self-reflection to improve client-centred practice. In V.G. Fearing & J. Clark (Eds.), *Individuals in context*. Thorofare, NJ: Slack Incorporated.

Sumsion, T. (1999). *Client-centred practice in occupational therapy: A guide to implementation*. London: Churchill-Livingston.

Sumsion, T., & Smyth, G. (2000). Barriers to client-centredness and their resolution. *Canadian Journal of Occupational Therapy, 67*, 15-21.

Suto, M. (1998). Leisure in occupational therapy. *Canadian Journal of Occupational Therapy, 65*, 271-278.

Townsend, E. (1996). Institutional ethnography: A method for showing how the context shapes practice. *Occupational Therapy Journal of Research, 16*, 179-199.

Townsend, E. (1998a). Client-centred occupational therapy: The Canadian experience. In M. Law (Ed.), *Client-centred occupational therapy* (pp. 47-65). Thorofare, NJ: Slack Incorporated.

Townsend, E. (1998b). *Good intentions overruled: A critique of empowerment in the routine organization of mental health services.* Toronto, ON: University of Toronto Press.

Townsend, E. (1999). Enabling occupation in the 21st century: Making good intentions a reality. *Australian Occupational Therapy Journal, 46,* 147-159.

Townsend, E., & Wilcock, A.A. (in press). Occupational justice. In C. Christiansen & E. Townsend (Eds.), *Introduction to occupation: The art and science of living.* New Jersey: Prentice-Hall Publishing, Inc.

Unruh, A., Versnel, J., & Kerr, N. (2002). Spirituality unplugged: A review of commonalities, contentions, and a resolution. *Canadian Journal of Occupational Therapy, 69,* 156-160.

von Zweck, C. (1999). The promotion of evidence-based occupational therapy practice in Canada. *Canadian Journal of Occupational Therapy, 66,* 208-213.

Vrkljan, B., & Polgar, J. (2001). Meaning of occupational engagement in life-threatening illness: A qualitative pilot project. *Canadian Journal of Occupational Therapy, 68,* 237-246.

Weinblatt, N., & Avrech-Bar, M. (2001). Postmodernism and its application to the field of occupational therapy. *Canadian Journal of Occupational Therapy, 68,* 164-170.

Westmoreland, M. (1999). Muriel Driver Lecture: Risk taking: An antidote to diffidence. *Canadian Journal of Occupational Therapy, 66,* 214-220.

Whalley Hammell, K. (2001). Intrinsicality: Reconsidering spirituality, meaning(s) and mandate. *Canadian Journal of Occupational Therapy, 68,* 186-194.

Whiteford, G., Townsend, E., & Hocking, C. (2000). Reflections on a renaissance of occupation. *Canadian Journal of Occupational Therapy, 67,* 61-69.

Wilcock, A.A. (1998a). An occupational perspective of health. Thorofare, NJ: Slack Incorporated.

Wilcock, A.A. (1998b). Doing, being, becoming. *Canadian Journal of Occupational Therapy, 65,* 248-257.

Wilcock, A.A., & Townsend, E. (2000). Occupational justice: Occupational Terminology Interactive Dialogue. *Journal of Occupational Science, 7,* 84-86.

Wilkins, S., Pollock, N., Rochon, S., & Law, M. (2001). Implementing client-centred practice: Why is it so difficult to do? *Canadian Journal of Occupational Therapy, 68,* 70-79.

Wood, W., Nielson, C., Humphry, R., Coppola, S., Baranek, G., & Rourk, J. (2000). A curricular renaissance: Graduate education centered on occupation. *American Journal of Occupational Therapy, 54,* 586-597.

Yerxa, E. (1998). Occupation: The keystone of a curriculum for a self-defined profession. *American Journal of Occupational Therapy, 52,* 365-372.

Background

CHAPTER ONE

Introduction

Purpose

To set the conceptual and historical stage for *Enabling Occupation* from an occupational therapy perspective.

Objectives

To introduce Enabling Occupation by summarizing:
- Occupational therapy concepts, history, and language
- The purpose of writing new guidelines;
- The intended audiences;
- Canada's history of collaboration in developing client-centred practice in occupational therapy;
- An overview of the document.

Summary

Enabling Occupation: An Occupational Therapy Perspective introduces core concepts and processes that demonstrate the important contributions of occupational therapy to the everyday lives of Canadians and others around the world. Beginning with a summary of occupation, client-centred practice and occupational therapy, the Introduction clarifies what these guidelines intend to do. A brief history summarizes how national guidelines for client-centred practice in occupational therapy have developed in Canada, and an overview explains the order and general purpose of the chapters to follow.

ORIENTING CONCEPTS, HISTORY, AND LANGUAGE

*O*ccupational therapy is a health profession whose members collaborate in enabling occupation with clients, who may be individuals, groups, or organizations. The profession emerged from occupational work into occupational therapy when it was organized to address the occupational problems experienced by returning soldiers (Driver, 1968; Dunton, 1919; Schwartz, 1992; Trent, 1919).

Occupational therapy developed historically in hospitals, rehabilitation centres, mental health facilities, special care residences, and special employment settings (Robinson, 1981). In these settings, occupational therapists have worked primarily with individuals and groups. The emphasis has been with people whose lives have been disrupted by illness, disability, addictions, the effects of aging, or social disadvantages (Canadian Association of Occupational Therapists (CAOT), 1991, 1993). Occupational therapy is less known but has long been practised in homes, work places, schools, correctional facilities, businesses, governments, universities, recreational settings, and the community (Frank, 1992; Law, 1991; LeVesconte, 1935; Polatajko, 1992; Townsend, 1993a).

From the 1940s to the 1980s, occupation was not central to occupational therapy; instead occupational therapists adopted terms such as tasks or activities, as in activities of daily living. As well, ideas about occupation were overshadowed by interests in specialized equipment and by techniques aimed at performance components. It also became popular to speak about function to capture the practical orientation of this profession.

Since the 1980s, occupation has been re-emphasized in occupational therapy theory and practice. Occupational performance is becoming widely known by occupational therapists as an important core concept for practice. Ideas about enablement and enabling are being discussed to clarify that this is a participatory and action-based type of therapy. The occupational therapist is being described as an enabler, who facilitates clients rather than doing things for them. A growing interest in client-centred practice is evident in the articles being published in the Canadian Journal of Occupational Therapy and in presentations at Annual Conferences of the Canadian Association of Occupational Therapists (Townsend, 1993b; Townsend & Banks, 1992).

While occupational therapy has tremendous diversity, core concepts unify this profession and give it direction. These new guidelines emphasize two core concepts and the processes for implementing them in practice. The title *Enabling Occupation* means enabling people to choose, organize, and perform those occupations they find useful or meaningful in their environment.

Enabling refers to processes of facilitating, guiding, coaching, educating, prompting, listening, reflecting, encouraging, or otherwise collaborating with people so that they have the means and opportunity to be involved in solving their own problems. Occupation refers to groups of activities and tasks of everyday life, which are named, organized, and given value and meaning by individuals and a culture. Occupation is everything people do to occupy themselves, including looking after themselves (self-care), enjoying life (leisure), and contributing to the social and economic fabric of their communities (productivity). Occupation is the domain of concern and the therapeutic medium of occupational therapy.

Shifting towards occupation, occupational performance and client-centred practice means using these concepts and language to guide everyday practice. It may seem like professional jargon to use these terms with anyone other than occupational therapists, yet occupational therapists who consistently use these concepts will educate others about the occupational aspects of life and the importance of enabling people to have meaningful lives, just as other professions have educated people about medical, psychological, and legal aspects of living. Besides, occupational therapy's understanding of enabling processes is gaining favour as people seek more control over health and other aspects of life, and occupation appeals to people because they know that there are important ways of being occupied besides the occupations known as work.

PURPOSE

Enabling Occupation: An Occupational Therapy Perspective is a leadership document. It offers an occupational and client-centred perspective which makes occupation, occupational performance, and enablement the focus of client-centred practice. Presented in this document is a new Canadian Model of Occupational Performance (CMOP) capturing ideas about the concept of occupational performance. The CMOP portrays persons as spiritual beings who are active agents with the potential to identify, choose, and engage in occupations in their environment, and who are capable of actively participating as partners in client-centred practice.

Rather than providing protocols or standards, *Enabling Occupation* encourages reflective practice (Schon, 1983; 1987). Occupational therapists are encouraged to apply theory in everyday practice, and to use their experience of everyday practice to advance theory. A synthesis of theory and practice can then be used in many ways (see Chapter 6), such as marketing occupational therapy, defining criteria for accountability, and attracting innovative people to the profession of occupational therapy.

While an occupational and client-centred perspective may seem to be outside the boundaries of some occupational therapy practice, theory and practice are developing so rapidly that new insights are appearing as these guidelines go to press. The purpose of these guidelines, as summarized in Table 1, is to propose concepts, processes, and outcomes for occupational therapy well into the 21st century.

INTENDED AUDIENCES

Enabling Occupation: An Occupational Therapy Perspective is intended primarily for occupational therapists. Those who are affiliated with occupational therapy as clients, managers, or professionals may find these guidelines useful for seeing how occupational therapists describe the profession and its practice. The ideas presented in these new guidelines will be particularly useful in educating occupational therapists and explaining occupational therapy to others. Other uses may draw in readers who are concerned with programme planning, advocacy, policy development and research where the focus is on occupation and client-centred practice.

Table 1: Purpose of *Enabling Occupation: An Occupational Therapy Perspective*

To propose concepts, processes, and outcomes for occupational therapy well into the 21st century, by:

1. setting the conceptual and historical stage for enabling occupation from an occupational therapy perspective;

2. highlighting the societal context of occupational therapy;

3. presenting values and beliefs, the Canadian Model of Occupational Performance (CMOP), and client-centred practice as core concepts of occupational therapy;

4. linking core concepts with a process for enabling occupation with individual and organizational clients;

5. linking core concepts of enabling occupation with a process for organizing occupational therapy services;

6. accenting ways of using guidelines for enabling occupation in occupational therapy education, communication, advocacy, marketing, programme and policy development, documentation, research, and debates;

7. illustrating theory and practice through vignettes;

8. providing references and additional readings on occupation, occupational performance, and client-centred practice.

Enabling Occupation: An Occupational Therapy Perspective, CAOT 1997

As with all guidelines, this document should be adapted for use in particular cultural contexts. Canada's rich ethnic diversity requires that core concepts be interpreted with sensitivity. In applying these guidelines, readers are urged to be sensitive to culture as well as to age, gender, race, sexual orientation, and other characteristics. Occupational therapy is not a technique with standardized methods. The diversity of persons, environments, and occupations makes each person-environment-occupation interaction unique.

To be client-centred is to understand and develop particular types of relationships with clients with full awareness of the part played by the self. Occupational therapists, like clients and others are part of an ongoing, active process of change as all partners participate in enabling occupation. The implication is that the Canadian Model of Occupational Performance presents a view of humanity and the environment which is applicable to occupational therapists as well as to clients. Moreover, occupational therapists as well as clients experience change in their power relationship when practice becomes client-centred.

CANADA'S HISTORY OF NATIONAL COLLABORATION ON GUIDELINES

Five Guidelines Documents and the Canadian Occupational Performance Measure

From 1980 to 1993, five guidelines documents and one outcome measure were published in Canada, all advocating client-centred practice and a focus on occupational performance. The first three volumes of guidelines were produced, in French and English, by a series of national Task Forces funded jointly by the Department of National Health and Welfare (DNHW) and the Canadian Association of Occupational Therapists (CAOT) (Townsend, Brintnell, & Staisey, 1990; DNHW & CAOT, 1983, 1986, 1987). Acting on recommendations in the third guidelines document, *Toward Outcome Measures in Occupational Therapy* (DNHW & CAOT, 1987), the National Health Research and Development Programme (NHRDP) and the Canadian Occupational Therapy Foundation (COTF) funded a research team which produced the *Canadian Occupational Performance Measure* (COPM) (Law et al., 1990,1991,1994). The COPM is based on the 1983 Occupational Performance Model described in *Guidelines for the Client-Centred Practice of Occupational Therapy* (DNHW & CAOT, 1983).

CAOT funded its Client-Centred Practice Committee to consolidate the first three volumes of guidelines into a fourth, composite document, *Occupational Therapy Guidelines for Client-Centred Practice* (CAOT, 1991). Most recently, Health Canada (formerly Department of National Health and Welfare) & CAOT funded and published *Occupational Therapy Guidelines for Client-Centred Mental Health Practice* (CAOT, 1993).

These five guidelines documents remain useful because they describe concepts in occupational therapy such as the worth and holistic view of the individual, professionalization, the team concept, adaptation, spirituality, motivation, the therapeutic relationship, the teaching learning process, ethics, and principles of outcome measurement. *Occupational Therapy Guidelines for Client-Centred Mental Health Practice* (CAOT, 1993) "address special parameters concerning occupational therapy mental health practice with adults; however, their content is sufficient to cover developments and needs in occupational therapy across age groups and clinical specialties" (p.v). The 1993 guidelines contain important discussions of forces and models shaping mental health practice, mental health practice roles, guidelines for stages of client-centred mental health practice, a practice illustration, references, and future visions for occupational therapy's mental health practice.

Impact Study

Almost a decade after publication of the first three guidelines documents, CAOT funded an Impact Study to determine occupational therapists' perceptions of their uses and usefulness (DNHW & CAOT, 1983, 1986, 1987; Blain, Townsend, Krefting, & Burwash, 1992; Blain & Townsend, 1993). The Impact Study used a multi-method, ethnographic design with in-depth telephone interviews and a national survey of CAOT members. Findings from this study showed that the three volumes were most useful for educating occupational therapists, and for explaining occupational therapy to medical or other professionals. The importance of describing occupational therapy using the profession's own concepts of occupational performance and client-centred practice was emphasized. Three key recommendations made from the Impact Study were that:

1. the purpose and audience of new guidelines be clarified;
2. development of new guidelines be subject to national consultation and review; and,
3. the language and description of a model of occupational performance be clarified.

Analysis of the interviews, in particular, showed that Canada's guidelines documents have been extremely useful in creating a unified view of core concepts in occupational therapy. Generic conceptual guidelines have offered graphic illustrations and a language to describe theory and the processes required to make occupational therapy practice consistent with the fundamental concepts of this profession. It was clear from the Impact Study that occupational theory and practice were changing so rapidly that it was NOT sufficient just to update the original guidelines. As a result, CAOT funded the development and publication of a new guidelines document to capture the leading concepts and processes for occupational therapy into the 21st century.

Guidelines for the 1990s and Beyond

Enabling Occupation: An Occupational Therapy Perspective is being launched during the 1990s reform period when health, social services, education, employment, and other segments of life are changing. In these times of change, there is a need to articulate the core concepts of occupational therapy. With so many competing pressures, it is important for occupational therapists to clarify the common threads beneath diverse types of occupational therapy practice. Hence, CAOT supported the national process of collaboration described previously in acknowledging the multiple authors and reviewers of this document. Development of guidelines for the 1990s and beyond has raised questions and diverse views along with a growing sense of direction and pride even though occupational therapy has been a profession for almost 100 years.

Profile of Occupational Therapy Practice in Canada

A companion document to these new guidelines has emerged through a separate national consultation process. The two documents were not initiated as companions but became consistent because some of the same people were involved in both projects, and there has been a growing concern about core concepts in occupational therapy in Canada. As a result, the *Profile of Occupational Therapy Practice in Canada* (CAOT, 1996c) is congruent with the conceptual framework for enabling occupation even though terms and processes are described differently, given their different purposes. The Occupational Therapists' Key Role statement and the Units of Professional Competency in Occupational Therapy in the *Profile* are based on concepts of occupational performance and client-centred practice. Moreover, four Units of Professional Competency which refer to the process of practice are comparable to the seven stages in the Occupational Performance Process for working with clients, outlined in Chapter 4. The other three Units in the *Profile* are comparable to the six elements described in Chapter 5 as a Process for Organizing Occupational Therapy Services.

OVERVIEW OF THE DOCUMENT

PART I provides a background for these new guidelines, first through this Introduction (Chapter 1), then through a review of the Context of Occupational Therapy (Chapter 2).

PART II offers conceptual, process, and organizational guidelines for occupational therapy. Chapter 3, Core Concepts of Occupational Therapy, opens with a statement of Occupational Values and Beliefs. Then discussion of a new Canadian Model of Occupational Performance (CMOP) emphasizes the dynamic, person-environment-occupation relationship. In addition, client-centred practice is discussed with reference to individuals and groups, then to agencies, organizations and other clients, with ethical issues raised around questions of choice, risk and responsibility. Chapter 4, Linking Concepts to a Process for Working with

Clients summarizes interconnected processes in which theory shapes practice and practice shapes theory. Chapter 5, Linking Concepts to a Process for Organizing Occupational Therapy Services, discusses six organizational elements: plan, market, manage, educate, research, and evaluate.

PART III completes the document. Chapter 6, Using New Guidelines accents ten suggestions for using the document in enhancing quality and accountability, forming alliances, and building knowledge in occupational therapy. Implicit in suggesting uses for these guidelines is the assumption that occupational therapists work in teams which may include clients, families, friends, professionals, employers, and others as appropriate.

An Index, Key Terms, References and Additional Readings are provided at the end of the text. A large number of Figures and Tables have been included to facilitate learning and presentation of the key points in this document.

There is much to celebrate in occupational therapy. The dynamism in the Canadian Model of Occupational Performance (CMOP) portrays individuals and communities with an energy and potential to go beyond what is to what might be, to move from today to visions of tomorrow. The Occupational Performance Process, based on the CMOP, is an active, collaborative process which enables individuals and communities to pursue their visions. In essence, this document is infused with ideas of possibility and hope. Ideally, occupational therapists will use these new guidelines to foster a sense of pride in the profession and to enable clients of any kind to hope and to actually do what might be possible. Although set in the Canadian context, *Enabling Occupation* offers a vision of occupational therapy practice that will be of interest and assistance to others around the world.

CHAPTER TWO
Context of Occupational Therapy

PRIMARY AUTHORS:
Elizabeth Townsend
Sharon Brintnell

Purpose

To highlight the societal context of occupational therapy and occupational therapy clients.

Objectives

To highlight four major changes, including 16 contextual features, that are shaping and being shaped by occupational therapy, clients, and society including:
- Changing Health and Social Systems
- Changing Professional Knowledge
- Changing Demographics
- Changing Societal Values

Summary

Chapter Two outlines 16 contextual features related to four areas of social change which are critical for enabling occupation. Occupational therapy is developing knowledge of occupation and enablement in a multicultural environment with an aging population and growing poverty. Contextual features such as health promotion, privatization, managed programmes, citizen participation, gender equity and concerns for quality of life challenge occupational therapists but they also show the importance of occupation and client-centred approaches.

$\mathcal{O}$ccupational therapy clients and practice exist in a context. Occupational therapy looks like common sense, but it requires complex reasoning that takes the context into account (Mattingly & Hayes Fleming, 1994). Without contextual support, the potential for enabling occupation is confined. Conversely, the process (Chapter 4) and organization (Chapter 5) appropriate for enabling occupation will flourish if the context supports a broad view of occupation and the use of enabling approaches in professional practice, as described in Chapter 3. Contextual features are described separately while recognizing that each is interconnected with other features. Moreover, each feature simultaneously presents barriers and opportunities; viewed from different perspectives, the same feature may close some doors while opening others.

ORIENTING PRINCIPLES

Three principles are important in understanding the societal context of occupational therapy.

Visible and Invisible Aspects

Some people refer to the invisible macro context, while everyday practice is the visible micro context (Biklen, 1988). Others refer to the systems and structure of society, versus the lifeworld where people communicate and experience everyday life (Habermas, 1984). The explanation used here is that the invisible organization of health, education and other functions in society determines what can be done in the visible everyday world (Smith, 1987, 1990a, 1990b). Visible aspects of occupational therapy include the people, places, equipment and written materials of everyday practice; whereas invisible aspects are the values and beliefs which are embedded in organizing processes, such as policies which determine whose priorities prevail and whose decisions are respected. Invisible priorities are embedded in everyday decisions about who will be involved and what will be done. Using the example of health services, invisible values and beliefs determine priorities in funding, the degree of challenge versus protectionism embedded in risk management procedures, and the categories used in workload statistics.

Interconnectedness of Context and Practice

The contextual features described in this chapter are all interconnected and changing. Everyday practice shapes and is shaped by contextual features, and each contextual feature influences others. Contextual features are not external to everyday practice; rather, everyday practice is embedded in contextual features. Occupational therapists are active participants in either perpetuating or changing everyday practice and its context. The implication is that occupational therapists can influence change, in that they are not trapped in fixed environments, systems, routines or approaches.

Organization of Power

Power works in the dynamic relationships of everyday life, yet is invisibly organized by the way people conduct everyday occupations in their environment. One can experience power as an inner resource for living, observe power by watching everyday interactions of passivity, assertiveness, aggression, or cooperation, and organize power by establishing routines, policies, standards, and other ways of controlling what is done in everyday situations (Townsend, 1996a).

In Canadian society, power is organized in the policies, legislation, budgets, statistics, standards, protocols and other documents which invisibly control what can and cannot be done in a particular context (Smith, 1990b). Documents both record and display decisions that are invisible until one looks more closely at them. For instance, the categories on assessment forms provide a convenient check list to record information, but they also display decisions about what is and is not important to assess. Similarly, statistical forms create a context that determines how occupational therapists make themselves accountable. Although the decisions have become invisible, someone has determined what information is important to collect and how that information will be used. Decisions about funding, staffing, or quality management are now based mainly on documented information, not on face-to-face negotiation (Sutherland & Fulton, 1994).

Documents which typically control what occupational therapists can do in everyday practice include: admission records, client records, policies, workload data, quality management protocols, budgets, legislation, statistics, job descriptions, insurance reports, recruitment materials, occupational therapy textbooks, accreditation standards, managed care standards, reports, brochures, videotapes, audiotapes, public relations materials, business cards, and more (Townsend, 1996b, 1998). Small changes can be made by thinking about power differently, or by changing everyday practice within the existing context, whereas substantial changes are made by changing the documents that organize power.

CONTEXTUAL FEATURES

Good intentions for enabling occupation can be unwittingly overruled by the context of occupational therapy (Townsend, 1998). Reflection on contextual features helps to explain why occupational therapy practice occurs as it does. Mental health services offer an example where everyday practice is shaped by and also shapes contextual forces such as "changing definitions of mental health", the "growth of community mental health services", and the "relationship of mental health occupational therapy to psychosocial rehabilitation" (CAOT, 1993, pp.15). The 16 contextual features related to four forces of change in Table 2 and below, will vary across cultural groups, regions, and countries.

Table 2: Context of Occupational Therapy

Changing Health and Social Systems
- Health promotion
- Health reform
- Managed programmes
- Privatization

Changing Demographics
- Aging population
- Multicultural diversity
- Poverty
- Underemployment

Changing Professional Knowledge
- Knowledge of enabling
- Knowledge of occupation
- Paradigm shift
- Professional dominance

Changing Societal Values
- Citizen participation
- Gender equity
- Quality of life
- Social inclusiveness

Enabling Occupation: An Occupational Therapy Perspective, CAOT 1997

CHANGING HEALTH AND SOCIAL SYSTEMS
Health Promotion

Ideas about health promotion are creating a context in which health is understood as more than the absence of disease (World Health Organization (WHO), 1978, 1980, 1984, 1986a, 1986b, 1989). Instead, health is defined in relation to lifestyles, the environment, and the organization of health services as well as biology. Three Canadian landmark documents set out principles and components of health promotion: *Ottawa Charter for Health Promotion* (WHO, 1986b); *Achieving Health for All: A Framework for Health Promotion* (Department of National Health & Welfare (DNHW, 1986), and *Mental Health for Canadians: Striking a Balance* (DNHW, 1988a).

People know from their own experience that their health is strongly influenced by what they do in working, playing, and generally living; this common knowledge is gaining support from research which indicates that health improves when people are empowered to direct what they do each day (McKnight, 1989). Based on common sense and scientific knowledge about daily living, health promotion encourages healthy living so that hospital care is a last resort rather than a mainstay of health services. There is also advocacy for the development of health promoting policies and legislation in jurisdictions from education to industrial planning (Labonte, 1989a; 1989b).

Health promotion funding has been very limited, but the idea of health promotion has created a context in which enabling occupation makes sense (Grace, 1991; Lincoln, 1992). For instance, the 1986 document entitled, *Achieving Health for All: A Framework for Health Promotion* calls for self-care and mutual aid in healthy environments (DNHW, 1986). The implementation strategies, which are described as fostering public participation, strengthening community health services, and coordinating healthy public policy, are highly compatible with the participatory, enabling approaches in client-centred occupational therapy (Finlayson & Edwards, 1995; McComas & Carswell, 1994). In a context that supports both physical and mental health promotion, occupational therapists have many opportunities to contribute to wellness and quality of life (CAOT, 1993; Johnson, 1986; Madill, Townsend & Schultz, 1989).

Health Reform

Health reform is sweeping across Canada and many other parts of the World (Health & Welfare Canada, 1993; Rachlis & Kushner, 1992; Sutherland & Fulton, 1994). One of the trends is the re-organization of discipline-specific services into programmes which emphasize team work; another is the decentralization of responsibility for service delivery by the creation of regional bodies (Kieser & Wilson, 1995). In health services, the number of managers is being reduced and services are being privatized if they are not seen to be medical necessities. Trends to shift from institutional to community services are accelerating (Bassett, 1975; Canadian Hospital Association, 1993). The shift is moving health professionals from individualized services to community development, as hospital services focus on acute medical needs (Labonte, 1993).

There are many contradictions in health reform. On the one hand, health reform has created a context in which client-centred, family-centred, and other participatory approaches are favoured. Family involvement is seen to enhance healing, and to speed the transition from illness to wellness. There is also an increasing concern with community living and the quality of life. Citizen participation, personal responsibility, and family caregiving are emphasized as ways of reducing dependence on professionals. To address these issues, the International Classification of Impairments, Disabilities, and Handicaps (ICIDH) developed an internationally recognized system that brings daily living problems into public view (Townsend, Ryan, & Law, 1990; WHO, 1980). On the other hand, there are concerns that caregiving duties fall primarily to women. For instance, some women who have children or partners with disabilities are having to change their employment (and economic) situation in order to provide services which have previously been available from professionals. Home care and other community services are positive alternatives, but only small amounts of hospital funding have been transferred to the community (Alberta Health, 1994).

Health reform's emphasis on holistic approaches and community services creates a very positive context in which occupational therapists can show leadership (Brintnell, 1985; CAOT, 1994b; Carswell-Opzoomer, 1990) Holistic approaches are not only basic to occupational therapy but they are being incorporated so that the whole person is involved in prioritizing and documenting his or her occupational performance issues (Fearing, 1993;

McColl, 1994). The challenge of health reform for occupational therapists is to educate clients, the public and potential funders about the importance of funding programmes which address occupational performance through client-centred approaches.

Managed Programmes

Many fields, including health, are adopting systems for managing programmes rather than disciplines (Baptiste, 1993a, 1993b). In medical settings, managed programmes tend to be described as client-centred, client-driven, patient-focused or family-focused, and are known as Programme Management, Product Line Management, Case Management, or Managed Care. Case coordination, sometimes called case management, is the process used to coordinate and integrate individualized services. The term *case coordination* is preferable to case management since it conveys an enabling rather than a controlling approach. Important driving forces in introducing managed programmes are demands for efficiency, coordination, quality improvement and accountability (Appel, 1991). Also emphasized are standardization, integration, multi-skilled work forces, role blurring, site-based planning, and localized decision making with centralized budget control (Health & Welfare Canada, 1993).

There are both cautions and opportunities for occupational therapists in a context of managed programmes (Chilton, 1990). Occupational therapists need to be very careful to articulate why occupational therapy is included. What occupational therapists do looks simple even though occupational therapy knowledge is complex (Mattingly & Hayes Fleming, 1994). While the consumer focus and holistic approach are compatible with occupational therapy's client-centred practice, standardized protocols, policies and funding lack the flexibility needed to address the complex, diverse issues in enabling occupation. Yet, client-centred case coordination is well suited to occupational therapy (Krupa & Clark, 1995). The conceptual framework of occupational performance in a client-centred practice gives occupational therapists a very practical, integrated view of holistic, active people choosing and engaging in occupations in their environment. Occupational therapists who pursue excellence in enabling occupation, articulate the core concepts which direct their practice, and build flexibility into management processes, appear to be in great demand.

Privatization

The world is changing so that nations are losing control of their economies to global corporations which are using low cost human and natural resources in places other than Canada (Reich, 1991). For example, international free trade arrangements, such as the North American Free Trade Agreement (NAFTA), are decreasing national control over the generation and use of capital. As a result, Canada and other Western nations are losing the taxation revenue needed for public services such as health and social welfare.

As government funds decrease, public services are privatized. On the positive side, privatization offers efficiencies, flexibility and a consumer focus, features that are not always present in publicly-funded programmes. Nevertheless, some people are concerned that privatization is placing the agenda for health and other social programmes under private rather than public control. For occupational therapists, private business can create ethical and moral dilemmas when the need to make a living is pitted against other client needs. Dilemmas arise when private services exclude vulnerable people, such as those with disabilities or social disadvantages, who have traditionally been an important part of occupational therapy's clientele. Although concerns are important to address, privatization is opening many new doors for occupational therapists to enable occupation through consulting, educational, management or other businesses.

CHANGING PROFESSIONAL KNOWLEDGE
Knowledge of Enabling

Knowledge of enabling is contrasted here with knowledge about treatment and caregiving (see also Chapter 3). Enablement refers to helping approaches that involve people as active agents in learning to help themselves (Dunst, Trivette, Boyd, & Brookfield, 1994; Florin, & Wandersman, 1990; Kidd, 1973). The emphasis is on participation, collaboration, partnership, reflection, experiential learning, and related actions. In enabling approaches, helpers work with people, in contrast to treatment and caregiving approaches in which something is done to or for people (Lloyd & Maas, 1993; Townsend, 1998). Knowledge of enabling is a contextual feature that supports involvement over caregiving, empowerment over dependence.

The 21st century is approaching as a time for personal and community responsibility rather than dependence on governments or professional experts (Labonte, 1989a). Knowledge of enabling is proving to be invaluable, as people with disabilities and chronic illnesses, elderly people, youth, underemployed people, and many others want to gain control over their lives (Deegan & Brooks, 1985; Sherr Klein, 1995). In some situations, professionals who use enabling approaches may be viewed as lacking knowledge when they do not provide ready answers. However, top-down, authoritative approaches reduce motivation, increase dependence and are increasingly being met with resistance from the Canadian public. Enabling approaches which share power between professionals and their clients promote health because they also promote empowerment (Katz, 1984; Labonte, 1986; McKnight; 1989).

Occupational therapists' ideas about enabling are implicitly if not explicitly embedded in client-centred practice (Polatajko, 1992; Townsend, 1993a). Besides, participation has always been a trademark of occupational therapy. With almost two decades of commitment to client-centred practice, occupational therapy is a profession that can demonstrate how to use knowledge of enabling in practice (Polatajko, 1994; Yerxa, 1994).

Knowledge of Occupation

Occupational therapists have a broad understanding of occupation in a context where the term is popularly equated with jobs (Braverman, 1974). A powerful classification system, the National Occupational Classification (NOC) (Employment and Immigration Canada Staff, 1993), includes only those occupations which receive pay in the market place. The NOC excludes many occupations, such as parenting, home gardening, helping neighbours, or reading books. These occupations are recognized officially if they are re-defined as service jobs. In contrast to this official view of occupation, there is considerable common knowledge of occupation as in references to the importance of being occupied, or of retired people having a worthwhile occupation. Historically, it was common to ask about a person's main occupations in life without restricting the question to paid work.

In these changing economic and social times, youth, elderly people, people with disabilities, families, and others are seeking satisfying occupations. There is an awareness that doing, i.e., participation, is crucial to learning and empowerment (Bateson, 1989; Brosio, 1990), while occupation has been studied more in the context of labour, i.e., jobs, knowledge about occupation in relation to daily function is expanding (Bondar, 1990; Marx, 1943/1970; Toulmin, 1995). Besides being of concern to occupational therapy, occupation is of concern in fields as diverse as anthropology, economics, history, leisure, organizational management, political science, physiology, psychology, recreation and sociology.

Today, occupational therapists are generating knowledge of occupation for organizing time, creating balance, fulfilling particular purposes, prompting human development, expressing spirituality, coping with change, developing ability, enhancing performance, building competence, adapting the built environment, responding to stress, and transforming oppressive situations (see Chapter 3). Occupation is being explored as the day-to-day basis for quality of life, wellness, empowerment, and social equity. A significant body of knowledge is growing in occupational therapy for addressing problems and barriers in occupation - how to enable people to go forward when something goes wrong with occupational performance, occupational roles, or other elements of occupation (Creighton, 1992; Fossy, 1992). Overall a broad view of occupation is becoming very relevant in society (Yerxa, 1967, 1991, 1994; Yerxa et al., 1990).

Paradigm Shift

Kuhn is often cited with reference to the concept of a paradigm, a set of beliefs about what can be known (Guba, 1990). He made us aware that each paradigm develops a different body of knowledge and different ways of proceeding in everyday life (Kuhn, 1970). The prevailing paradigm is a contextual feature that determines how clients and occupational therapists can proceed in everyday situations.

Three main paradigms are associated with knowledge in the Western world (Bernstein, 1983; Frankel & Dye, 1991). The dominant paradigm since the Enlightenment has been Positivism, the theory and practice of empirical science. The emphasis is on objectivity and quantitative measurement as a basis for understanding and changing both humans and the natural environment. Positivist science operates through controlled experimentation to test hypotheses. Hierarchical classification systems create a hierarchical order of knowledge, which is reflected in practice. As an example, medical science ranks biomedical knowledge of disease higher, i.e., more powerful and important, than knowledge of adaptation and change in daily living (Forget, 1983).

Another way of thinking is expressed in Interpretive Social Science. Although this way of thinking has a long history, interest in Interpretive Social Science has been growing in the later part of the 20th century. Interpretive approaches recognize the importance of subjective experience, narrative reasoning, and multiple perspectives. Qualitative approaches are used to explore human relationships, intersubjective experiences, or other aspects of human existence that cannot be measured truthfully. The purpose is to develop grounded theory or interpretations about human experience (Krefting, 1989; Strauss & Corbin, 1990).

A third paradigm is Critical Social Science, sometimes associated with Constructivism (Guba & Lincoln, 1989). This is the science of critique. Rather than focusing on individuals, critical social science examines how systems shape and are shaped by everyday life, and either support or limit enlightenment, empowerment, and emancipation (Fay, 1987; Freire, 1985; Habermas, 1984). A critical analysis may examine everyday experience, statistics or policies with the purpose of explaining why some people are alienated or powerless while others remain dominant. The purpose of critique is to raise consciousness and to spark social change in the structure and organization of society, such as in health services. As a rule, critical analyses explore questions of discrimination related to disability, age, gender, race, social class, sexual orientation, religion or ethnicity, in light of an ideal of social equity.

A major paradigm shift is underway in the late 20th century as seen in trends to value qualitative as well as quantitative research, and to emphasize holistic as well as technical knowledge (Franklin, 1990). Positivist, empirical science is no longer viewed as the only legitimate science, and concerns are being expressed about the mechanistic and reductionistic approaches of empirical science. Interpretive and critical social sciences are on the rise as it becomes clear that empirical science cannot satisfactorily answer all questions.

As a profession that aims to be client-centred, and to attend to real problems in daily occupations, occupational therapy can show leadership in the paradigm shift. Occupational therapists understand the importance of measurement while also holding beliefs and values that are consistent with interpretive and critical social sciences (see Table 3, Chapter 3). Issues for measuring occupational performance and occupational therapy have been well described (Law, 1987; Law et al, 1994; Ottenbacher, 1986). Yerxa in particular has long advocated the use of narrative and other qualitative approaches in occupational therapy (1967, 1979, 1991). Now qualitative methods which draw on Interpretive Social Science are being used in assessment and research (Helfrich, Kielhofner, & Mattingly, 1994; Krefting, 1989; Mattingly & Hayes Fleming, 1994; Spencer, Krefting, & Mattingly, 1993). Occupational therapists are also developing critiques of empowerment for clients and occupational therapists (Ellek, 1991; Frank, 1992; Kari & Michels, 1991; Pizzi, 1992; Townsend, 1993a, 1996b, 1998).

Professional Dominance

Professionalization has created a practice context that is generally characterized by professional dominance (Navarro, 1986). Professional control over education, credentials, and standards make professional expertise elite, prestigious and more powerful than the expertise that people develop through real life experience (Freidson, 1986; Pinderhughes, 1983, 1989). Typically, professionals have the power to determine who has access to services, and to define policies and programmes (Butterill, O'Hanlon, & Book, 1992; Illich, Zola, McNight, Caplan, & Shaiken, 1977). Official documentation is generally done by professionals who can decide whether or not to include client interpretations and perceptions (Fisher & Todd, 1986).

In the major institutions of health services, education, social services and employment, professional dominance is sustained by hierarchical practices (Hearn, 1982). An example is that medicine is more dominant in the hierarchy of health services than other health professions (Crompton, 1987). Hierarchies also make professionals dominant over clients so that they are dependent on professionals rather than being collaborating partners (Moyers, 1991).

The context of professional dominance is particularly important for occupational therapists to consider if client-centred practice is to become more pervasive (Donovan & Blake, 1992; Sumsion, 1993). Clients have said that occupational therapists dominate them with little awareness of how dominant they are (Abberley, 1995; Sherr Klein, 1995). However, occupational therapists face difficulties in shifting processes of dominance with clients since this profession is itself dominated by other professions (O'Shea, 1977; Parham, 1987). The tendency towards professional dominance makes it imperative for occupational therapists to become aware of power in their relationships with individual and organizational clients (Sherr Klein, 1995). Certainly occupational therapy's 20 years of history of advocating client-centred practice provides an important framework and incentive to move beyond professional dominance.

CHANGING DEMOGRAPHICS
Aging Population
The Canadian population is aging, the fastest growing age group being persons over 85 years (Macpherson, 1995; Schulz & Ewen, 1993). By the year 2020 there will be more people who are 85 years than 14 years old, meaning that there will be more seniors than young people. In Canada, approximately 75% of persons over 65 years are well and living without special assistance in the community; the other 25% are considered to be frail (Rockwood, Fox, Stobe, Robertson, & Beattie, 1994). Frail people are functionally dependent for some type of practical help (Raphael et al., 1995). Of these seniors, 10% may live in long-term care facilities. At issue here is the quality of life of seniors. It is important that seniors sustain active participation in self-care, leisure and productive occupations in whatever ways they can inside and outside special facilities. Seniors also need opportunities to choose occupations which are within their capabilities and resources, and which give meaning to their life.

This demographic shift has major implications for occupational therapists. There are many occupational therapy services that can help both well and frail elderly people (Bowlby, 1993; Judd, 1982). Occupational therapists are needed to enable seniors to engage in meaningful occupations even though their abilities are changing (Bondar & Wagner, 1994). Seniors are increasingly vocal about their needs and resist being viewed as a homogeneous group. Where appropriate, occupational therapists can advocate as allies with Grey Power and other organizations (Crabtree & Caron-Parker, 1991). Alternately, occupational therapists can educate the caregivers of seniors in the purpose and importance of adapting homes and seniors' residences so that they can sustain some involvement in meaningful occupations. Especially important is an emphasis on being client-centred even as people lose mental or physical ability.

Multicultural Diversity
Canada espouses a multicultural ethic that seeks to make services such as occupational therapy accessible and relevant to all cultural groups. Aboriginal peoples are increasingly making their needs known. Moreover, immigration policy and changing world conditions have resulted in people from many countries settling in Canada (Dyck, 1989; 1992). Many of these new Canadians are not white nor from European backgrounds, as used to be the case (Dillard et al, 1992). They are faced with adjusting to a different social, economic and political world. In occupational therapy practice, multicultural issues are interconnected with the culture of disability, and with cultural views on aging and social disadvantage

(Brisenden, 1990). These demographic changes require occupational therapists to reflect on the cultural implications of this profession's core concepts (Schusky & Cullbert, 1987).

Occupation is a highly cultural concept, with meanings of specific occupations differing with respect to culture and age. Moreover, culture is fluid and ever changing so that there is an ongoing cultural transformation of society (Khoo & Renwick, 1989). The meanings people give to particular occupations will be derived from their cultural world views and from their experiences of immigration and colonialism (Baptiste, 1988). As occupational therapists explore cultural variations in the meaning and perceived roles of occupation in everyday life, new opportunities will arise for addressing occupation in relation to differing views of health (Paul, 1995).

Client-centred practice, like occupation, is a cultural concept, and is based on the idea of active client participation and shared power between clients and professionals. Cultural values will determine how individuals, families or organizations participate with occupational therapists. For instance, some people may have greater authority than others in seeking health services. In addition, Canadian occupational therapists have traditionally been socialized to value individualized approaches based on clients' self-directed goals, whereas many situations may require community approaches based on goals that emphasize interdependence. Since concepts about the importance of individuals versus communities vary culturally, groups or communities may challenge occupational therapists to rethink traditional frames of reference, goals and methods (DeMars, 1992; Dyck,1993; Wieringa & McColl, 1987).

A multicultural context offers tremendous opportunities for occupational therapists to develop culturally diverse practices, or to specialize in working within a particular cultural milieu. Awareness of multiculturalism will help occupational therapists to advocate for flexibility and diversity rather than standardization, particularly in managed programmes. Another advantage of a multicultural context is that it prompts occupational therapists to critically evaluate their personal and professional assumptions about culture.

Poverty

An increasing number of people in Canada are facing poverty which impinges on their health (Cohen, 1994; Reutter, 1995). To some extent, poverty is fuelled by technologies that reduce the need to pay people for certain occupations. Poverty cannot be relieved by individuals, groups or even governments acting in isolation (Labonte, 1986, 1989a; O'Connor, 1989). Health, social and economic reforms create a context that emphasizes economic production despite individual, group and government efforts to relieve poverty (Navarro, 1991).

Poverty is addressed to some extent through corporate philanthropy and social programmes for those who demonstrate serious needs. As well, community volunteers raise funds for food banks or special projects. Certainly, these efforts are important because they demonstrate kindness and concern for others, and they protect people from the worst effects of poverty. The problem is that those who receive this type of assistance are dependent on others to help them. Rather than creating a fair society, handouts, social programmes and volunteer efforts keep those who are poor, even more dependent (Labour Participation Advisory Committee, 1993; Whitmore & Kerans, 1988).

In the context of growing poverty, occupational therapists are challenged to help communities move away from dependence on this type of help. It makes sense for occupational therapists to develop client-centred approaches that enable people to reduce their own poverty. Poverty creates a context that calls occupational therapists to enable people with little means to participate more fully in public decision making (Alberta Premier's Council On The Status Of Persons With Disabilities, 1995). Although this issue may not directly concern some occupational therapy clients, many clients who are aging or have disabilities live in poverty (Human Resources Development, 1994). A well defined role is emerging for addressing poverty as occupational therapists work with both individual clients who live on social assistance, and with agency personnel such as boarding home owners (Babiski, Sidle & McColl, 1996). As with each contextual feature, change in poverty requires collective, community approaches which build on the talents of the individuals involved.

Underemployment

Global economies are changing employment patterns with the result that western societies are facing massive underemployment. In part, traditional employment patterns are shifting away from resource-based industries to technology and service industries (Beck, 1992). As well, technological changes and competition in power, telephone and other infrastructure services have changed employment opportunities. Some managers and professionals are losing their employment alongside unskilled workers, with work intensifying for some people while others are at a loss for something meaningful to do, making them too busy or underemployed (Reich, 1991). One response has been to turn hobbies into paid work, and to create new services that address today's personal and community needs. Those who are underemployed for long periods of time experience psycho-emotional as well as physical impacts, with the impact affecting the soul as well as the body (Mason & Boutilier, 1995).

Society could benefit from occupational therapists' knowledge of occupational performance and enabling approaches in addressing underemployment. Occupational therapists could enable individuals and communities to make personal and environmental changes which would enhance social as well as economic productivity. For instance, occupational therapists could use their knowledge of coping, balancing occupations, and finding meaning in daily occupation to facilitate communities which are seeking new employment ideas. In a context where underemployment and unemployment are prevalent, occupational therapists could enable community partnerships, such as bringing together bankers, managers, workers and underemployed people to generate ideas for employment.

CHANGING SOCIETAL VALUES
Citizen Participation

Throughout Canada as well as the rest of the world, there are many examples of people wanting to participate in shaping their own lives (Coady, 1939; Freire, 1985): women are seeking participation in decisions about their health (Belenky, Clinchy, Goldberger, & Tarule, 1986); seniors are participating in decisions to increase the types of housing, recreation, and family options available to them (Hubbard et al., 1992; Kari & Michels, 1991); and workers are seeking participation with management in determining everything from wages to the investment of profits (Beck, 1992). Besides, people with disabilities are redefining their place in society, and advocating for independent living rather than rehabilitation (Active Living Alliance for Canadians with a Disability, 1995; Canadian Association of Independent Living Centres, 1992; De Jong, 1993; Status of Disabled Persons Secretariat, 1991; Walters & Ternette, 1994).

The increase in citizen participation in Canada is producing self-help and mutual aid approaches that put decision-making control in the hands of citizens. With the support of self-help groups, people are learning to help themselves and each other, and to participate more in their relationships with professionals (Banks, 1987; Katz & Bender, 1987; Powell, 1987). Self-help and mutual aid approaches recognize subjective knowledge based on experience, and they question expert professional knowledge. When citizens participate in self-help and mutual aid approaches, they reap many personal, economic and social benefits (Scott, 1992; Sherr Klein, 1995; Warner & Polak, 1995).

In Canadian health services, health promotion emphasizes participaction, the idea that health is enhanced through active physical participation. With participation has come an emphasis on collaboration between consumers and professionals in health services (George, 1990; Health & Welfare Canada, 1993). Mental health services have been particularly adamant in stressing the importance of consumer participation (DNHW, 1988a; CAOT, 1993; Rose & Black, 1985; Woodside, 1991). Although some people in health services need to be looked after, others are seeking ways to participate in shaping their own lives (Jongbloed & Crichton, 1990a). In this context, occupational therapy has tremendous opportunities to show leadership, as citizen participation is not new in occupational therapy, nor is it an add-on; rather it is the basis of client-centred practice.

Gender Equity

Gender equity refers to fairness in opportunities for men and women, whereas gender equality describes an equal relationship but does not necessarily account for differences in opportunity (Hare-Mustin & Marecek, 1988). To varying degrees in Canada and elsewhere, women are developing their own voice and raising awareness of women's invisible work (Daniels, 1987). There is also growing awareness of invisible elements of the masculine experience (Kimmel, 1993). Issues around gender equity differ from community to community, family to family, and individual to individual, depending on the cultural context.

Gender equity is a contextual feature of great relevance to occupational therapy. Client-centred practice respects the worth of all persons regardless of gender or other characteristics. Ideally, all clients have equal access to quality health, social, education and other services. Besides, occupational therapists' broad view of occupation is consistent with the broad view of unpaid and paid work put forward by those who are advocating for gender equity (Primeau, 1992; Wharton, 1994). In other words, the Canadian Model of Occupational Performance (Chapter 3) provides a reference point for discussing gender equity in terms of occupation.

Gender equity is also relevant since approximately 95% of Canadian occupational therapists are female, even though the work of enabling occupation is not gender specific. Occupational therapy is not women's work, as demonstrated in some African, Asian and other countries where most occupational therapists are men. In other words, the gender distribution in occupational therapy is influenced more by culture and economics than by the nature of the work itself (Reece, 1987). Until recently, salaries and career opportunities for Canadian occupational therapists have been limited, and thus less attractive to men (Readman, 1992; Turgeon & Hay, 1994). Besides, occupational therapy has developed mostly in the patriarchal world of medicine where males were more likely to become physicians (Frank, 1992). All told, gender is an issue related to the empowerment of occupational therapy as a profession which is still viewed as largely attractive to females (Litterst, 1992). In a context like Canada, where gender equity is a public issue, one might see a more equal number of female and male occupational therapists. In fact, the percentage of male occupational therapists in Canada is slowly increasing from 4% in 1988 to 5.25% in 1995 (CAOT, 1989, 1996h).

Quality of Life

There is increasing concern for quality of life in Canada (Renwick, Brown, & Nagler, 1996). Quality is typically defined with reference to people having choice and control in their lives, and having goals that they define as meaningful. Quality of life is also defined as having the power to participate in important personal and community decisions (Alberta Health, 1994). To some extent, the North American concern for quality of life is fostered by medical technologies that can preserve a quantity of life that may have little quality, at the same time that people are increasingly seeking a life with occupations that have meaning.

Those interested in quality of life are often concerned with spirituality (Blazer, 1991). Meaningful occupation is important in the spiritual aspects of life, as occupation allows self-expression and connection with others, while assisting in the making of meaning in everyday life (Egan & DeLaat, 1994; Urbanowski & Vargo, 1994). It seems that quality of life depends on individuals and cultural communities recognizing the spiritual element of occupations. Concerns for quality of life create a context in which meaningful occupations are being recognized as an important foundation for living, and client-centred approaches are valued by those who want more control in their lives and communities.

Social Inclusiveness

Social inclusiveness is an issue of legal and human rights, and refers to people having fair opportunities in society regardless of ability, gender or other defining characteristics (Young, 1990). There is an increase in social inclusiveness when people who have been segregated are included as participants and leaders in their communities (Alberta Premier's Council On The Status Of Persons With Disabilities, 1995; Kuyek, 1990).

A strong force for social inclusiveness is the Canadian Charter of Rights and Freedoms (Government of Canada, 1982). Disadvantaged groups, such as people with disabilities and seniors, have been able to use the Charter to advocate against discriminatory policies, and in favour of greater opportunity. With this legislation, individual rights, worth and respect have been given legal standing in Canada (Kyserlink, 1985).

The idea of social inclusiveness has helped people with physical, mental, and learning disabilities to reject demeaning or stigmatizing labels (Deegan & Brooks, 1985; De Jong, 1979). For example, rather than referring to people as crazy, there is an emphasis on referring to people with mental health problems; people who have been described as crippled are asking to be called people with physical disabilities or people who are physically challenged; and, those who have been labelled as stupid or lazy are raising awareness that they are people with learning disabilities or learning challenges (Active Living Alliance for Canadians with a Disability, 1995). These and other groups also want to remove dehumanizing labels which treat them as objects, as in the mentally retarded, the disabled, and the elderly. Instead, they want to be known as people first, with descriptors added only if these are necessary or appropriate in specific situations.

Occupational therapists stress the worth of each individual and recognize the importance of accessible, supportive environments (CAOT, 1991; Law, 1991). They also foster connectedness and belonging by including those who are marginalized in some way, as well as other people in meaningful occupations (Townsend, 1998). This is a profession which has declared its commitment to building inclusive communities where all people can realize their potential (Grady, 1995). When occupational therapists enable individuals to improve their occupational performance, they are indirectly preparing them to be more integrated in their communities, whereas advocacy for social integration policies and programmes directly promotes social inclusiveness (Jongbloed & Crichton, 1990b). Occupational therapists who work towards social inclusiveness can do so most effectively by strengthening alliances with people who have been socially excluded (Sherr Klein, 1995).

Occupational Therapy Concepts and Practice

PART II

CHAPTER THREE

Core Concepts of Occupational Therapy

PRIMARY AUTHORS:
Mary Law
Helen Polatajko
Sue Baptiste
Elizabeth Townsend

Purpose

To present core values, beliefs, and concepts of occupational therapy.

Objectives

To present an occupational therapy perspective on:
- Values and beliefs about occupational therapy;
- The Canadian Model of Occupational Performance;
- Client-centred practice.

Summary

Occupational therapy is a health profession which makes an important contribution to the everyday lives of Canadians. Members of this profession possess an occupational and client-centred perspective based on a particular set of values and beliefs. The profession's concern is for the occupational needs of individuals and society. Occupational needs are everything people need to do to look after themselves and others, enjoy life, and contribute to the social and economic fabric of their communities. A new Canadian Model of Occupational Performance (CMOP) illustrates the relationship between persons, their environment and occupation. The new Model provides a direction for addressing occupational needs through client-centred practice with individuals, groups, agencies, organizations and other clients. In occupational therapy, client-centred practice means that occupational therapists and clients collaborate to meet occupational performance goals that clients define as meaningful.

OCCUPATIONAL THERAPY VALUES AND BELIEFS

$\mathcal{O}$ccupational Therapy Values and Beliefs (Table 3) underpin a perspective on occupational performance and client-centred practice. From this perspective, the primary role of occupational therapy is that of enabling occupation. Occupation is everything people do to occupy themselves, including looking after themselves (self-care), enjoying life (leisure), and contributing to the social and economic fabric of their communities (productivity). Enabling occupation means collaborating with people to choose, organize and perform occupations which people find useful or meaningful in a given environment. This primary role of enabling occupation constitutes a necessary and sufficient condition for the practice of occupational therapy. Enabling change in performance components and elements of the environment is thus a secondary role.

Occupational therapy's client-centred practice is described as promoting health by enabling occupation (Polatajko, 1992). Enabling occupation contributes to the empowerment of those with limited occupational performance (Townsend, 1993a). Through collaborative partnerships, occupational therapists enable persons to achieve satisfactory performance in occupations of their choice. The emphasis is on enabling occupation with clients rather than doing things for clients. In working with people, occupational therapists recognize the dynamic relationship between persons, environments and occupation (Law et al., 1996). Changes in any of these areas will influence a person's performance in, and satisfaction with their occupations.

CANADIAN MODEL OF OCCUPATIONAL PERFORMANCE

Occupational performance is the result of a dynamic relationship between persons, environment, and occupation over a person's lifespan.

> **Occupational performance refers to the ability to choose, organize, and satisfactorily perform meaningful occupations that are culturally defined and age appropriate for looking after one's self, enjoying life, and contributing to the social and economic fabric of a community.**

Over the past two decades Canadian occupational therapists have developed a particular perspective on occupational performance. An early conception of occupational performance describes the therapeutic use of activity in a client-centred framework (DNHW & CAOT, 1983). Occupational performance was depicted in three concentric circles. Four performance components of persons, including spirituality, were in the centre circle and areas of occupation were in the middle circle. Elements of the environment were in the outside circle. Problems with this model included: occupational performance looked static; the environment appeared to be external and unconnected to the person; and spirituality was

Table 3: Occupational Therapy Values and Beliefs

About occupation,
We believe that:
- occupation gives meaning to life
- occupation is an important determinant of health and wellbeing
- occupation organizes behaviour
- occupation develops and changes over a lifetime
- occupation shapes and is shaped by environments
- occupation has therapeutic effectiveness

About the person,
We believe that:
- humans are occupational beings
- every person is unique
- every person has intrinsic dignity and worth
- every person can make choices about life
- every person has some capacity for self-determination
- every person has some ability to participate in occupations
- every person has some potential to change
- persons are social and spiritual beings
- persons have diverse abilities for participating in occupations
- persons shape and are shaped by their environment

About the environment,
We believe that:
- environment is a broad term including cultural, institutional, physical and social components
- performance, organization, choice and satisfaction in occupations are determined by the relationship between persons and their environment

About health,
We believe that:
- health is more than the absence of disease
- health is strongly influenced by having choice and control in everyday occupations
- health has personal dimensions associated with spiritual meaning and life satisfaction in occupations and social dimensions associated with fairness and equal opportunity in occupations

About client-centred practice,
We believe that:
- clients have experience and knowledge about their occupations
- clients are active partners in the occupational therapy process
- risk-taking is necessary for positive change
- client-centred practice in occupational therapy focuses on enabling occupation

(Adapted from: Polatajko, 1992; and Law, Baptiste, & Mills, 1995)
Enabling Occupation: An Occupational Therapy Perspective, CAOT 1997

depicted as a performance component, parallel to mental, physical, and socio-cultural performance.

Occupational therapy theory, research and practice are showing that occupational performance is not static as the circles imply. Occupational performance is the result of an interdependent and changing person-environment-occupation relationship (CAOT, 1991; Christiansen & Baum, 1991; Law, 1991; Law et al., 1996; Law, Baptiste & Mills, 1995; Polatajko, 1994). This dynamic interaction exists among people, their occupations and roles, and the environments in which they live, work and play over their lifespan. As knowledge about the dynamic processes involved in occupational performance continues to expand, it is important

Figure 1: Canadian Model of Occupational Performance

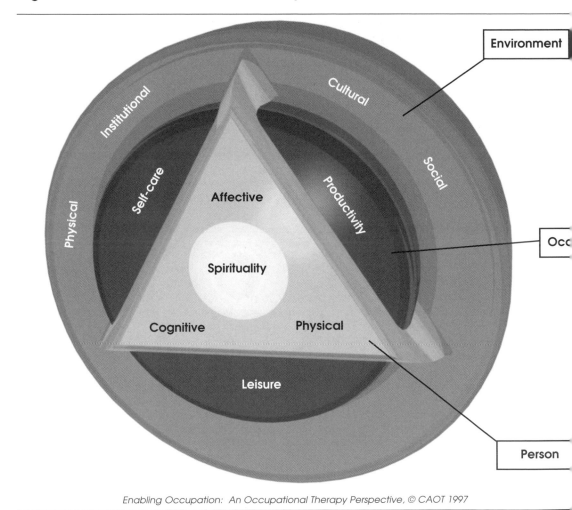

Enabling Occupation: An Occupational Therapy Perspective, © *CAOT 1997*

Chapter 3 - Core Concepts of Occupational Therapy

to incorporate emerging ideas into a new conceptual model for occupational therapy practice (Blain & Townsend, 1993).

The new Canadian Model of Occupational Performance (CMOP) (Figure 1) graphically illustrates an occupational therapy perspective on the dynamic relationship between persons, environment and occupation. The CMOP provides a framework for enabling occupation for all persons. A significant feature of the CMOP is its three-dimensional illustration of the dynamic interdependence between person, environment, and occupation. The person is connected to the environment, and occupation occurs in the interaction between persons and their environment. Change in any aspect of the Model would affect all other aspects. The Canadian Model of Occupational Performance portrays occupational therapy's occupational perspective by highlighting the focus on occupation. Spirituality is embedded as a core in all parts of person-environment-occupation interactions. Spirituality resides in persons, is shaped by the environment, and gives meaning to occupations.

The Canadian Model of Occupational Performance, with a person at its centre, conveys occupational therapy's client-centred perspective. Client-centred practice with individuals attends to the individual's occupational needs in his/her specific environment. Client-centred practice with communities or other organizations attends to occupational needs of groups of persons.

OCCUPATION

As the name implies, occupational therapy is concerned with what people do in their environment - namely occupation. The word occupation derives from the general concept of occupying oneself and seizing control of one's life (Clark et al., 1991). The historical roots of occupational therapy are in occupational work accomplished by occupational aides employed in 19th century mental asylums (Driver, 1968). When the profession of occupational therapy began in the early 20th century, occupation was defined as both the domain of concern and the therapeutic medium of occupational therapy (Dunton, 1919; Meyer, 1922). From the 1940s to the 1980s, both the term and therapeutic use of occupation were rarely used in occupational therapy. The first Canadian occupational therapy guidelines on client-centred practice did not explicitly refer to occupation, but rather to the "therapeutic use of activity" (DNHW & CAOT, 1983, pp.18-19).

The term occupation tends to be used interchangeably by occupational therapists with two other terms: task and activity. Neither term has been consistently defined or precisely used in occupational therapy (Christiansen & Baum, 1991). Task is defined as a set of purposeful activities in which a person engages (Law et al., 1996). An example of a task is writing a report. Activity is the basic unit of a task. An activity is a singular pursuit that contributes to the completion of a task. Activities in the task of writing a report include developing an outline or reviewing the report for coherence. Occupation is much broader than either task or activity. Occupations encompass more than one task, while tasks encompass more than one activity. Whereas tasks or activities may fulfil specific purposes, occupations bring meaning to life.

Despite the efforts of Canadian and other national occupational therapy associations, there is no single definition of occupation that is acceptable to everyone in occupational therapy. Using literature on occupation inside and outside occupational therapy, including dictionary definitions, this document proposes that:

> **Occupation refers to groups of activities and tasks of everyday life, named, organized and given value and meaning by individuals and a culture. Occupation is everything people do to occupy themselves, including looking after themselves (self-care), enjoying life (leisure), and contributing to the social and economic fabric of their communities (productivity).**

The definition proposed here indicates that occupation is more than work. Occupations are any human activities or tasks organized to fulfil a particular function (Clark et al., 1991). Occupations are also described as "chunks of activity within the ongoing stream of human behaviour which are named in the lexicon of the culture" (Yerxa et al., 1990, p.5). Occupation is embedded in life (Clarke, 1993). Occupation is a complex process in which persons fulfil needs and purposes as they interact in their environment. This complexity may not be visible because the meanings, purposes, values and beliefs behind what people do are not directly observable.

Table 4: Key Features of Occupation

Occupation is a:
- basic human need
- determinant of health
- source of meaning
- source of purpose
- source of choice and control
- source of balance and satisfaction
- means of organizing time
- means of organizing materials and space
- means of generating income
- descriptor
- therapeutic medium

Enabling Occupation: An Occupational Therapy Perspective, CAOT 1997

Chapter 3 - Core Concepts of Occupational Therapy

Occupational therapists have a very broad understanding of occupation. Eleven key features of occupation are highlighted in Table 4 and the summaries that follow.

Basic Human Need

Occupational therapists understand that occupation is a basic human need (Wilcock, 1993). An early Credo for Occupational Therapists (Dunton, 1919) states that:

- occupation is as necessary to life as food and drink
- every human being should have both physical and mental occupations
- all should have occupations which they enjoy

In this Credo, occupation is identified as essential to life, to health, and to enjoyment. Ideally, occupations can provide people with a flow experience (Csikszentmihalyi, 1991). Flow is achieved when the demands of an occupation are in harmony with the skills of the person and the environment in which the occupation is performed (Law, 1991). Flow also contributes to a sense of personal resonance in which there is personal growth and expression of the self.

Occupations offer many benefits for the person since individuals engage in various occupations throughout the life span. Occupations serve to organize behaviour, and to enable the expression and management of self-identity, social connectedness and management of time (Laliberte, 1993).

Determinant of Health

Occupational therapy is concerned with occupation in relation to health. Health is viewed in occupational therapy as more than the absence of disease, and is understood to be strongly influenced by what people do in everyday life (CAOT, 1994a). Occupation has been linked with health for centuries. Those with mental health difficulties have been encouraged to work or enjoy themselves in serene places, such as country estates, or segregated places, such as asylums. In the 20th century, occupation was discovered to have a motivating effect or a calming influence on soldiers returning from World War I. Injured soldiers were rehabilitated into meaningful employment through curative workshops that returned them to healthy living.

The Alma Ata Declaration of Health for All by the Year 2000 gave world recognition to the importance of people having the resources and opportunities that provide decent housing, employment, community support, and enjoyment (World Health Organization, 1978). Although the term occupation is not used, this Declaration makes it clear that health depends on people having meaningful occupations which provide them with housing, employment, community and enjoyment. Occupation is recognized implicitly as an important determinant of health.

Source of Meaning

Occupation brings meaning to life. Occupations are meaningful to people when they fulfil a goal or purpose that is personally or culturally important (Egan & DeLaat, 1994). In addition, psychological motivation and volition are dependent on people finding meaning in the occupations that comprise their everyday life (Kielhofner, 1995). The implication is that the occupations that seem meaningful to occupational therapists may fall outside the values and beliefs of their clients.

In occupational therapy, the term activity is often prefaced with the terms meaningful or purposeful. Sometimes this is done to distinguish between those activities that are or are not occupational in nature, i.e., to exclude random involuntary, non-meaningful, non-purposeful activity from the domain of occupation (Nelson, 1988). Sometimes this is done to emphasize the assumption that the therapeutic potency of an activity is directly related to the degree of meaning or purpose an activity holds for a person. The meaning of an occupation is individually and culturally determined.

Meaning differs from purpose in occupation (Ferguson, 1995). Occupations can be meaningful to individuals or groups without the occupations having any identifiable purpose. What is meaningful to some may not be to others even though the occupation fulfils the same purpose. For example, driving a car for employment or visiting neighbours may serve the same purpose for many people, but only some people will find meaning in those occupations.

Source of Purpose

Since occupation is a cultural concept, there is no universal classification of the purpose of occupation. In 1983, Canadian occupational therapists classified three main purposes of occupation: self-care, productivity, and leisure (DNHW & CAOT, 1983) as defined in Table 5. Nevertheless, purpose is determined by individual needs and desires within an environmental context. In addition, occupations take on diverse purposes in different contexts. Using a telephone can be work or leisure, depending on the specific purpose to the client; dental care is typically self-care but is productivity for dental personnel. Therefore, classes of the purpose of occupation are arbitrary. Classification offers a convenient and manageable way of explaining occupation to clients, professionals and others. Classifying purpose also prompts occupational therapists to think about the full range of occupations in a life. Prompting is important in health services where there is a tendency to focus on self-care, and possibly leisure, but to pay less attention to productivity (DNHW & CAOT, 1987; McColl, 1994).

Occupational therapists around the world have adopted differing classes of occupation. For simplicity and familiarity, this document supports the continued use of three classifications of purpose but advocates that they be

Table 5: Purposes of Occupation

Leisure
Occupations for enjoyment. Examples include socializing, creative expressions, outdoor activities, games and sports.

Productivity
Occupations that make a social or economic contribution, or that provide for economic sustenance. Examples include play in infancy and childhood, school work, employment, homemaking, parenting, and community volunteering.

Self-Care
Occupations for looking after the self. Examples include personal care, personal responsibilities, functional mobility and organization of personal space and time.

Enabling Occupation: An Occupational Therapy Perspective, CAOT 1997

used in ways that are culturally appropriate. American occupational therapists, like the Canadians, have adopted three classes of occupation. However, they have named the categories differently: activities of daily living (ADL), work, and play. While this classification seems similar to the Canadian one, the concepts are not synonymous. In particular, productivity occupations are viewed differently than work. In the Canadian classification, productivity in children includes (but is not limited to) play and school work. Productivity in adults includes employment, housework, or parenting. Productivity in seniors includes volunteer work, grand parenting, or hobbies. A fourth class of occupation has been suggested in Canada as community-building (Banks, 1991). Australian occupational therapists identify occupations as work, activity, self-care, leisure, play and rest (Australian Association of Occupational Therapists, 1994, p.1).

Source of Choice and Control

Occupations are more likely to be effective if they give the person a sense of control and fit the personal and environmental resources of the individual (Laliberte, 1993; MacGregor, 1995). People have choice, and can exercise control in their life, when they have opportunities to decide what they will do. People can express choice by deciding whether to continue, change or stop what they are doing. Locations, timing, scheduling, resources and organization are all aspects of occupation that offer choice.

Control is more than choice. People may make choices about their occupations but have little control to act on choices. There is an element of personal control when people show persistence or find creative ways of following up on their choices. Control is dependent on opportunities provided by the environment (Townsend, 1998). For example, some people may choose the occupation of skiing but they need snow to act on that choice. Others may choose to be welders but can only do so if the training programme fits their budget, schedule and family circumstance, and if the requirements for admission recognize their background experience and personal characteristics.

Source of Balance and Satisfaction

Balance in occupations refers to the pattern of occupation over days or years (Bateson, 1989; Csikszentmihalyi, 1991). Personal experiences of satisfaction or fulfilment are strongly linked to the organization of time throughout life. Balance is not a mathematical division of life into equal, eight-hour parts of self-care, productivity and leisure in all stages of life. A student might experience balance if there is a small amount of time for self-care and leisure and sufficient time to excel in school work. A retiree might experience balance if a few hours of time are spent in community volunteer occupations that satisfy needs to feel productive.

Personal views on balance are influenced by cultural and other environmental expectations. Work-oriented cultures encourage people to balance their lives by spending large amounts of time on productivity, with less time for leisure. The opposite is true in cultures where more socialization and leisure are part of a balanced life.

Means of Organizing Time

Through occupations, people organize time into patterns, habits and roles (Kielhofner, 1985, 1992, 1995). If one observes those who lose their employment, retire, or take on new routines, it is clear that changes in temporal patterns of occupation have an important effect on people's lives (Peloquin, 1991). Ideally, time is organized so that people look after themselves, enjoy life, and contribute to the social and economic fabric of their communities.

Time is organized to emphasize different occupations over the life course (Laliberte, 1993). For example, early life stages are usually characterized by play, then schooling. In adolescence, time for social occupations with peers is important. Adults may organize time around employment, parenting, homemaking, and other occupations for productivity. Later in life, time may be organized to emphasize personal care, family, and community volunteer occupations.

Means of Organizing Materials and Space

Besides organizing time, people organize the materials and space for their occupations. Since occupations involve doing, they occur in what is described as the material conditions of life - using materials and equipment in time and space (Marx, 1943/1970). Materials refer to the tools, technology, substances, facilities or other aspects of the physical environment in which occupations are done. Occupations are a means of organizing space, in that certain occupations require specific locations and equipment. From work spaces to sports arenas, space is organized into facilities that have specific purposes; locations are further organized into rooms or compartments, then into areas. Persons organize space by choosing and organizing their immediate or broad surroundings. The organization of space can itself be an occupation involving design, construction and decoration.

Conversely, the organization of space determines what occupations can and cannot be done. Space is organized in part by ideas and attitudes about how it is best used. Ideas and attitudes are embedded in funding, policies and regulations about the use of space in buildings, parks or other locations. For occupations to be performed satisfactorily, it is necessary to select materials and locations, and analyze how space can be used or adapted.

Means of Generating Income

Occupational therapists know that occupation is more than work and more than a means of generating income. For instance, occupation contributes to health, gives life a sense of meaning, fulfils various purposes, and organizes time and space. Nevertheless, some occupations are a means of generating income. Each culture names and gives an economic value to occupations. Occupations which generate income in an industrial society are largely those that produce manufactured goods. In contrast, agrarian societies value the occupations required to manage the land and animals which sustain life.

Those who are paid for their performance of occupations generate income through their employment. Some occupations may generate economic value that is not counted as part of the formal economy (Toulmin, 1995). An example is the informal, local economy that operates by trading baby sitting labour amongst families and neighbours, or the informal trading practices of aboriginal peoples. Other occupations, particularly those in the National Occupational Classification, become part of local, national, and international markets (Employment and Immigration Canada Staff, 1993).

Descriptor

Occupation can be used as a descriptor of human behaviours to provide new perspectives about occupation. For example, occupational therapists are concerned with occupation and development, but when one talks about occupational development, development is given a new quality, and occupation is seen from a new perspective.

Table 6 describes five examples which show how occupation is a descriptor: occupational behaviour, occupational competence, occupational development, occupational performance, and occupational function. Each represents a different aspect of occupation and evokes a different orientation and focus.

Table 6: Occupation as a Descriptor

Occupational...

Behaviour	is that aspect or class of human action that encompasses mental and physical doing
Competence	is adequacy or sufficiency in an occupational skill, meeting all requirements of an environment
Development	is the gradual change in occupational behaviour over time, resulting from the growth and maturation of the individual in interaction with the environment
Performance	is the actual execution or carrying out of an occupation
Function	is the usual or required occupations of an individual

Enabling Occupation: An Occupational Therapy Perspective, CAOT 1997

Therapeutic Medium

Enabling occupation is accomplished by using occupation as a therapeutic medium (Hopkins & Smith, 1988; Kielhofner, 1983, 1995; Meyer, 1922; Reilly, 1962; Yerxa, 1967). The idea that occupation is a therapeutic medium underpins occupational therapy. Assessment of clients' occupational needs and assets enables clients to name, validate and prioritize occupational performance issues (see Chapter 4, Linking Concepts to a Process for Working With Clients). Occupational therapists also analyze the characteristics of occupations as a basis for implementing plans using occupation. Occupational analysis, traditionally described as activity analysis, is a way of identifying the complexity of personal and environmental demands of an occupation (Cynkin, 1979; Cynkin & Robinson, 1990).

Occupational analysis provides information for classifying occupations according to their complexity. Occupations may be designated as simple or complex based on the number of individuals or groups involved. Complexity can also be defined in terms of the time span or duration and diversity of sites in which an occupation occurs, and it increases when there is a multiplicity of methods. For instance, a simpler occupation might be the basic process of bathing for a person whose physical, cognitive, and affective performance components are intact. Simple bathing has few cognitive, affective or physical requirements. There are few tools other than soap, a towel and possibly a wash cloth or sponge. Usually, bathing occurs in a single location. The complexity of bathing increases if there are special personal needs, complex water or bathtub arrangements, or elaborate cultural routines. Occupational therapists use occupational analysis to identify a step-by-step process for planning just-right-challenges for people to engage in occupations in a given environment.

Occupation can be a therapeutic medium with an individual client. An occupational therapist might facilitate client participation in occupational therapy by asking an adolescent female who is unable to concentrate in school to show the occupational therapist what she does best. In other words, the adolescent would be drawn into defining her occupational performance difficulties by demonstrating her current occupational performance in occupations that she has chosen as having some meaning in her life. If the assessment shows that the adolescent has learning difficulties compounded by a disruptive home situation, the occupational therapist and client would analyze occupations that are familiar and meaningful to the adolescent. Sports occupations might be considered if the adolescent indicates that sports are a source of success. Occupational analysis of the learning opportunities, social requirements, and environmental demands of soccer might show this sport to have therapeutic potential in this situation. The occupational therapist might then help the adolescent to work out a schedule for practising soccer while the occupational therapist is present to verbally reward success, to encourage the development of concentration in a sports routine, and to use soccer as a focal point for enhancing family communication. The occupational therapist might gain consent from the adolescent and family to work with the soccer coach so that the team supports the sense of excitement and importance of including this adolescent on the team.

Occupation can also be a therapeutic medium with groups, agency personnel or corporations. For example, an occupational therapist invited to organize a workshop on interpersonal communication for a corporate client could use occupation as a learning medium. The workshop would possibly include a simulated action project that requires communication. Then the group might organize a meeting of managers who are raising controversial issues. A meeting would be used for experiential practice followed by reflection on the positive and difficult communication exhibited during this occupation. The corporation might then request an analysis of the environment. The occupational therapist would examine the cultural, institutional, physical and social barriers to productive occupation for various groups of workers. Occupations would be observed in the workers' environments. Change could then be tried in the workplace.

PERSON

Occupational therapists believe in the worth of all persons, regardless of disability, age, developmental difficulty, or social condition (DNHW & CAOT, 1983, p.16), and have traditionally viewed persons from a holistic framework. The implication of holding this holistic view is that occupational therapists understand how meaningless it is to attend to parts of a person in isolation from other people and from elements of the environment. The new Canadian Model of Occupational Performance presents the person as an integrated whole who incorporates spirituality, social and cultural experiences, and observable occupational performance components. Since socio-cultural performance is shaped by the environment, performance components are defined more simply as feeling, thinking and doing - that is, as affective, cognitive and physical performance. The person is depicted in a dynamic relationship with occupation, and with an environment which now includes an institutional element.

Spirituality

The importance of spirituality has always been highlighted in Canadian occupational therapy views of persons. The original triangular badge worn by early Canadian occupational therapists depicts the integration of mind, body, and spirit (Trent, 1919). Discussions continue about occupational therapy's concern for spirituality. Some occupational therapists recommend removal of spirituality. Others recommend that spirituality be highlighted as a central feature of the person rather than as a performance component (Blain & Townsend, 1993; Egan & DeLaat, 1994; Urbanowski & Vargo, 1994). While discussions continue, guidelines for considering spirituality within the occupational therapy process are offered.

The Canadian Model of Occupational Performance places spirituality as a central core, as the essence of the self. Table 7 outlines key ideas about spirituality. The spirit is seen as our truest self, and as something which we attempt to express in all of our actions (Egan & DeLaat, 1994; Gutterman, 1990). Because people are spiritual beings, each individual is appreciated as a unique person. Recognizing people as spiritual beings means recognizing their intrinsic value and respecting their beliefs, values and goals, regardless of ability, age or other characteristics. When occupations are used as a therapeutic medium, care is taken to ensure that the occupations have relevance and meaning for each client, and that people have opportunities to choose how they will participate in occupations.

"Spiritual means uniquely and truly human" (Frankl, 1988, p.40). It is the manifestation of a higher self, a spiritual direction or greater purpose which nurtures people through life events and choices. How a person chooses to envision this guiding principle depends upon how they evolve as individuals. For some, spirituality is a religious vision, for others it is much less clear, being purely a feeling or sense of meaning. Another way in which to see this distinctly human attribute is to state it as the capacity for self-determination. This idea is illustrated by Zimmerman through the eyes of Heidegger:

> "...the human way of manifesting itself is to be engaged with things, in making and doing and using, and with others, in speaking and acting and sharing, and with oneself in deliberating and thinking and choosing" (Zimmerman, 1990, p.140).

Table 7: Ideas about Spirituality

- innate essence of self
- quality of being uniquely and truly human
- expression of will, drive, motivation
- source of self determination and personal control
- guide for expressing choice

Enabling Occupation: An Occupational Therapy Perspective, CAOT 1997

Spirituality is viewed as the personal experience of meaning in everyday life (Urbanowski & Vargo, 1994). In times of difficulty, individuals face new ways of being and doing. The implication is that personal meaning is important to good quality of life (do Rozario, 1992, 1993, 1994). Occupational therapists explore spirituality by listening to people speak of their lives (Kirsh, 1996), and by reflecting with people on the occupations which held and continue to hold meaning for them.

Consideration of spirituality is a way of developing a clear appreciation for the uniqueness of each person in the occupational therapist-person relationship (Peloquin, 1993). An occupational therapist who considers the spirituality of each person is prompted to reflect on her or his own spirituality, and personal values and beliefs (Egan & DeLaat, 1994; Urbanowski & Vargo, 1994).

Social and Cultural Experience

Social and cultural experiences are important, subjective aspects of life. They influence people's view of themselves, bring meaning to everyday life, and connect people with others in their environment. Social relationships and their cultural context influence a person's family, ethnic, religious, educational, and other experiences. Conversely, people shape their social, cultural, physical and institutional environment as they relate to others. Like spirituality, social and cultural experiences are understood by listening to clients, observing how they go about daily life, and reflecting on the media, statistics, and other documents that are part of a culture.

Performance

Occupational therapists have traditionally attended to the performance components which contribute to successful engagement in occupation. Four performance components have been labelled for over a decade as mental, physical, spiritual and socio-cultural (DNHW & CAOT, 1983).

In keeping with the principles of clarity and shared meaning, this document uses an adaptation of Bloom's Taxonomy: affective, cognitive, and physical performance (Woolfolk & Nicolich, 1980) which are described in Table 8. While three performance components have been

Table 8: Performance Components of a Person

Affective	(feeling) the domain that comprises all social and emotional functions and includes both interpersonal and intrapersonal factors
Cognitive	(thinking) the domain that comprises all mental functions both cognitive and intellectual, and includes, among other things, perception, concentration, memory, comprehension, judgement and reasoning
Physical	(doing) the domain that comprises all sensory, motor and sensori-motor functions

Enabling Occupation: An Occupational Therapy Perspective, CAOT 1997

identified for ease of understanding, it must be remembered that none operates in isolation of the other, and that all three are interdependent (Payne & Isaacs, 1991).

ENVIRONMENT

The term environment is defined as those contexts and situations which occur outside individuals and elicit responses from them (Law, 1991). The environment is the context within which occupational performance takes place.

Several ways of classifying elements of the environment have been created to assist in studying the interaction between individuals and the environment. Shalinsky (1986) describes environmental factors as physical (the built and natural environments), and psychosocial (the psychological and social factors such as attitudes, family and government). This classification is similar to others in which environments have been described as inanimate (physical) and animate (social) (Knapper, Lerner, & Bunting, 1986). Environment can be classified by location, from home to neighbourhood, community, province and country. Alternately, the environment can be classified by attribute, including cultural, institutional, physical and social elements (Law, 1991). Analysis of the influence of specific environmental elements in relationship to environmental location can be used to determine what factors are enabling or hindering occupational performance. As well as considering the external environment, Kaplan (1983) and Baker and Intagliata (1982) have emphasized the internal environment of the individual. They point out that individuals' perceptions, particularly of past experiences, affect their performance.

Occupational therapists' view of the environment has changed over the past 20 years. Relationships between people and the environment are no longer seen to occur in a linear cause-effect direction with the person and environment existing independently of one another. Instead, it is recognized that person, environment and occupation are inseparable. Interactions between persons and their environment are dynamic so that change within any part affects the other parts.

In the past, occupational therapists as well as other health professionals have recognized environmental influences; however, the focus has been on environmental elements within the immediate and intimate environment of the individual. These ideas are changing so that the environment is viewed in a much broader way, to include community, provincial, national and international factors which may need to be changed as part of enabling occupation.

The environment influences occupation, and in turn is influenced by the behaviour of persons acting individually or collectively. The environment is dynamic and can have an enabling or constraining effect on the performance of occupations. Optimal occupational performance requires the ability to balance occupation and views of self and environment that sometimes conflict, and to encompass changing priorities. Over a lifetime, individuals are constantly renegotiating their view of self and their roles as they ascribe meaning to occupation and the environment around them.

Previously, occupational therapists in Canada classified elements of the environment as cultural, physical and social (DNHW & CAOT, 1983). While these three elements remain important, many documents on health indicate that economic, legal and political elements of an environment have a strong influence on everyday life. These last elements have been described collectively as the institutional environment (Bellah, Madson, Sullivan, Swidler, & Tipton, 1991). The Canadian Model of Occupational Performance adopts this term and defines the environment as having cultural, institutional, physical, and social elements (Table 9).

OCCUPATIONAL PERFORMANCE

The Canadian Model of Occupational Performance (Figure 1) is useful for illustrating the connections between persons, the environments in which they live their daily lives, and the occupations which they perform. The result of this relationship, occupational performance, is not visible. Occupational performance is the result of a dynamic relationship between persons, environment and occupation. Occupational performance refers to the ability to choose and satisfactorily perform meaningful occupations that are culturally defined, and appropriate for looking after one's self, enjoying life, and contributing to the social and economic fabric in a community.

A person constantly engages in occupations in interactions with an environment. The environment provides the context within which occupations are accomplished. Occupational performance represents the actual execution or carrying-out of occupation and is the experience of a person engaged in occupation within an environment. There is a natural

---

Table 9: Elements of an Environment

Cultural	ethnic, racial, ceremonial and routine practices, based on ethos and value system of particular groups
Institutional	societal institutions and practices, including policies, decision-making processes, procedures, accessibility and other organizational practices. Includes economic components such as economic services, financial priorities, funding arrangements and employment support; legal components such as legal processes and legal services; and political components such as government-funded services, legislation and political practices
Physical	natural and built surroundings that consist of buildings, roads, gardens, vehicles for transportation, technology, weather, and other materials
Social	social priorities about all elements of the environment, patterns of relationships of people living in an organized community, social groupings based on common interests, values, attitudes and beliefs

Enabling Occupation: An Occupational Therapy Perspective, CAOT 1997

permeability assumed at the boundary points between the person, an environment and occupation. This interaction may or may not create person-environment congruence (Knapper et al., 1986; Michelson, 1976; Shalinsky, 1986). Person-environment congruence suggests the interdependence of human beings and the environment, with neither dominating the other. Compatibility or congruence between persons, their environment, and their occupations helps to ensure optimal occupational performance (Law, 1991).

Using Figure 2, the relationship between persons, their environment, and their occupations can be demonstrated. The person can be highlighted as a focus for change. Change in persons will affect their environment and their occupations and occupational performance. Alternately, occupation or the environment can be highlighted as a focus of change. Change in any part of the person-environment-occupation interaction will affect occupational performance.

Occupational therapists work with clients to enable achievement of individual, group, agency or organizational goals in occupational performance. They analyze the potential for change in each aspect of a person-environment-occupation relationship: components of the person; elements of the environment; and features of occupation. The analysis of occupational performance provides a framework for choosing an effective and efficient course for change.

OCCUPATIONAL LIFE COURSE: A DEVELOPMENTAL PERSPECTIVE

Occupational therapy takes a developmental perspective on the dynamic, evolving interaction between persons, the environment, and occupation. The relationship between persons, the environment and occupation changes over a lifespan in response to the opportunities and challenges that shape each person's occupational life course. In addition, changes occur within persons over time. An enlarging spiral (Figure 3) shows that one's cumulative experience in occupational performance grows over time, even if the number and diversity of occupations diminishes because of aging, disability, environmental change, personal growth, or other circumstances. People expand their repertoire of occupational experience by developing some occupations and abandoning others as long as life continues.

Figure 3 portrays the cumulative experience in an occupational life course as a simple spiral. In reality, an occupational life course is not a simple

---

Figure 2: Occupational Performance

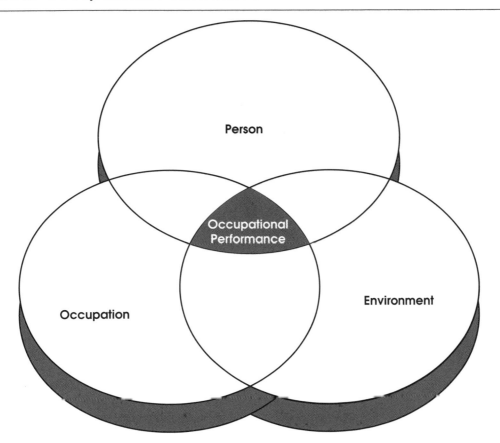

(Adapted from Law et al, 1996. Canadian Journal of Occupational Therapy, 63, p. 18)
Enabling Occupation: An Occupational Therapy Perspective, CAOT 1997

Figure 3: Cumulative Experience Across an Occupational Life Course

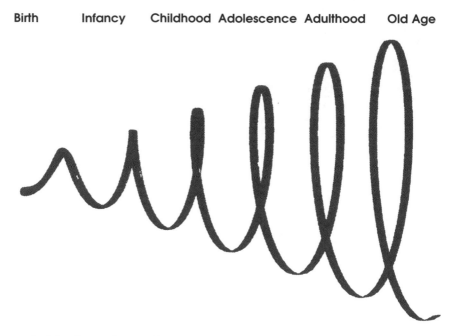

Birth   Infancy   Childhood Adolescence Adulthood   Old Age

Enabling Occupation: An Occupational Therapy Perspective, CAOT 1997

spiral. Occupational development may result in increasing complexity in some occupations but not others; development of self-care occupations may advance more quickly than development in productivity occupations; or leisure occupations may be omitted when self-care and productivity are overwhelming.

Developmental delay, disability, illness, injury, aging or other personal difficulties will shape an occupational life course into changing patterns that may not resemble the course of those around them. Personal growth may take people into unexpected realms of life. The result is that life stages may not progress from stage to stage as depicted. Environmental threats, from natural disasters to political and economic change, will require people to take unexpected (welcome or unwelcome) turns in an occupational life course. Occupations may also change. For instance, the physical and mental demands of an occupation shift when technology is introduced. Occupations may become culturally or economically inappropriate. People will likely be challenged to discover untapped potential or unforeseen paths in their occupational life course.

Over time and with changes in person-environment-occupation interactions, a person's occupational life course will evolve, adapt, or be transformed into new patterns. As people proceed through their occupational life course, occupational therapists may enable environmental change in order to enhance occupational performance, or enable persons to restore, develop, maintain, or discover their occupational potential in their environment. An occupational therapy interaction represents only a part of an individual's occupational life course.

CLIENT-CENTRED PRACTICE

In developing a framework for Canadian occupational therapy, the concept of client-centredness has been a constant theme since 1983. In the 1990s, the basis for client-centred practice has been described as enablement (Polatajko, 1992). The term client-centred practice was coined by Rogers in *The Clinical Treatment of the Problem Child* (Rogers, 1939), in which he referred to client-centred practice as emanating from the client's perspective. From the 1940s to the mid-1960s, the client-centred movement grew, primarily in social work (Rogers, 1951, 1969). Canadian occupational therapists describe client-centred practice as collaborative approaches of working with people (CAOT, 1991; CAOT, 1993). There are ongoing discussions about the term client-centred. Some occupational therapists are debating whether people should be called clients or patients (Reilly, 1984; Sharrott & Yerxa, 1985). Others are debating whether to describe practice as client-centred or client-driven (Gage & Polatajko, 1995). Person has been suggested as a generic term for recognizing that people are active agents with the power to participate in occupational therapy and their lives (Townsend, 1993a). These debates will help to clarify what client-centred practice means in occupational therapy. In the meantime, this document offers continuity with the past by using the term client-centred practice.

Client-centred practice in occupational therapy embraces a philosophy of respect for, and partnership with, the people who are engaging in occupational therapy services. Underlying client-centred practice is a recognition of the autonomy of the individual person even though persons are understood to be interdependent in their environment (Polatajko, 1992; Townsend, 1993a). There is also recognition of the strengths that clients bring to occupational therapy, of the need for client choice, and of the benefits of client-therapist collaboration (Law et al., 1995; Sumsion, 1993). Client-centred practice represents an ethical stance by occupational therapists based on democratic ideas of empowerment and justice (Townsend, 1993a). In occupational therapy:

> **Client-centred practice refers to collaborative approaches aimed at enabling occupation with clients who may be individuals, groups, agencies, governments, corporations or others. Occupational therapists demonstrate respect for clients, involve clients in decision making, advocate with and for clients in meeting clients' needs, and otherwise recognize clients' experience and knowledge.**

To encompass the diversity of Canadian occupational therapy practice, the definition of a client is:

Clients are individuals who may have occupational problems arising from medical conditions, transitional difficulties, or environmental barriers, or clients may be organizations that influence the occupational performance of particular groups or populations.

Occupational therapy's philosophy of client-centred practice is translated into practice through processes of enablement. Enablement differs from treatment in which things are done to or for rather than with people. While the processes of enabling have long been used in occupational therapy, the term has not been defined. Enabling is a process that involves clients as participants in occupational therapy.

Enabling may involve individual clients in therapeutic processes, particularly when they are very ill or recuperating from a traumatic injury. In these situations, enablement aims to elicit motivation and to prompt people to engage in their rehabilitation. Enabling processes may involve people in addressing issues over the loss of occupational performance and their sense of integrity as humans. In other situations, enabling processes are educational, as in health promotion or in occupational therapy programmes which educate people to use adaptive technology or to discover new ways of living. Therapeutic and educational processes of enablement are complementary and may be blended to meet the needs at hand. In any case, enabling is the type of helping that is most appropriate when the goal is occupational performance (Polatajko, 1992). Enabling processes recognize that people are active participants in occupational performance, whereas treatment and caregiving forms of helping are applied to people who are dependent on their helper (Townsend, 1998). In this document:

Enabling refers to processes of facilitating, guiding, coaching, educating, prompting, listening, reflecting, encouraging, or otherwise collaborating with people so that individuals, groups, agencies, or organizations have the means and opportunity to participate in shaping their own lives.

Drawing on occupational therapy values and beliefs (Table 3), 12 guiding principles for enabling occupation in client-centred practice are presented in Table 10. Such principles can be applied in various ways depending on whether practice is with individual or organizational clients. Essentially, client-centred practice re-defines and shifts power. Individual, group, agency, organizational, and other clients participate actively in defining their priorities. Clients engage as partners in the occupational therapy process. There is also partnership with client representatives who

Table 10: Guiding Principles for Enabling Occupation in Client-Centred Practice

- Base practice on client values, meaning, and choice as much as possible

- Listen to client visions

- Facilitate processes for clients envisioning what might be possible

- Support clients to examine risks and consequences

- Support clients to succeed, but also to risk and fail

- Respect clients' own styles of coping or bringing about change

- Guide clients to identify needs from their own perspective

- Facilitate clients to choose outcomes that they define as meaningful even if the occupational therapist does not agree

- Encourage and actively facilitate clients to participate in decision-making partnerships in therapy, programme planning, and policy formation

- Provide information that will answer clients' questions in making choices

- Offer services that do not overwhelm clients with bureaucracy

- Foster open, clear communication

- Invite clients to use their strengths and natural community supports

Enabling Occupation: An Occupational Therapy Perspective, CAOT 1997

participate in organizing occupational therapy services that are appropriate to their needs and communities.

Client-Centred Practice with Individual and Group Clients

Taken overall, the guiding principles outlined in Table 10 acknowledge a respect for self-determination. A "holistic view of the individual", and the "worth of the individual" are beliefs that have already been highlighted in occupational therapy (DNHW & CAOT, 1983, p. 16). Each individual is unique and brings a unique perspective to the occupational therapy experience. This is true even though clients' views of rights and autonomy are culturally determined.

To be client-centred with individuals and groups is to ensure that clients receive information to enable them to make decisions about the services that will most effectively meet their needs. It is important for clients to know that their opinions, wishes and needs will be sought, that their values will be respected and that they will maintain their dignity and integrity throughout the occupational therapy process. Respecting individual self-determination means encouraging client responsibility, and drawing on clients' resources.

The goal of the client-therapist relationship with individuals and groups is an interdependent partnership which will enable the solution of occupational problems and the achievement of occupational goals. Plans and action are based on clients' visions and values, taking into account their roles, culture, and environments. Action is implemented to build on clients' strengths. Client-centred practice challenges occupational therapists to recognize their own values and not impose them on clients. What may seem to be irrational choices by clients may be exactly what is needed, based on what clients know about their situations.

Client-centred practice with individuals or groups is characterized by flexibility. Services are ideally organized to be timely, accessible, and to meet the needs of the client rather than fitting into professional schedules and approaches. Contextual congruence emphasizes the importance of clients' roles, interests, environments and culture in the occupational therapy process. Clients are participants in deciding where and when they will work with occupational therapists.

A client-centred practice is variable, with differing degrees of participation by clients and the occupational therapist. For example, people with little experience in making decisions around health issues may begin by making choices from a small range of options proposed by the occupational therapist. The process is dynamic because the nature of this partnership can change as the client and occupational therapist proceed. Client-centred practice is open to perspectives from all who are involved, and allows a broader choice for solutions to occupational problems. Clients can expect to have their opinions sought and listened to by occupational therapists and to be supported in the level of participation they choose. It is also important that occupational therapists discuss clearly with clients whether or not they can provide the services requested by them.

Key principles in client-centred practice include determining who the client is; respecting the client's value system; facilitating the client in setting occupational goals; providing education and information to facilitate personal choices and problem solving; and using occupational therapists' skills to help clients achieve their goals through meaningful occupation.

Important client-therapist partnership issues to be addressed in a client-centred practice are as follows: defining the nature of the occupational performance issues; discussing targeted occupational performance outcomes and actions from a client's perspective; and deciding how to implement plans through occupations that have meaning to an individual or organizational client. Processes of applying the client-therapist partnership principles effectively in practice are outlined in Chapter 4 (working with clients) and Chapter 5 (organizing occupational therapy services).

Research examining the use of some of the principles of client-centred practice with individuals has demonstrated that providing respectful and supportive services leads to improved client satisfaction and adherence to health service programmes (Greenfield, Kaplan & Ware, 1985; Hall, Roter & Katz, 1988; Wasserman, Inui, Barriatua, Carter & Lippincott, 1984). Provision of information results in both improved functional outcomes and improved client satisfaction (Greenfield et al., 1985; Moxley-Haegert & Serbin, 1983). The development of a client-therapist partnership has been demonstrated to increase client participation, increase clients' sense of control and enhance satisfaction with services (Dunst, Trivette, Boyd & Brookfield, 1994; Greenfield et al., 1985). An individualized, flexible approach in which the client defines goals improves functional outcomes and satisfaction (Law et al., 1994).

Client-Centred Practice with Agencies, Organizations and Other Clients

Occupational therapists work with agencies, organizations and other clients who are not directly experiencing occupational performance issues. An organization may have individuals with occupational performance problems, but the occupational therapist will become involved at a different point. For example, occupational therapists may work with organizational clients in their roles as consultants, managers, educators, researchers, programmers, or business people.

In these situations, occupational therapy clients may be the managers of employment programmes, housing services, or social support systems. Some clients may be human rights organizations or independent living groups which are advocating for those with occupational issues. An increasing number of occupational therapists work with clients who are lawyers, architects, engineers, rehabilitation agencies, insurance companies, governments, or businesses. These clients may need contractual services for occupational assessment, programming, or evaluation. Whereas occupational therapists have traditionally worked mostly with individual or group clients, there is a growing trend to become involved in population health. Here, clients may be community health or other agencies which recognize the importance of assessing or meeting the occupational needs of a particular population. New clients are emerging, as policy analysts and planners address occupational crises which communities may be experiencing because of industrial shutdowns or other economic and social change. Where occupational therapists develop continuing education workshops or consulting businesses, they are finding various professional and non-professional clients. An untapped group of clients may be consumers who need special services.

The guiding principles for enabling occupation in client-centred practice as outlined in Table 10 apply when using a client-centred approach with agencies, organizations or other clients. The occupational therapist respects the opinions of the group or organization involved and participates in a collaborative process to achieve the client's goals. As with all clients, the occupational therapist respects and collaborates with the client in decisions. To date, client-centred approaches with communities or organizations have not been researched in occupational therapy. However literature on community and organizational development indicates that participation, choice and other features of client-centred practice are key elements of success.

Choice, Risk, and Responsibility in Client-Centred Practice

Occupational therapists adhere to a professional Code of Ethics (CAOT, 1996b), which requires them to protect client interests and safety, and to advocate for client respect and fairness. Documents and writings on ethical issues can help occupational therapists who are faced with challenging situations.

In client-centred approaches, an occupational therapist facilitates the identification and operationalization of a client's goals. Sometimes these are not shared by other health professionals or by others significant to the client. A client's goals may be judged to be unrealistic, unsafe or placing people at risk for injury or illness. Conversely, client goals may be perceived by occupational therapists as too simple; in this case, occupational therapists could actively encourage the risk-taking needed for clients to achieve their goals.

The National Advisory Council on Aging (NACA) has taken a proactive role in educating the public about the necessity of people being free to choose options which others may perceive as potentially harmful. Dickson states that "...The right of older or disabled seniors to choose to live 'at risk' is sometimes questioned in a way that would never be acceptable in the case of younger adults." (1993, p.2). To operationalize the client-centred model of practice, occupational therapists need to discuss and participate in values clarification with clients. The issue of individual rights, whether it be the right to die or the right of elderly people to decide not to accept assistance with homemaking, will continue to challenge occupational therapists. Questions about what is best for individuals versus communities or organizations are also challenging.

Occupational therapists attend to a client's rights, values and priorities in a non-judgemental manner. Some professionals view clients as having insufficient knowledge and insight to understand the implications of the decisions they are making. To be client-centred does not mean to abandon this concern. If clients' goals appear to be unsafe or to place people at risk for injury or illness, occupational therapists need to exercise legal and ethical responsibilities for identifying potential harm if clients decide to engage in clearly dangerous or socially irresponsible actions. Enabling clients to make choices does not remove occupational therapists' responsibility for alerting them to dangers and guiding them as safely as possible.

If occupational therapists believe that clients are making potentially unsafe decisions, they are obliged to assist clients in the detailed examination of the potential risk. Occupational therapists have a responsibility to help individual or organizational clients to explore and identify the potential consequences of their decisions. This identification serves several purposes. It demonstrates to the occupational therapist, team and significant others that the client has considered and understood the implications of a decision. Identifying risks also allows the client and the occupational therapist to deal with potential problems in a realistic and empowering fashion, and allows occupational therapists to fulfil their ethical and legal responsibilities.

In client-centred practice with an individual client, the dialogue between an occupational therapist and individual client would not be, "...you have to use a walker around the home or else you will fall and end up in the hospital." Rather, the individual would be engaged in active problem identification and planning. For instance, a client-centred occupational therapist might say: "You have stated you do not wish to use a walker at home. I have concerns about what you will do if you fall. Would you like to talk about your plans if this happens?" In some situations, an occupational therapist may need to refuse to carry out a client's request if it is believed to be unethical or constitute malpractice.

In client-centred practice with an organizational client, the occupational therapist might guide managers to develop policies which encourage collaborative decision making with those served by the organization. Here, the occupational therapist would be encouraging an organization, such as industry, to consult with workers. Consultation might be around policies and environmental conditions which are putting people at undue risk. In this example, issues of worker as well as employer choice, risk and responsibility would be raised. To engage employees and employers in a meaningful occupation, an occupational therapist might facilitate the joint development of safety policies that take into account their differing perspectives.

Client-centred occupational therapists incorporate an understanding of the environmental context in which the client is making a decision. What appears to be objective, scientific clinical judgement is influenced by the unacknowledged factors of economics, politics, service tradition and social values (Biklen, 1988; Townsend, 1998). There are also tensions between the needs of clients and the scarcity of available resources (Picard-Greffe, 1994). The challenge is to uncover these unacknowledged forces that determine the judgment of clients and others.

Occupational therapists analyze person-environment-occupation interactions. In doing so, they assume a key ethical and legal role in facilitating a comprehensive review of risk, consequences and responsibilities. Some ethical and legal issues relate to an individual's competency to make decisions. Other ethical and legal issues relate to the locus of responsibility for actions, and the right to participate in or refuse services. There is an overriding responsibility for occupational therapists to respect the dignity and worth of individuals in all situations. This means ensuring that there are sufficient checks and balances in the decision making process to ensure that an occupational therapist's personal biases are not driving client choices.

Working with organizational clients raises additional issues of choice, risk and responsibility. Some occupational therapists are faced with the dilemma of working with organizational clients who pursue unsafe practices with the workers, residents, or others for whom the organization is responsible. There are often no easy answers, and those that emerge in one situation may not suit another situation.

Endnote

Key references describing occupational performance, or the development of conceptual frameworks of occupational performance include Blain & Townsend, 1993; CAOT, 1991, 1993; Department of National Health and Welfare (DNHW) & CAOT, 1983, 1986, 1987; Law, 1991; Law, et al., 1990; Law, et al., 1994; Law, Baptiste, & Mills, 1995; Law, Cooper, Strong, Stewart, Rigby, & Letts, 1996; McColl, Law, & Stewart, 1993; and, Townsend, Brintnell & Staisey, 1990.

Important references on occupation in occupational therapy include: Christiansen & Baum, 1991; CAOT, 1994b; Clark et al., 1991; Cynkin & Robinson, 1990; Dunton, 1919; Hopkins & Smith, 1988; Kielhofner, 1983, 1985, 1992, 1995; Leakey & Lewin, 1978; LeVesconte, 1935; Mayers, 1990; Meyer, 1922; Nelson, 1988; Primeau, Clark, & Pierce, 1989; Reilly, 1962; Rogers, 1984; Yerxa et al., 1990; Townsend, 1996b; and, Wilcock, 1993.

References to occupational therapy's developmental perspective include Breines, 1989; CAOT, 1991; DNHW & CAOT, 1983, 1986, 1987; and, Christiansen & Baum, 1991. References on client-centred practice include Blain & Townsend, 1993; CAOT, 1991, 1993; DNHW & CAOT, 1983, 1986, 1987; Law, 1991; Law, et al., 1990; Law, et al., 1994; Law, et al., 1995; McColl, et al., 1993; Polatajko, 1992; Townsend, 1993a; and, Townsend, et al., 1990.

PRIMARY AUTHORS:
Sue Stanton
Tracey Thompson-Franson
Christine Kramer

Purpose

To demonstrate how the core concepts of occupational performance and client-centred practice are applied in working with individual and organizational clients.

Objectives

- To emphasize key features of an Occupational Performance Process;
- To apply concepts of occupational performance and client-centred practice to seven stages of an Occupational Performance Process.

Summary

Chapter 4 links the core concepts in Chapter 3 to an Occupational Performance Process for working with clients. Key features of the process are emphasized and the partners in the process are identified, prior to describing each stage. Two illustrations show how to apply the process, one with an individual client, and one with an organizational client. Reflective questions are posed for each stage to guide occupational therapists in applying the core concepts.

Occupational therapists assume diverse roles; some occupational therapists are educators, managers, researchers, policy developers, and/or business people. Nevertheless, working with clients remains at the centre of what occupational therapists do (CAOT, 1996b). This chapter describes a process and guiding principles for enabling occupation based on the Canadian Model of Occupational Performance (CMOP) and client-centred practice as outlined in Chapter 3.

OCCUPATIONAL PERFORMANCE PROCESS

Canadian occupational therapists previously described an occupational therapy process as a systems approach which includes referral, assessment, programme planning, intervention, discharge, follow up and programme evaluation (CAOT, 1991). Similar generic problem-solving models of an occupational therapy process have been developed, particularly in the United States (Christiansen & Baum, 1991; Kielhofner, 1995; Reed & Sanderson, 1992); however none of these models state explicitly how the concepts of client-centred practice, or occupational performance are applied, or how client strengths and resources are considered in a process for working with clients.

The Occupational Performance Process that is described in this chapter has been adapted from the process developed by Fearing (1993), and Fearing, Law and Clark (1997). This process is a practice model because it shows how to apply the concepts of the Canadian Model of Occupational Performance in practice. This feature, its client-centred focus, and consideration of clients' strengths and resources for planning and implementing occupational therapy, address the limitations of past process models. Since it is a generic process model, it can be used with all clients in many different environments or situations.

The seven stages of the Occupational Performance Process appear to be simple, but as Fearing et al. (1997) point out, occupational therapists need a complex set of knowledge and skills to work through the stages with clients to enable occupation. This complexity is reflected in the competencies described in a companion document, the *Profile of Occupational Therapy Practice in Canada* (CAOT, 1996c). The Occupational Performance Process and the units of the *Profile* are congruent although there are some differences in terminology.

Key Features of the Process

Important features of the Occupational Performance Process are highlighted in Table 11, and many of these are evident in the descriptions of the seven stages, which are listed in Table 12. Others, although equally important, are described following the review of the stages because they flow from the process.

Table 11: Key Features of the Occupational Performance Process

- Reflects occupational therapy values and beliefs

- Applies the Canadian Model of Occupational Performance

- Guides the development of collaborative partnerships in client-centred practice

- Recognizes the expertise of the client and the occupational therapist in the process

- Integrates theory with practice

- Is flexible and dynamic

- Is action-oriented

- Leads to client outcomes

- Guides the evaluation of client outcomes

- Can be used with all clients (individual, organizational, etc.)

- Can be applied in diverse environments

- Guides documentation

- Fosters accountability

- Differentiates occupational therapy from other disciplines

Enabling Occupation: An Occupational Therapy Perspective, CAOT 1997

Partners in the Process

The partnership between the client and occupational therapist is essential to the Occupational Performance Process. Each party brings different expertise to the process and participates to varying degrees depending on circumstances, choices or the situation.

Clients in the Occupational Performance Process may be individuals, groups, organizations, governments, and communities. Family members, associates or others may also need to participate in the process (Canadian Council on Health Services Accreditation (CCHSA), 1995; Stanton & Jongbloed, 1993). Clients are encouraged to take an active role as partners in the Occupational Performance Process; however it is recognized that clients' values and beliefs, difficulty in making their needs or wishes known, or other factors may influence the extent to which this choice is exercised. Graded decision-making or advocacy with client representatives are options when clients cannot participate fully in the process (Hobson, 1996). In Chapters 4 and 5, the term client is understood to mean the actual client and/or selected client representatives.

All clients, representatives of clients and other participants bring expertise about their occupational performance, environment and/or life experiences to the Occupational Performance Process. Clients' descriptions of their circumstances, their perspectives on possible actions that could be taken to resolve the issues they have brought to occupational therapy, and ongoing feedback,all contribute to the decision-making that occurs with the occupational therapist throughout the process.

Occupational therapists bring their expertise about enabling occupation to the Occupational Performance Process with all clients. This expertise comes from professional education and experience. An experienced occupational therapist can draw on a repertoire of client stories when working with clients. Knowledge from recent academic and fieldwork experiences, continuing education programmes and/or research can also provide fresh perspectives and ideas for problem-solving. Day-to-day reflections on practice assist occupational therapists to identify the actions that enabled or did not enable occupation and why. These reflections ensure that their knowledge about occupation continues to build and strengthen as a resource for clients.

As facilitators of the Occupational Performance Process, occupational therapists assume responsibility for answering clients' questions and ensuring that clients have sufficient information to participate as a partner in decision making. Occupational therapists' self-knowledge, and awareness of their active influence in working with clients are important strengths in creating client-centred partnerships.

The expertise of the client and the occupational therapist are combined when they work in partnership within the Occupational Performance Process. It is this interdependent client-occupational therapist partnership that leads to the best solutions to the issues that clients bring to occupational therapy.

The Context of the Occupational Performance Process

The effectiveness of clients and occupational therapists when using the Occupational Performance Process is influenced strongly by the service environment and the societal context in which the process takes place. Chapter 5 describes how occupational therapists can organize occupational therapy services within the societal context to support rather than constrain the Occupational Performance Process. Two illustrations, one for working with an individual client, and one with an organizational client, follow the descriptions of each stage of the process in this chapter. These illustrations, and the five vignettes in Chapter 7, show how to apply the

Figure 4: Occupational Performance Process Model

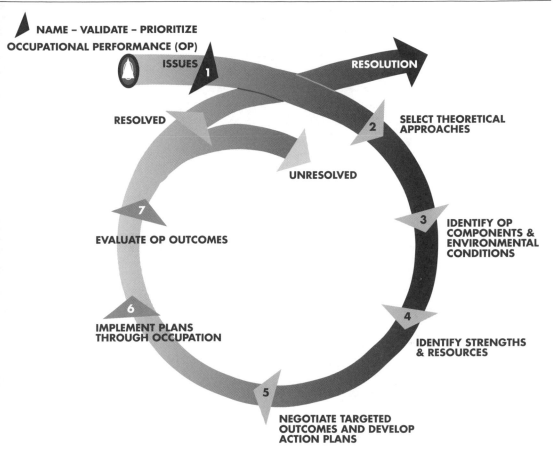

NAME – VALIDATE – PRIORITIZE
OCCUPATIONAL PERFORMANCE (OP)
ISSUES **1**

RESOLUTION

RESOLVED

2 SELECT THEORETICAL APPROACHES

UNRESOLVED

7

EVALUATE OP OUTCOMES

3 IDENTIFY OP COMPONENTS & ENVIRONMENTAL CONDITIONS

6

IMPLEMENT PLANS THROUGH OCCUPATION

4

IDENTIFY STRENGTHS & RESOURCES

5

NEGOTIATE TARGETED OUTCOMES AND DEVELOP ACTION PLANS

(Adapted from: Fearing, Law & Clark, (1997).
Canadian Journal of Occupational Therapy, 64, p. 11)
Enabling Occupation: An Occupational Therapy Perspective, CAOT 1997

seven stage Occupational Performance Process within different service environments and societal contexts.

SEVEN STAGES IN A PROCESS OF PRACTICE

The Occupational Performance Process is graphically presented in Figure 4 and summarized in Table 12. It is client-centred and focuses on occupational performance. Depicted is a seven stage, clockwise process which starts on the left and ends on the right side of Figure 4. A review of the seven stages in Table 12 shows that Stages #1, #3 and #4 are different stages for gathering information, and Stage #5 sets target client outcomes and develops plans for occupational therapy. Implementation of plans and evaluation of outcomes follow in Stages #6 and #7. Information gathered

Table 12: The Seven Stages of the Occupational Performance Process

Stage #1:   Name, Validate and Prioritize Occupational Performance Issues
Occupational performance issue(s) related to self-care, productivity and leisure occupations are named, validated and prioritized with the client. When no issues are identified, the process ends.

Stage #2:   Select Theoretical Approach(es)
When an occupational performance issue is named, validated and given priority, the occupational therapist selects, with client input, one or more theoretical approach(es) that will guide the remaining stages of the process.

Stage #3:   Identify Occupational Performance Components and Environmental Conditions
The occupational therapist and client identify the occupational performance components and environmental conditions that are contributing to the occupational performance issue(s).

Stage #4:   Identify Strengths and Resources
The strengths and resources that the client and the occupational therapist bring to the Occupational Performance Process are identified.

Stage #5:   Negotiate Targeted Outcomes, Develop Action Plan
The client and the occupational therapist negotiate the client outcomes to be targeted in occupational therapy, and develop action plans. The plans specify what the client and occupational therapist will do to resolve or minimize limitations to occupational performance in order to achieve the targeted outcomes.

Stage #6:   Implement Plans Through Occupation
Plans are implemented, reviewed, and modified on an ongoing basis. The plans address occupational performance issues by taking action to remove or reduce limitations in the occupational performance components and/or environmental conditions.

Stage #7:   Evaluate Occupational Performance Outcomes
The outcomes of the occupational performance process are identified. If the targeted outcomes have been achieved, services are completed. If the targeted outcomes have not been achieved, the targets are reviewed. If continuation of the process is perceived to be beneficial to the client, parts of the process are repeated.

Enabling Occupation: An Occupational Therapy Perspective, CAOT 1997

from Stage #1 is analyzed to select the potential theoretical approach(es) (Stage #2) that will guide Stages #3 to #7. Selecting theoretical approaches is an addition to past process models and is consistent with the need for evidence-based practice (CAOT, 1996c). The titles specify the actions and outcomes that are required for each stage.

The process ends when occupational performance issues are RESOLVED, unless new occupational performance issues are identified to begin another process. Issues are resolved when an occupational performance issue has been changed, eliminated or minimized to enable occupation. When UNRESOLVED issues persist after evaluating occupational performance outcomes (Stage #7), clients have two choices. They may choose to repeat parts of the Occupational Performance Process until the unresolved issues have been resolved, or until it is clear that there are no further benefits for continuing occupational therapy. Alternatively, clients may choose to discontinue occupational therapy.

Figure 4 also shows the Canadian Model of Occupational Performance (from Figure 1) inside the Occupational Performance Process (represented by a symbol). A cross-section of the process loop at any point would also reveal the Canadian Model of Occupational Performance. Consequently, the Canadian Model of Occupational Performance is a constant reference point for occupational therapists who use the Occupational Performance Process.

Identifying Clients

Identifying clients is a pre-requisite for initiating the Occupational Performance Process. Requests for service or referrals may come from many sources. Examples include self-referring individuals, physicians, health professionals and agencies, government agencies, schools, corporations, unions, vendors of home health care equipment, insurance and rehabilitation companies, and lawyers. The occupational therapist may be able to determine the appropriateness for initiating the Occupational Performance Process by reviewing the nature of, and reasons for the service request. A decision about the potential value of occupational therapy to a client often cannot be made until occupational performance issues have been explored (Stage #1). In some situations, provincial legislation governing occupational therapy practice and/or other regulations specify that a referral is needed from a designated source (e.g., a physician) prior to starting the process.

Stage #1: Name, Validate and Prioritize Occupational Performance Issues (Screening)

Purposes

The title of this stage cues the occupational therapist to three actions that are required to identify the occupational performance issues of importance to the client, and negotiate an agreement or contract that will guide subsequent process stages. Fearing et al (1997) use the term *occupational performance* problem in this context. Use of the term *issues* here acknowledges that not all clients who seek the services of occupational therapists may view or want their situations viewed as a problem or concern. The term *issues* is perceived as less emotionally laden and gives clients greater flexibility in choosing their own terms to describe their situation.

Not all requests for service require the assistance of an occupational therapist. Since this is an initial assessment stage, it serves to screen service requests. Whether a client is an individual or an organization, this screening function enables the client to judge whether or not an occupational therapy service would be of benefit. Similarly, it enables the occupational therapist to predict whether or not the available services would likely meet a client's needs.

This first stage of the process is extremely important. It sets the stage for the development of the collaborative, interdependent partnership in which the expertise of the client and occupational therapist begin to be shared. If the process is not client-centred or focused on occupation at this point, occupational performance outcomes that are valued by the client are unlikely.

Naming Occupational Performance Issues
Methods:
Pertinent information about occupational performance is gathered with the client and others, such as employees, community and/or family members with the client's consent. The occupational therapist chooses methods that will enable the client to identify important self-care, productivity, or leisure issues (Fearing et al., 1997).

A variety of methods may be used to gather information. The Canadian Occupational Performance Measure (COPM) is an excellent method to use with individual clients because it focuses on identifying issues that are important to the client. The COPM "is an individualized measure designed for use by occupational therapists to detect change in a client's self-perception of occupational performance over time" (Law et al., 1994, p. 1).

When clients are organizations or groups, diverse methods may be used. For example, a combination of semi-structured interviews and focus groups may be used to identify occupational performance issues with managers and employees in a corporation. Community visits, a review of community resource information, and environmental rating scales are other examples of possible methods. The occupational therapist selects the best method(s) for achieving the outcomes of this stage.

Actual Versus Potential Occupational Performance Issues:
Clients may identify actual or potential occupational performance issues.

Issues that are occurring at the time of a screening assessment are described as actual occupational performance issues. A potential occupational performance issue is one which places the client and/or others in the client's environment at risk. Dilemmas occur when the occupational therapist's and client's perspectives of potential risks differ (see Chapter 3, Choice, Risk, and Responsibility in Client-centred Practice). If the methods used to screen the request for service do not identify actual or potential occupational performance issues, the Occupational Performance Process ends.

Validating and Prioritizing Occupational Performance Issues

Occupational performance issues must be validated with the client. This means confirming with the client that each occupational performance issue accurately reflects what the client has said about the situation. When more than one issue is validated, the client and occupational therapist determine priorities for action after considering all available information (Fearing et al., 1997).

When occupational performance issues are named, validated and prioritized, potential conflicts of interest that could affect the quality of service may be identified. Conflicts of interest between the occupational therapist and client may be raised by either party, or by others. If necessary, the client may seek (or be referred to) another occupational therapy service. Similarly, when available services are insufficient or not suitable for addressing the prioritized issues, it is necessary to re-direct the client to other services. If there are no occupational performance issues, the Occupational Performance Process ends.

Stage #2: Select Theoretical Approach(es)

Role of Theoretical Approaches

The purpose of Stage #2 is to select a theoretical approach. This means selecting a conceptual system to guide and justify decisions throughout the process. Approach is a general term used here to include developing models, existing models and tested theories. Other terms used may be theory, model, framework, or paradigm, although each may have different interpretations in different situations (Fawcett & Down, 1992; Krefting, 1985; McColl, Law & Stewart, 1993; Reed, 1984; Reed & Sanderson, 1992).

Theoretical approaches guide actions and reasoning and assist in deciding how the assessment and intervention process should proceed. They also explain or predict how concepts work in practice (McColl & Pranger, 1994). In doing so, they can be useful in explaining the relevance of an approach to clients, enabling them to participate as partners in the process.

With increasing pressure for evidence-based practice, occupational therapists are encouraged to use theoretical approaches that have been validated through research (Cosman & Heinz, 1996). When practice has a clear theoretical rationale, outcomes can be evaluated with confidence. Theory-based practitioners run less risk of being found professionally negligent in working with clients.

Generic Versus Specific Theoretical Approaches
The Occupational Performance Process is what McColl and Pranger describe as a practice model, in that it serves to "instruct therapists about how to intervene to produce a desired effect" (1994, p.251). Both the Occupational Performance Process and the Canadian Model of Occupational Performance are generic because they can be applied in working with all occupational therapy clients. Other generic approaches that define concepts like interdependence and supervision, can also be helpful in the process.

Alone, a generic conceptual or practice model is not sufficient to guide practice (Kielhofner & Barris, 1986). An occupational therapist needs to select specific theoretical approach(es) for use with particular clients. Specific approaches can only be applied in some occupational therapy situations; for example, with children whose occupational performance issues are related to their social environment, or with adults whose occupational performance issues arise from physical components that are related to neurological problems. Specific approaches guide actions for changing occupational performance components and environmental conditions that are unique to each client.

McColl, Law, and Stewart (1993) provide annotated bibliographies for six categories of specific theoretical approaches which are consistent with the Canadian Model of Occupational Performance: physical-rehabilitative; psycho-emotional; neuro-integrative; socio-adaptive; developmental; and environmental (Figure 5). The theoretical approaches within the categories can be selected to guide practice with clients. Examples include biomechanical, group, psychosocial, sensori-integrative, rehabilitative, neurodevelopmental, cognitive development, learning, community health, health promotion, and psychoanalytic approaches. Approaches that are consistent with the Occupational Performance Model and client-centred practice are advocated in this document.

Selecting, Adding or Changing Approaches
The client's occupational performance issues direct the selection of the theoretical approaches that will guide the Occupational Performance Process. The relevance of possible approaches is discussed with a client where possible, in language that has meaning to clients. A client's goals and past experience contribute to the selection of a theoretical approach. In practice, use of more than one theoretical approach is common. Using only one theoretical approach is risky because important information that can contribute to the resolution of the occupational performance issue may be missed (Fearing et al., 1997).

Figure 5: Occupation: A classification system for theory

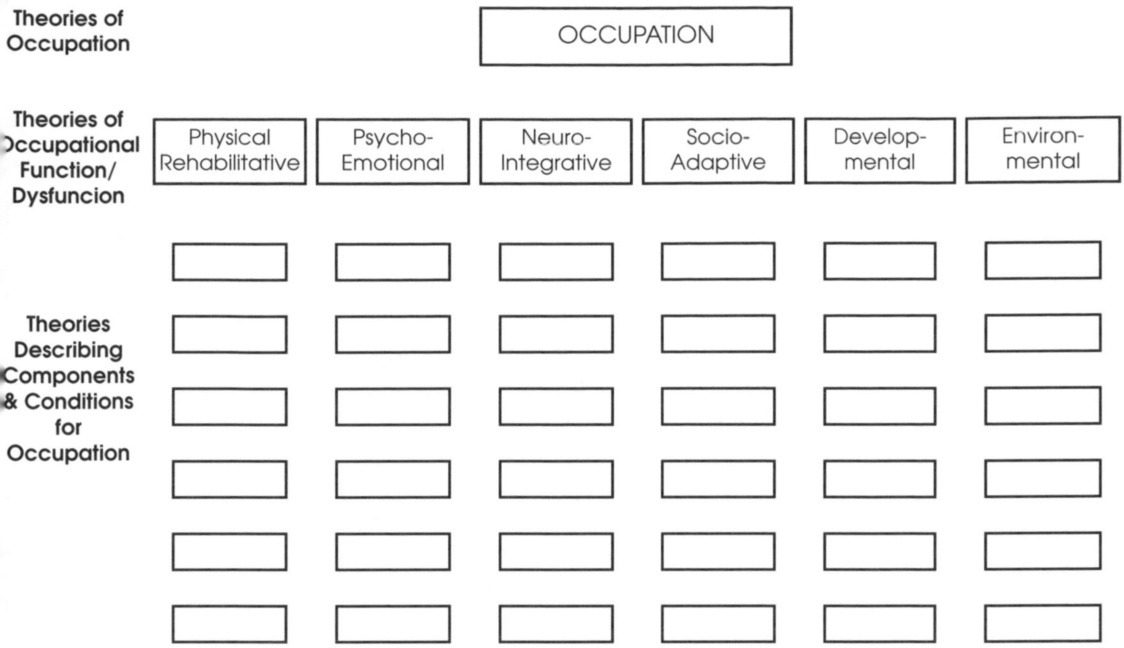

Theories of Occupation	OCCUPATION				

Theories of Occupational Function/ Dysfuncion	Physical Rehabilitative	Psycho-Emotional	Neuro-Integrative	Socio-Adaptive	Develop-mental	Environ-mental

Theories Describing Components & Conditions for Occupation						
	☐	☐	☐	☐	☐	☐
	☐	☐	☐	☐	☐	☐
	☐	☐	☐	☐	☐	☐
	☐	☐	☐	☐	☐	☐
	☐	☐	☐	☐	☐	☐
	☐	☐	☐	☐	☐	☐

(Reproduced from: McColl, Law & Stewart, (1993), p. 7. With permission of Slack Inc.)
Enabling Occupation: An Occupational Therapy Perspective, CAOT 1997

As new information emerges or a situation changes, the occupational therapist may need to change or add theoretical approaches. For example, if an affective occupational performance component (e.g. fear and coping with pain) emerges as an unanticipated barrier to occupational performance, psycho-emotional approaches might be added to guide planning and implementation stages.

Stage #3: Identify Occupational Performance Components and Environmental Conditions

Purpose
At this third stage, the occupational therapist addresses the question: What occupational performance components and/or environmental conditions are contributing to the actual or potential occupational performance issue(s)? Occupational performance components are unique to each person, and are influenced by environmental conditions.

The assessment process used to identify the components and conditions that influence occupational performance needs to be relevant to the environments in which occupational performance is or will be occurring. For example, if an assessment of individuals involved in meal preparation in an unfamiliar environment reveals poor organization skills (cognitive component), this may or may not mean that they would have poor organization skills in a familiar home environment. Considering the context of the assessment situation is extremely important in achieving accurate and meaningful results that will enhance decision-making and occupational therapy outcomes.

Determining What to Assess

It is rarely necessary to assess every occupational performance component (of persons) or every aspect of the environment (CAOT, 1996c). The goal in this stage is to identify the occupational performance components and environmental conditions that are relevant to the prioritized occupational performance issue(s). Identification of components and environmental conditions occurs in the process of assessing occupational performance. For example, when an occupational performance issue is related to self-care, an assessment of self-care will uncover the components and conditions that limit, or have the potential to limit occupational performance.

Decisions about what to assess and how this will be done are also guided by the theoretical approach(es) selected in Stage #2. For example, when it is anticipated that occupational performance is being limited by joint changes and organization of the environment, both biomechanical and environmental analysis approaches may be used to identify the components and/or conditions in a client's home, workplace or community.

Selecting Methods

Many sources of information are useful in choosing potential methods for assessing occupational performance components and environmental conditions (Asher, 1989; Letts et al., 1994; McDowell & Newell, 1987; Spencer, Krefting, & Mattingly, 1993; Yerxa, 1991). Typically, evaluation methods are categorized as qualitative or quantitative.

Qualitative methods describe and analyze occupational performance based on interviews, observations, client narratives (stories), review of documents, questionnaires that use open-ended questions, or other methods. One purpose may be to describe what people are doing, or to describe where, when and how occupations are being done. Qualitative methods are used to seek input or opinions from clients, service personnel or others who can provide information on an occupational performance issue.

Quantitative methods measure occupational performance components using standardized tools, and are the most common way of demonstrating change over time. Use of a standardized assessment of motor function or self-concept, and The Assessment Tool (Maltais, Trickey, Robitaille &

Rodriguez, 1989) are examples of methods that can be used to assess performance components or environmental conditions.

Usually, more than one method is used. For example, clients may be interviewed about their interpretation of the influence of environmental conditions on occupational performance in a particular situation. Some observation, testing or review of documents (e.g. records) would likely be added to gather other perspectives or measure environmental conditions.

The choice of methods is made in collaboration with the client, bearing in mind the questions that need to be answered to guide occupational therapy and to demonstrate occupational performance outcomes. The time and resources available also influence the choice of methods. Information to demonstrate occupational performance outcomes is gathered from this point on, particularly if there is a desire to evaluate change over time.

Analyzing Findings

Analysis focuses on the influences of occupational performance components and environmental conditions on the occupational performance issues which clients have identified as priorities. Table 13 illustrates one way to analyze self-care, productivity and leisure occupational performance issues that could be named by individual or organizational clients. With each occupational performance issue are examples of identified occupational performance components and/or environmental conditions that could be changed or modified through the Occupational Performance Process. Client's perspectives of occupational performance components and environmental conditions are reflected in the quotations. The Canadian Model of Occupational Performance can be used to guide the analysis of the occupational performance issues, and the occupational performance components and/or environmental conditions.

Typically, there are many influences on occupational performance. Since occupational therapists work with clients to enable occupation, targeting an occupational performance component or environmental condition that cannot be changed or modified in some way would not be effective. Therefore, the crucial aspect of analysis is to identify which occupational performance components and environmental conditions should be targeted for action by the client and occupational therapist in order to resolve or minimize the occupational performance issues. These decisions provide direction for subsequent stages.

Stage #4: Identify Strengths and Resources

The purpose of this stage is to summarize the client's strengths and resources for resolving prioritized occupational performance issues. Typically, information gathered in Stages #1 and #3 is a source for identifying client strengths and resources. Client strengths and resources

---

Table 13: Analysis of Occupational Performance Issues

Occupational Performance Issue	Occupational Performance Components and/or Environmental Conditions
Unable to maintain routines for personal care	• Ruminating about personal losses • "No-one cares about me"; "I don't care about myself" • Feels unsafe sharing the bathroom in boarding home
(individual self-care)	*(affective occupational performance component - quotes; worry about personal safety; cognitive component - ruminating; physical environmental condition - safety in bathroom)*
Unable to shop for groceries	• Person lacks strength to carry bags which are large and heavy • Cannot remember grocery items • No delivery services from local grocery • Fear of shopping alone
(individual productivity)	*(physical and cognitive occupational performance components - strength, memory; affective component - fear; physical environmental condition - large, heavy bags; social environmental condition - no delivery)*
Unable to access community recreation centre	• Building entrance ramp too steep (1:6) and broken • Upper extremity strength insufficient to use a ramp with a slope that is more than 1:12 • "I feel embarrassed in public in a wheelchair, none of my friends are in wheelchairs"
(individual or population leisure)	*(physical environmental condition - lack of access, ramp too sleep; physical performance component - lacks strength to use ramp; social environmental condition - community attitudes; ramp broken, no action to repair it; affective performance component - embarrassment)*

continued on page 71

Table 13 (continued): Analysis of Occupational Performance Issues

Occupational Performance Issue	Occupational Performance Components and/or Environmental Conditions
Potential for re-injury at work	• Lack of worker and management knowledge about safe work practices • No mechanical lifting devices • Low level of worker physical fitness in relation to work demands • Worker apathy and loss of sense of control over work conditions
(individual and/or organizational productivity)	*(affective occupational performance component - worker apathy; cognitive occupational performance component - lack of knowledge; physical performance component - lack of fitness/weakness; physical, institutional, social and cultural environmental conditions - lack of equipment to complete work safely, managers do not enforce safety standards, attitudes of workers and work traditions do not support machine `assists'*
Workers cannot complete a team project	• Workers unwilling to share their resources to complete project • Workers' lack of knowledge and skills in conflict resolution
(organizational productivity)	*(affective occupational performance component - attitude, values and beliefs re sharing resources; cognitive occupational performance component - lack of knowledge re conflict resolution).*
Lack of options for gym sports for people with disabilities in a community	• Lack of community awareness about disability • Lack of community awareness re the link between leisure and health • Lack of adapted gym facilities
(community leisure)	*(Physical, institutional, and social environmental conditions - lack of adapted facilities, lack of funding for such facilities and lack of social awareness about the needs of people with disabilities)*

Enabling Occupation: An Occupational Therapy Perspective, CAOT 1997

are summarized and documented in an Occupational Profile that is explained following the description of the seven stages.

Some occupational therapy services may end at this stage if the agreement is for assessment but not action. In these situations, outcomes (Stage #5) need to be negotiated when prioritizing occupational performance issues in Stage #1. For example, the targeted outcome may be that a client receives a summary of assessment findings (Stages #1, #3 and #4) in an Occupational Profile. In this stage, the strengths and resources of the occupational therapist are also considered to determine whether they are sufficient for the occupational therapist to enable the client to resolve the occupational performance issues.

Client Strengths

The occupational therapist and client identify a client's strengths for resolving the named occupational performance issues. People who participate in the Occupational Performance Process as individuals or representatives of organizations bring personal strengths and skills. They have experience in solving problems in their particular situation, so occupational therapists can learn much from them (Fearing et al., 1997).

Personal strengths are identified in affective, cognitive, and physical occupational performance components. For example, an individual's strong motivation to return home and resume valued occupations after an amputation, would be important in dealing with difficulties that arise. It would also represent an important spiritual strength. Representatives of organizations may bring strong communication skills and a history of empathetic, collaborative leadership. Coping style, sense of humour, and interest in taking an active role in the Occupational Performance Process are additional examples of client strengths.

Client Resources

Whereas client strengths lie within persons, client resources lie in environmental conditions. Many clients have social, familial, community and organizational supports that may work well for them and assist in resolving occupational performance issues (Fearing et al., 1997). A supportive team-oriented environment in a manufacturing plant where there is cultural, social, and institutional support would be an important resource in reducing the rate of injuries among workers. Informed family and friends, and funding for architectural changes may be an important resource for assisting a client to return home after hospitalization. The strong commitment of a community to improve housing conditions for seniors is an environmental resource for changing the self-care, leisure and productivity occupations for many seniors in the community. A well-funded seniors' housing programme and generous pension legislation would also be positive resources for enabling occupation with seniors.

Occupational Therapists' Strengths and Resources

The strengths and resources of occupational therapists are relevant to client-centred practice to the extent that they contribute to the resolution of a client's occupational performance issues. Occupational therapists bring their expertise and experience with them when enabling occupation. The availability of resources to the occupational therapist may be critical in resolving the client's occupational performance issues. Examples include knowledgeable colleagues, professional guidelines, books, and research findings. Universities with occupational therapy programmes may also be a useful resource. Organizational planning, marketing, management, education, research, and evaluation (see Chapter 5) are resources which can support occupational therapists' work with clients.

Stage #5: Negotiate Targeted Outcomes, Develop Action Plan
Targeted Outcomes and Goals

A targeted outcome is a more precise term for a goal. Targeted outcomes represent a client's and occupational therapist's best estimates of what may result from occupational therapy.

In the past, occupational therapists have defined goals using terms such as restore, develop and maintain function, or prevent dysfunction (CAOT, 1991). Although occupational therapists may find these terms useful in explaining the goals of occupational therapy to co-workers, managers or clients, they do not represent clients' goals for the Occupational Performance Process. For example, a client may hope to resume participation in weekly curling events with family members. The occupational therapist's goals (within the partnership) may be defined as helping the client to restore lost strength and develop new ways of participating in curling. Restoring and developing reflect the occupational therapist's rather than the client's goals. In client-centred practice, targeted outcomes are related to the occupations that the client wants to be able to do.

Identifying Targeted Outcomes

Mattingly and Hayes Fleming showed that while occupational therapists consider a current disability and situation, they focus more on possibilities for occupational performance (1994). Fearing et al., (1997) noted that "this ability to coach people from a present problem to a possible future requires a shared vision with a destination that is achievable" (p. 12). In a partnership, it is vital for all parties to be working towards the same vision (outcome).

When an individual client cannot make her or his goals known, a client representative may be able to develop targeted outcomes with the occupational therapist. Legislation on the status of a proxy or health care directive may be required to legitimize this representation.

Determining Priorities for Action

Priorities for action are decided jointly by an occupational therapist and client as much as possible. During discussions, the client and occupational therapist may revise the priorities for addressing the occupational performance issues that were set in Stage #1. Whether revised or not, the agreed upon priorities for the occupational performance issues need to match the priorities for the targeted outcomes. These are the primary outcomes in enabling occupation.

Interim or short term goals or objectives provide a framework for defining specific actions related to occupational performance components or environmental conditions. Each goal may address a particular barrier to occupational performance, enabling a client to progress through graded steps which provide a path towards targeted outcomes. These short term goals are secondary outcomes in enabling occupation. Like targeted outcomes, they should specify behaviours that can be observed and/or measured, and be realistic, understandable and achievable.

Defining Targeted Outcomes for Evaluation

Targeted outcomes need to be defined clearly and include the features noted previously, to facilitate the evaluation of occupational performance outcomes in Stage #7. Specifying how evidence will be gathered to evaluate client outcomes is particularly important. At this point, the occupational therapist and client decide whether the information from the assessment is sufficient or appropriate for evaluating outcomes in occupational performance. For instance, before implementing plans related to a targeted outcome, it is important to decide whether knowledge of a client's current level of occupational performance (gathered in Stages #1 and #3) is sufficient to enable later comparison with occupational performance outcomes that are evaluated in Stage #7. Later discovery of missing information may mean that targeted outcomes cannot be evaluated. Evaluation of client outcomes contributes to evaluation of service outcomes (see Chapter 5). Typically, evidence is required to demonstrate how client outcomes were, or were not met.

Developing Action Plans

Action plans are developed to meet targeted outcomes. The selection of theoretical approaches is likely reviewed at this point, and changed if necessary. Since occupational therapy is active rather than passive, participation of the client in developing the action plans is crucial for implementation to be successful. Plans reflect a focus on occupation, whether as a medium for therapy with individuals or groups, or in various consultation, policy development or other roles.

Planning to Enable Change in Occupational Performance

Strategies for enabling change in occupational performance components and/or environmental conditions are explored with the client. Risks, benefits, responsibilities and resources are discussed so that the best options can be identified. The occupational therapist facilitates an open discussion with the client, acknowledging potential ethical, moral or legal implications. The action plan must be compatible with the chosen theoretical approaches and logically lead to the achievement of targeted outcomes. It must be congruent with the client's values and beliefs, and expectations. Action plans may include strategies to develop, restore, maintain or promote occupational performance, or to prevent occupational dysfunction.

<u>Enhancing Occupational Performance Components:</u>
Enhancing occupational performance components may be necessary to achieve primary outcomes in occupational performance, i.e., targeted outcomes. For example, increasing knowledge about safety at work may resolve the occupational performance issue related to unsafe work practices (see Table 13). Another part of the action plan may be to engage individuals in meaningful occupations which increase muscle strength. In an organizational context, an occupational performance issue may be that workers cannot complete a team project as shown in Table 13. Action to enhance skills of communication and conflict resolution may be a step in resolving this occupational performance issue.

<u>Overcoming Environmental Barriers:</u>
When the physical environment limits occupational performance, the strategies may be to remove physical barriers through adaptations such as raising the height of chairs, lowering counters, or purchasing mechanical lifting devices. The occupational therapist may also seek funding for these changes, or enable individuals in this environment to develop new skills for managing the environment.

Strategies may also be developed to compensate for, or change cultural, social or institutional barriers to occupational performance. Working with families and community groups may help to address social or cultural barriers to occupational performance. Likewise, involvement in corporate planning may help to create environments that support safe and productive work. Linking clients with social action groups, or becoming involved in policy development committees may lead to changes in the social, cultural and/or institutional environment. Since each client is unique, the occupational therapist and client choose the strategies that are most relevant to the situation and the targeted outcomes.

Finalizing Action Plans
Part of developing action plans is deciding on the location, timing (schedule), frequency, materials, and estimated duration of implementation (Stage #6). The theoretical approach(es) guiding the process can be used to explain the reasoning for the plan. If implementation is contingent on funding, confirmation of its availability is necessary before proceeding. Methods of evaluation and accountability are built into the action plan.

A plan may include follow-up, as appropriate, so that funding and time can be allocated to determine if targeted outcomes have been reached or sustained. A follow-up plan may be made at this stage or later if this is preferred by a client. In any case, actions to implement or intentions to discuss follow-up need to be included in the plan. A mechanism for ongoing review and revision of the plan is also discussed with the client, as conditions may change.

Stage #6: Implement Plans Through Occupation

Actions are implemented in accordance with the plan. The occupational therapist continually adapts and grades occupations to enable progress towards the targeted outcomes. Grading refers to the technique of categorizing tasks and activities according to their degree of difficulty or complexity (Reed & Sanderson, 1992). The occupational therapist recognizes that implementating the plan is a process of change for clients, and is sensitive to the issues that may arise for clients. Throughout implementation of the plan, the occupational therapist monitors the client's satisfaction with the process and outcomes, and makes changes to enhance satisfaction when needed.

The extent to which all occupational performance issues are resolved, relative to the targeted outcomes, is assessed on an ongoing basis with each client. Even though a targeted outcome may remain the same, the methods for reaching the target may vary from day to day as conditions change. Client perceptions, the occupational therapist's experience, and research results are all used to guide decisions to retain or modify a plan. When changes are made, they are communicated to team members and others. The occupational therapist strives to ensure that the best methods available for resolving or minimizing the occupational performance issue(s) are used.

Stage #7: Evaluate Occupational Performance Outcomes

Before the occupational therapy service is completed, the occupational performance outcome(s) are reviewed to determine the effectiveness of the Occupational Performance Process. This stage is essential for demonstrating professional accountability. Changes in occupational performance and the processes that contribute to change can be determined through evaluation. The importance of evaluating occupational performance outcomes cannot be over-emphasized.

The most important aspect of client-centred evaluation is determining whether the targeted outcomes have been met. The occupational therapist can compare actual outcomes with targeted outcomes, and decide whether to continue or end the Occupational Performance Process. Evaluation may also measure the degree of change in occupational performance over time. Occupational performance outcomes may be compared in simulated versus real settings to determine whether outcomes differ in these settings.

Outcome research may compare the changes in people with similar occupational performance issues who have and have not participated in occupational therapy.

One step in evaluating outcomes is to evaluate the process. A process evaluation documents what was and was not done along with the reasoning for decisions. A client and an occupational therapist might review how occupational performance issues were prioritized, theoretical approaches were selected, and strengths and resources in occupational performance were identified. The client-centredness of these stages might be discussed in order to determine the extent of client involvement. A process evaluation might also identify who was involved, where action took place, and how occupation was incorporated into assessment and implementation. The availability of environmental resources and service supports would be noted. Evaluation of the process is important because it helps to provide clues regarding how and why the successful or unsuccessful outcomes occurred.

Selecting Evaluation Methods

Choices about approach and methodology are based on the evaluation questions that need to be answered. Planning for the evaluation begins in Stage #1. When prior planning has not occurred, the choice of evaluation methods is dependent on the type of documentation that is available.

If client narratives (stories) are recorded from the beginning, and if the process steps, reasoning or the conditions of practice are documented throughout practice, there is a foundation for qualitative evaluation (Guba & Lincoln, 1989). Observation notes and a review of various types of documentation, including statistics can be included in a qualitative evaluation.

Similarly, if the results of standardized testing are recorded at various stages in the process, there is a foundation for quantitative evaluation. Quantitative evaluation might also use statistics on the time, frequency, costs, numbers of people involved or other quantifiable information on the Occupational Performance Process. Additional information on evaluation methods is presented in Chapter 5 in the section, Element #1: Plan Services, Develop a Plan to Evaluate Outcomes.

Completing the Occupational Performance Process

Evaluation completes the Occupational Performance Process unless there is agreement to pursue unresolved or new occupational performance issues; sometimes resolution of one issue leads to others (Fearing et al., 1997). If funding, interest and other resources are present, the process may continue until all occupational performance issues are resolved.

An Occupational Performance Process may end for various reasons. Ideally, services are completed when clients agree that target outcomes have been achieved and no new occupational performance issues require action. The occupational therapist informs the client how services can be re-activated (re-accessed) if necessary in the future, and refers the client to other resources as needed.

Completion and follow-up should be part of the action plan. If there has been partnership among clients, occupational therapists and pertinent others throughout the process, completion of services will not be a surprise. Sometimes services end unexpectedly due to changes in funding, priorities or other factors. Clients and occupational therapists then need to decide whether to accept, revise or challenge these circumstances.

In some situations, follow-up may be implemented by another occupational therapy service. When this occurs, the Occupational Performance Process may be continued in a new setting with a different occupational therapist. For example, the first cycle of the Occupational Performance Process may occur in a hospital setting, with the second and third cycle occurring in a client's home; or three cycles may occur in one industrial setting over a period of years in the same or different settings. Any combination of cycles is possible - the process belongs to and goes with the client and can occur in diverse environments. Since the process is client-centred, clients may wish to pursue the same targeted outcomes when a process cycle is continued by a new service. Ideally, some aspects of assessment may not need repeating if there is good communication and agreement by a client that information can be shared with a new service. In an organization, one set of managers may agree to share information with other managers so that a process may be continued rather than repeated for different parts of the organization. When service is expected to continue in a different setting, recommendations are communicated to future services with the client's consent and/or as documentation and privacy laws indicate.

ADDITIONAL FEATURES AND GUIDELINES FOR THE OCCUPATIONAL PERFORMANCE PROCESS

Occupational Therapy Reasoning in the Process

Schon (1983, 1987) and Rogers (1983) indicate that using a linear process aids reasoning for students and novice occupational therapists. In contrast, experienced occupational therapists tend to use the non-linear approach to reasoning that is reported by Mattingly & Hayes Fleming (1994). They may alter the sequence of the stages to follow the reasoning of the client, or combine stages. The stages in the Occupational Performance Process are presented here as a linear sequence to provide an easy guideline for practice. In reality though, some stages may occur concurrently and others may not occur because the process ends before Stage #7.

Even when the sequence of the stages in the process are similar, the actions of an occupational therapist in each stage are unique. Each person-environment-occupation interaction produces unique priorities for addressing occupational performance issues. For example, when new occupational performance issues arise during the implementation of plans, an occupational therapist will alter the process to address these new issues. The process stops if no occupational performance issues are identified, or the client chooses to exit the process.

While there are variations in the process, there are also commonalities. Information gathering (Stages #1 and #3) precedes the development of action plans (Stage #5); planning precedes implementation (Stage #6); and the plan is implemented before client outcomes can be evaluated (Stage #7). Stages are rarely discrete. It is common for planning, action, implementation, and evaluation to occur simultaneously. In these days of continuous quality improvement, evaluation of outcomes is a stage that pervades all others.

Spirituality and the Process

References to spirituality are noticeably absent in the descriptions of each stage. However, spirituality is not missing from the process; rather it is reflected in the entire process. The Occupational Performance Process respects the uniqueness of all persons, whether as individuals or members of an organization or community. The views of the clients (or their representatives) are essential to the process. The development of a collaborative partnership between the client and occupational therapist not only guides the process, but more importantly provides greater assurance that occupational therapy will reflect clients' values, beliefs and preferences. Spirituality is at the heart of assessing which occupations are meaningful to clients, and in building meaningful occupation into targeted outcomes, action plans and implementation. Spirituality is a fundamental, central part of the process of enabling self-determination, relating services to life experiences, and making occupation meaningful.

Ethics and the Process

Working with clients inevitably raises ethical issues. Ethical decisions, for which occupational therapists are accountable, are often required in everyday practice situations. One ethical issue may be to decide who is the primary client. If an individual is the primary client, then family or community members may be secondary clients. Alternatively, corporate managers may be the primary client, while the workers are secondary clients.

Another ethical issue may arise when an occupational therapy assessment is used in liability or insurance claims. The occupational therapist may be placed in a conflict of interest situation between the insurance company and the person being assessed. The *Codes of Ethics* of the Canadian

Association of Occupational Therapists and provincial regulatory bodies are important guides in making ethical decisions (CAOT, 1996a).

Accountability in the Process

Occupational therapists who are accountable give "satisfactory reasons or an explanation" for the decisions they make (Guralnik, 1984, p. 9). The CCHSA (1995) defines accountabilities as "responsibilities that may not be delegated" (p. 39). With increasing demands for accountability it is important that the Occupational Performance Process guide the delivery of effective and accountable occupational therapy services.

Accountability may be demonstrated in many ways. Examples include:
- adhering to professional codes of ethics and standards;
- documenting the Occupational Performance Process;
- maintaining professional competence;
- using research findings to justify decisions about practice approaches;
- participating in research and education;
- making changes to practice based on feedback from clients and others; and
- being proactive in addressing service or societal issues that limit the occupational performance of clients (see Chapter 5).

These examples of accountability influence the Occupational Performance Process. The process also facilitates accountability. By specifying the outcomes of each stage in the titles of the stages, major responsibilities of the occupational therapist in the Occupational Performance Process are identified. The importance of occupational therapists' accountability for every stage of the Occupational Performance Process cannot be overemphasized.

Documentation of the Occupational Performance Process

Documentation is a common method for demonstrating accountability. An occupational therapist's records should be in sufficient detail to meet legal requirements, professional responsibilities, and standards, such as those published by the CCHSA (1995) and other regulatory bodies (Cosman & Heinz, 1996). The format used to document the Occupational Performance Process will depend on the nature of the service request, the type of service offered, the needs of the client, and the environment in which service occurs. Canadian law now gives individuals the right to review and photocopy their health records unless it is legally determined that access to a record would have harmful effects on the individual or other parties (Rozovsky & Rozovsky, 1990, 1992). Documentation is also subject to local, provincial, national and agency regulations.

Documentation requirements vary from setting to setting; however it is typical to document the outcomes of each stage, whether or not occupational therapy continues. Key recommendations related to the documentation of the stages are outlined.

Stage #1:

The occupational therapist ensures that documentation of an occupational performance issue accurately reflects the client's validation and priorities. In some situations, the issue may be recorded as quoted or written down by the client. Otherwise, where possible, the occupational therapist reviews with the client what was documented. At the end of Stage #1, written contracts are recommended if the process continues (Cosman & Heinz, 1996). An initial contract at this stage would outline information such as prioritized occupational performance issues, possible theoretical approaches, available services, who can participate, and payment arrangements.

Stages #1-#4

Occupational Profile:

The Occupational Profile summarizes the client's prioritized occupational performance issues, occupational performance components and environmental conditions, and strengths and resources for resolving the prioritized issues. That is, key information and outcomes of Stages #1-#4. An Occupational Profile provides a record of assessment findings and the reasoning for actions taken to that point. Documentation of an Occupational Profile is necessary for accountability and also guides the remainder of the Occupational Performance Process.

Sufficient information should be included in an Occupational Profile to facilitate negotiation of the targeted outcomes with the client. The information is also needed to develop and implement action plans. Strengths and resources for resolving the identified issues are outlined, pointing out current or potential opportunities for removing barriers to occupational performance. Where appropriate, a client should develop the Occupational Profile in partnership with the occupational therapist. In some situations, a client might prefer only to review and comment on the Profile. The written Occupational Profile may be supplemented with photographs, maps of the environment, audio or videotapes and other materials.

Stages #5 & #6:

The targeted outcomes and action plans (Stage #5) are documented and signed ideally by a client and occupational therapist prior to implementation. Client signatures on plans may not be typical but they are important in client-centred practice. They provide a tangible way of ensuring that the client knows and agrees with the plan. Client representatives may need to sign in some situations. Stage #5 may be the second contractual stage if an agreement was signed after naming, validating and prioritizing occupational performance issues in Stage #1. The agreement forms a contract of partnership between the occupational therapist and client. The agreement indicates that ongoing discussion of progress with modification of the plan as needed, is part of implementation. This is another opportunity for accountability. Documentation of the targeted outcomes and the action plan provides evidence that there is a clear purpose and plan to end occupational therapy.

Progress, changes in the plan, reasons for the changes, and referrals to other resources are also documented. Where appropriate, implementation and changes in plans are communicated to those who are coordinating client services. If the occupational therapist is coordinating services (with as much client involvement as possible), information from other service personnel may be included in the occupational therapy documentation.

Stage #7:
When the process is being completed (Stage #7) significant aspects of the process and practice conditions that have not already been documented are recorded to enable evaluation of the processes that contributed to client and service outcomes (see Chapter 5). Qualitative and quantitative evaluation findings for clients are also documented, ensuring that assessment information gathered during the process meets all accountability and legal requirements. Occupational performance outcomes for the client, as well as future plans and recommendations are identified.

Two vignettes demonstrate how the stages of the Occupational Performance Process are applied with an individual and organizational client. They reflect what the occupational therapist does in partnership with clients during the process. The vignettes are based on real situations, with names, locations and other identifiers changed to preserve anonymity.

APPLICATION #1: WORKING WITH AN INDIVIDUAL CLIENT (Mr Elliott)
Scenario
Mr Elliott was discharged from a hospital to a care facility 6 months after his stroke. He did not work with occupational therapists in the hospital but told the care facility occupational therapist about his desire to return home. The Occupational Performance Process guided the occupational therapist, Mr Elliott and Mrs Elliott, and others in determining what would be required for Mr Elliott to return home, and the actions needed for that to occur (the first targeted outcome). Once home, he had additional occupational performance issues that he wanted to address with an occupational therapist. It is these issues that are noted in Stage #1.

Stage #1: Name, Validate, and Prioritize Occupational Performance Issues
Mr Elliott identified the following occupational performance issues in order of priority on the *Canadian Occupational Performance Measure*

(COPM): Potential inability to travel by air to visit friends and family; Inability to continue to edit a community newspaper; and Inability to manage family finances. Application of the process for the first occupational performance issue (travel) follows. Although not essential for successful travel, Mr Elliott indicated that his goal was to be independent in the mobility and self-care tasks associated with travel.

Stage #2: Select Theoretical Approach(es)

To address the issue of being unable to travel by airplane, neuro-integrative, biomechanical and environmental approaches were used. These approaches guided the occupational therapist in deciding what to assess and how assessment would be done. Planning and implementation were consistent with these approaches, incorporating the leisure occupation of visiting and related tasks and activities as a central focus.

Stage #3: Identify Occupational Performance Components and Environmental Conditions

Assessment in his home indicated that Mr Elliott required one person to assist with all transfers from his wheelchair to his car, an ordinary chair, etc. Less assistance was required to use the toilet because grab rails had been installed in the bathroom. Although he required assistance to bathe, this was not a concern related to the first occupational performance issue. He could walk with a quad cane (cane with four prongs) with one person assisting, but used a wheelchair for distances of more than 3 metres. His wife provided assistance on request. Help with hook fastenings on his clothing, particularly the zipper on his pants, was required. Mr Elliott had mastered one-handed techniques and could feed himself but could not open small individual serving food containers (like the ones used by airlines).

Analysis of his occupational performance in self-care occupations showed that weakness in all four limbs contributed to his difficulties (limited physical performance component). There was generalized atrophy of all muscles. He had not exercised in hospital but demonstrated some promise of gaining strength as he had become more active since returning home. His ability to transfer to and from the toilet using a grab rail indicated that with improved strength and a supportive physical environment in an airport he might be able to meet his goal of independence in the self-care tasks related to his travel.

The local airport was found to have an accessible entrance and washrooms. A brief visit to the airport revealed that long terminal hallways could be traversed using airport wheelchairs, although these were not always available at the entrance. A conversation with family members and airline personnel at the potential travel destination indicated that the destination airport met accessibility requirements. Family and friends at the destination stated that their homes had some accessible features but all had stairs. In summary, the analysis of all findings showed that the occupational performance issue, i.e. potential inability to travel by air to visit family and friends, was related to: lack of knowledge and skill in using one-handed techniques to open small individual food packages and to close hook fastenings on clothing; lack of muscle strength and activity tolerance to walk more than 3 metres and transfer independently; potential lack of an adapted physical environment and a supportive social environment during travel.

Stage #4: Identify Strengths and Resources

Mr Elliott had a strong desire for independence, and was highly motivated to acquire the needed knowledge and skills. He was also realistic, as he did not want to travel until his physical stamina was the best it could be, and all preparations were made. As a retired mechanical engineer, he was an active problem-solver. His wife, other family members and friends were very supportive. Community disability organizations and airline personnel offered to provide information and assist with travel. Airline personnel were trained to provide boarding assistance and a wheelchair if needed, and family members and airport staff offered to assist with luggage at the destination. The occupational therapist had experience working with people following a stroke, and the resources, procedures and insurance of the service enabled the occupational therapist to visit the airport with Mr Elliott.

Stage #5: Negotiate Targeted Outcomes, Develop Action Plan

Targeted Outcome:

Within 6 months, Mr Elliott will have travelled successfully by air to visit his family

Criteria for measuring success from Mr Elliott's perspective included:

- Identification of acceptable methods that enable use of the aircraft as well as the airport terminal toilet facilities (e.g. for transfers, walking, dressing);
- Ability to gain wheelchair access to terminals, through security, and to/from departure/arrival gates;
- Ability to open food containers on the aircraft.

Plans for occupational therapy action included:

- The occupational therapist will refer Mr Elliott to a physiotherapist to improve muscle strength and stamina;
- The occupational therapist will demonstrate one-handed skills for opening food containers, closing fastenings, and independent transfers; and coach Mr Elliott in practising these techniques;
- Mr Elliott will contact the airport to confirm that the information about airport and aircraft access, facilities and resources is accurate;
- The occupational therapist will provide information to Mr & Mrs Elliott on how to obtain a community resources handbook on

travelling with a disability;

- With the Elliotts, the occupational therapist will test access and identify potential environmental barriers at the airport, and devise strategies for overcoming actual and potential barriers to travel.

Stage #6: Implement Plans Through Occupation

The plans were carried out. Mr Elliott and his wife obtained resource information and visited the airport. The occupational therapist interpreted the information and assisted in developing the travel plan (related to the occupational performance issue). Other plans were carried out jointly. With the exception of the visit to the airport, meetings with the Elliotts occurred in their home. When difficulties arose in testing the travel plan at the home airport, these were analyzed and strategies for preventing these and other potential difficulties were devised. Progress was documented regularly with Mr Elliott's participation. Mr Elliott requested that a follow-up meeting with the occupational therapist occur after he had completed the travel.

Stage #7: Evaluate Occupational Performance Outcomes

Following completion of the travel plan, Mr Elliott travelled out of province with his wife to visit his family. The follow-up meeting upon his return indicated that the trip had not been without difficulties, but the strategies discussed before the trip enabled the couple to solve the problems as they occurred. The targeted outcome had been achieved and the Elliotts were satisfied with the service from the occupational therapist. They discussed the additional occupational performance issues that Mr Elliott was now ready to address, and a new cycle of the Occupational Performance Process began.

APPLICATION #2: WORKING WITH AN ORGANIZATIONAL CLIENT (A Fish Filleting Plant)
Scenario

A private occupational therapy practice was asked to assess the factors that were contributing to the high injury rate among workers at a fish filleting plant. The initial contract was only for assessment and recommendations. As assessment proceeded, the contract was extended to implement recommendations.

Stage #1: Name, Validate, and Prioritize Occupational Performance Issues

Interviews with union and management representatives, and with workers at the fish filleting plant identified one common occupational performance issue: 60% of workers at the fish filleting plant are unable to complete all or parts of their scheduled shifts.

Workers were unable to complete all or parts of their shifts because of injuries. These included painful wrists for fish filleters, shoulder and back injuries for workers who sorted and drenched fish prior to freezing, and sore feet for many workers who stood for long periods at a variety of work stations.

The initial occupational therapy contract with the plant specified that within four weeks, the occupational therapist was to:
- Identify factors that were contributing to the high injury rate
- Recommend changes to minimize or eliminate these factors
- Provide a full written report of the assessment and recommendations
- Present recommendations to management and workers.

Stage #2: Select Theoretical Approach(es)
A biomechanical approach (physical-rehabilitative theory), human factors theory (environmental theory), theories of coping and adaptation (psycho-emotional theories) and role and group theory (socio-adaptive theories) guided the assessment that sought to answer the question: Why are workers unable to complete part or all of their scheduled shifts?

Stage #3: Identify Occupational Performance Components and Environmental Conditions
Assessment methods included:
- Review of data re injury types and rates at the 15 different work stations
- Interviews with management representatives and workers
- Individual assessments of workers at their stations to identify occupational performance components and environmental conditions related to their work (productivity occupations) at the plant
- Occupational analysis of the 15 work stations on several shifts

Observation and interviews confirmed that there was a strong relationship between workers' habits, the environment, and injuries. That is, a poor person-environment-occupation fit.   For example:
- Workers used poor posture and incorrect body mechanics
- Methods used to lift baskets of wet fish placed heavy demands on workers' shoulder muscles, increasing risk of injuries
- The physical environment did not match workers' needs (e.g., heights of work stools and tables were not adjustable; fish filleting knives were not sized for different workers needs, and some work stations were very cold)
- Aspects of the institutional environment at the plant such as the policies about scheduling, assigning work shifts and payment for quotas encouraged fast, unsafe work without sufficient breaks.

The injury rate was highest amongst the fish filleters. Interviews with these workers indicated that there was a lot of culture, ritual and tradition about use of a particular type of fish filleting knife. The workers seemed to know that the use of the knife contributed to their injuries but were reluctant to change knives. The fish filleters received the highest pay of all workers. They acknowledged that they would not last long as fish filleters but since the pay was high they wanted to continue in those roles as long as possible even if their health suffered.

For most workers, being able to carry out their jobs without injuries was extremely important. Although the financial compensation for their work was valued, it was evident in the interviews that there was high camaraderie among workers and many social activities were shared after work. The workers placed high value on these social aspects. Injured workers missed the support from these activities that went with the job. As one worker stated, "not being at work makes me feel that I'm not a member of the club".

Interviews revealed a lack of knowledge by management and union workers concerning the effect of work scheduling and the lack of variety in work tasks on repetitive motion injuries. It was noted that basic Workers' Compensation Board safety standards were being met.

Analysis of the findings indicated that the occupational performance issue, i.e., 60% of workers at the fish filleting plant are unable to complete all or parts of their scheduled shifts was related to: Workers used methods and equipment that lead to injuries; Management and workers lacked knowledge of how workers' methods and the physical, cultural and institutional environment contributed to the injury rate; Workers' fitness level was below that required to meet the physical demands of the work; The physical environment did not support workers in meeting work expectations without injury; and, Organizational policies encouraged unsafe work.

Stage #4: Identify Strengths and Resources

Workers and management were highly motivated to resolve the plant difficulties so that workers could resume employment, and injuries to others could be prevented. Their readiness to give comments and suggestions and to ask questions reflected their interest in collaborating to solve the problems. The occupational therapist's experience as a consultant in other assembly plant situations was an asset.

A comprehensive Occupational Profile written in a report format, detailed all assessment findings and recommendations. The latter included the need for:
- Changes to methods and equipment at work stations that would improve the person-environment-occupation fit

- Changes in work scheduling and work station rotations to prevent injuries
- Education to enhance knowledge about injury prevention
- A programme to increase the physical fitness of workers to reduce injuries
- A graded return to work programme for injured workers

Highlights and recommendations in the Occupational Profile report were discussed with management, and then with management and workers together. Based on the recommendations in the report, satisfaction with the service, available funding, and the positive response of workers, management decided to extend the contract by negotiating targeted outcomes and developing action plans to address the occupational performance issue.

Stage #5: Negotiate Targeted Outcomes, Develop Action Plan
Targeted outcomes:
- Within 12 weeks, recommended adaptations will be made to work stations and new equipment will be purchased and installed, to the extent that plant funding is available, in consultation with the occupational therapist.
- Within one month, changes in work scheduling will be made by management and workers to reduce injuries, and a plan for work station rotations will be developed with plant managers and worker representatives in consultation with the occupational therapist, for discussion with all workers.
- Within 12 weeks, plant workers will be leading a workers' physical fitness programme three times per week with a view to increasing awareness of the physical demands of plant jobs and the need for a high level of fitness on the job
- Within one month, the plant Industrial First Aid Attendant and workers will be ready to coordinate a plant injury prevention programme that they have developed, in consultation with the occupational therapist
- In one month, a graded return to work programme for injured workers will be provided by the occupational therapist upon request
- After 6 and 12 months, the Industrial First Aid Attendant (and other workers recommended by management) will have evaluated the extent to which the programmes have been successful in reducing injuries, with coaching provided by the occupational therapist as needed

Action plans:
- Work station adaptations will be made and new equipment installed to the extent that funding is available from the plant.
- The occupational therapist will consult with plant management

and workers in planning for work scheduling changes and work station rotations.

- A qualified physiotherapist or fitness expert will be hired for 12 weeks to educate workers in developing and offering the on-site fitness programme during working hours.
- The physical fitness expert will be responsible to the occupational therapist.
- An injury prevention programme will be developed and targeted to all current workers and new employees.
- The Industrial First Aid attendant and workers will be coached by the occupational therapist in developing and implementing the plant's injury prevention programme.
- Resource materials for work station training will be identified by the occupational therapist and workers.
- A graded return to work programme will be provided by the occupational therapist for individual workers upon request by the plant, in one month, when other plans have been initiated. When this occurs, the occupational therapist and each worker will use the seven stage Occupational Performance Process to guide the development of each worker's programme.
- A plan for evaluating the effectiveness of the programmes will be developed and implemented in collaboration with the plant management and workers.

Stage #6: Implement Plans Through Occupation

Plans were implemented and monitored on a continuing basis. Implementation emphasized actions that engaged management and workers in new approaches to their occupations in the plant.

Stage #7: Evaluate Occupational Performance Outcomes

After one year, injured workers who participated in the graded return to work programme spent less time off work. Those who returned to full-time work had lower re-injury rates than other injured workers who had not participated in the graded return to work programme. Injury rates were lowest among new and continuing workers who participated in the new injury prevention and fitness programmes, and who worked in the adapted work stations. Although work scheduling changes were made, the workers would not support a work station rotation system.

Workers and managers' satisfaction with the occupational therapy consultation were assessed at the end of the consultation by questionnaire. Anecdotal comments were also recorded from completion interviews with plant and union managers who were interviewed separately, then together. The results of these evaluations were very positive. Individual outcome measures were administered before and after occupational therapy consultation. They demonstrated changes in individual workers' use of injury prevention methods to enhance their occupational performance.

REFLECTIVE QUESTIONS

Each client and practice situation raises unique questions. Nevertheless, a client-centred, occupation-focused practice is subject to questions that examine how occupation is kept in focus while collaborating with clients. These reflective questions guide occupational therapists in using the Occupational Performance Process with clients and can stimulate thinking about application of the core concepts outlined in Chapter 3.

Stage #1: Name, Validate, and Prioritize Occupational Performance Issues

- Who is the primary client? Secondary clients?
- What choice does the client have for participating in the Occupational Performance Process?
- Have risks and responsibilities for the client and occupational therapist been openly discussed and clearly documented? Signed and dated as appropriate?
- Have the method(s) used in a screening assessment focused on identifying the client's perceptions of actual or potential occupational performance issues?
- Have occupational performance issues been named, validated, and prioritized by the client? Are issues related to self-care, productivity, leisure?
- How are occupational performance issues related to health? Quality of life? Fair opportunities for living?
- What is the purpose of this first stage? To begin the Occupational Performance Process with an individual client? To plan the organization of occupational therapy or other services? To initiate decision making about housing, employment?
- How is the screening part of Stage #1 coordinated with Stage #3 assessments?
- What enabling methods were used by the occupational therapist? Group facilitation, coaching during occupations, listening and supporting, etc.?
- Is service complete at this stage? Why? Are reasons for completing service documented?
- How is this stage documented? How is the client's point of view reflected in the documentation? Signed?

Stage #2: Select Theoretical Approach(es)

- How will decisions about theoretical approaches involve the client?
- What theoretical approaches will guide assessment of occupational performance? Identification of targeted occupational performance outcomes? Development of action plans and their implementation through occupation? Evaluation of occupational performance outcomes related to self-care, productivity, and leisure?

- How will theoretical approaches be used to explain assessment findings? With clients? In interprofessional or 'team' situations? With others?
- What is the research base for the selected theoretical approaches? How does research justify the use of these approaches in practice?
- How is this stage documented? Are client concerns or agreement with the theoretical approaches documented?

Stage #3: Identify Occupational Performance Components and Environmental Conditions

- How is the assessment related to the identified occupational performance issues? How is the client involved in assessment decisions? How will assessment information be used? Guiding the Occupational Performance Process? Research? Legal purposes? Are the reasons for assessment clear to the client, occupational therapist, pertinent others?
- Is the information focussed on identifying the occupational performance components and environmental conditions that are contributing to the occupational performance issues? How much information needs to be gathered?
- How is the information best collected? What options for assessment are possible?
- How is occupation being used in assessment? What occupations are being observed? Tested? Described? Analyzed? Where? Why?
- What qualitative methods are appropriate?
- What quantitative methods are appropriate?
- Will the methods provide the information needed to guide subsequent stages of the Occupational Performance Process?
- How might assessment information be used for research?
- What are potential legal uses? Evidence in court? Protective evidence in a malpractice suit?
- What ethical, moral or legal restrictions apply to the assessment process or information?
- Have ethical, moral or legal issues in assessment information been discussed with the client?
- Will the assessment information provide sufficient baseline information for judging whether or not occupational performance outcomes have been achieved later in the process?
- Has the impact of performance components and environmental conditions on occupational performance been identified?
- How is this stage coordinated with assessments being done by others?
- How is this stage documented? How is the client participating in documentation? Is there a signed contract outlining the plan?
- Does documentation of the assessment specify the occupational performance issues, theoretical approaches, occupational

performance components and environmental conditions?

- If the occupational therapy contract with the client is completed at this stage, is documentation complete? Are the reasons for completing the contract identified in the documentation?

Stage #4: Identify Strengths and Resources

- What performance components and environmental conditions do the client and occupational therapist view as the client's resources for resolving the prioritized issues?
- What social and cultural resources are available to the client? Personal friends? Family? Organizations?
- What physical or institutional resources are available? e.g., space to work at home; an adapted environment
- What financial resources are available?
- What are the occupational therapist's personal and professional strengths for enabling the client to resolve the prioritized occupational performance issues?
- What resources are available to the occupational therapist? Assistance from peers? Professional team? Non-professional workers? Self-help groups? Equipment and materials? Human resources? Management support? Access to funding? Educational opportunities?
- How are client and occupational therapy resources coordinated with team and other resources?
- Have opportunities and barriers for supporting current or potential occupational performance been identified?
- Does the Occupational Profile summarize all assessment information about priority occupational performance issues, occupational performance components and environmental conditions, strengths, resources, opportunities, barriers?
- Have ethical issues or potential conflicts of interest been identified in the Occupational Profile?
- How is the Occupational Profile documented? Is documentation through film, photographs, or other methods besides a written report? Is the client co-signing the Occupational Profile or providing an alternate, written point of view?

Stage #5: Negotiate Targeted Outcomes, Develop Action Plan

- What occupational performance outcomes are meaningful to the client?
- What other outcomes are being pursued with the team, consulting group, community, etc?
- In identifying the targeted outcomes and discussing plans for reaching them, how was the client encouraged to envision new possibilities?
- Does the wording of the targeted outcome accurately reflect the targeted outcome(s) which were discussed and negotiated with the

client(s)?

- Do targeted outcomes state what occupation(s) a client will be able to perform upon completion of the Occupational Performance Process?
- Are targeted outcomes measurable? What will be measured?
- Can targeted outcomes be described or otherwise recorded (if not measured)? What will be described or documented?
- What methods are being used to measure, describe, or record targeted outcomes?
- Can the client describe the targeted outcomes and the plan chosen to reach them?
- Are options for the action plans being discussed with the client in developing the plan?
- How are occupational therapy plans coordinated with those of others involved in the situation?
- Does the plan specify what the occupational therapist and the client(s) will do to reach the targeted outcomes? Who is responsible for what and when? Were responsibilities discussed jointly?
- Is the plan realistic and achievable? Are the resources available to provide the occupational therapy and other services in the plan? Can the plan be implemented in the time available, and with the available human, material and financial resources? Is planning information documented?
- How will occupations that have meaning for the client be used in implementing the plan?
- Will the plan lead logically to the targeted outcomes?
- Does the plan include strategies to take advantage of opportunities and reduce barriers to occupational performance?
- Does the plan acknowledge and utilize the strengths and resources of the client?
- Is the plan documented in a manner that is understandable to the client, occupational therapist, service reviewers, and others who may be legally entitled to have access to it?
- Is a mechanism for ongoing review and revision of the plan being decided with the client?
- Is follow-up related to occupational performance included in the plan if needed?
- Does the evaluation plan include outcomes that are focused on occupational performance and client-centred practice?
- How is the occupational therapy evaluation coordinated with other evaluation strategies?
- Is some type of agreement or contract being signed and dated by the client and occupational therapist?
- How will the targeted outcomes, plans, and changes be documented? What has the client documented or signed in relation to the plan?

Stage #6: Implement Plans Through Occupation

- Is implementation following the plan?
- What decisions and actions is the client taking in implementation?
- How are the actions that address occupational performance components and environmental conditions relevant to occupational performance issues?
- How are targeted occupational performance outcomes being reviewed and revised (if appropriate) during implementation?
- Is the action plan being implemented in a safe, efficient and timely manner?
- Is implementation based on current research about effective approaches?
- How is the theoretical basis for implementation being reviewed by the occupational therapist and the client?
- Is the equipment required to implement the action plan in working order? Are facilities or locations for implementation accessible - physically, financially, socially, culturally?
- How is implementation of the occupational therapy plan coordinated with other actions, programmes, services?
- How is implementation being documented? Are clients documenting perceptions of progress alongside occupational therapy progress notes?

Stage #7: Evaluate Occupational Performance Outcomes

- Is evaluation being done according to the action plan?
- What will be evaluated? What is the purpose of evaluation? To show change? To demonstrate accountability? To monitor the process? To determine service costs?
- How is the client collecting and analyzing evaluation information?
- What is the difference between evaluating individual client occupational performance outcomes and targeted outcomes of an organizational client?
- What is the relationship between evaluating client outcomes and evaluating service outcomes?
- How will the evaluation be done? By whom? When and where?
- What will be done with evaluation findings? Reflection with client? Research? Programme evaluation? Circulation to pertinent participants or funding agents? Legal proceedings?
- How are targeted outcomes compared with actual outcomes?
- How is occupational therapy evaluation linked to other evaluations?
- How is evaluation being documented? What evaluation evidence is being documented by the client? How is the client participating in analyzing evaluation information?

CHAPTER FIVE

Linking Concepts to a Process for Organizing Occupational Therapy Services

PRIMARY AUTHORS:
Sue Stanton
Christine Kramer
Tracey Thompson-Franson

Purpose

To demonstrate how the core concepts of occupational performance and client-centred practice are applied in organizing occupational therapy services.

Objectives

- To present six elements of a process for organizing occupational therapy services; and

- To show how each element interacts with the societal context of practice to support or constrain the Occupational Performance Process described in Chapter 4.

Summary

Chapter 5 links features of the Context of Practice (Chapter 2), Core Concepts of Occupational Therapy (Chapter 3), and the Occupational Performance Process (Chapter 4) to the organization of an occupational therapy service. Six service elements are described: plan, market, manage, educate, research, and evaluate. Depending on how it is organized within the societal context, each element either supports or constrains the Occupational Performance Process used in working with clients. Examples and reflective questions guide occupational therapists in organizing services to support the Occupational Performance Process and enable occupation.

$\mathcal{A}$n occupational therapy service is defined here as a set of activities that are designed and organized by occupational therapists to enable occupation with individuals, organizations and communities. Services are organized when a need for an occupational therapy service is identified, and resources are available to meet that need.

Each occupational therapy service has distinct features because it is organized in a particular context to meet the occupational performance needs of clients in that context. The types of settings in which services occur, the scheduling of programmes, the amount of funding, and the numbers and types of clients and service personnel can vary considerably. Furthermore, a service may or may not be called an occupational therapy service. Occupational therapists may work in group practices with personnel from a variety of disciplines.

Despite these differences, the services offered by occupational therapists have common features. Occupational therapy services that enable occupation:

- reflect occupational therapy values, beliefs and core concepts;
- enable persons to perform occupations which are meaningful to them;
- use occupations to promote the achievement of self-care, productivity and/or leisure occupations;
- follow a client-centred Occupational Performance Process such as the one described in Chapter 4; and
- are tailored to meet the specific needs of each client.

The examples listed in Table 14 reflect occupational therapy's focus on enabling occupation.

A FRAMEWORK FOR LINKING CLIENTS, SERVICES AND SOCIETY

Effective application of the Occupational Performance Process (described in Chapter 4) is only one ingredient of an occupational therapy service that enables occupation. The organization of an occupational therapy service and the societal context in which it occurs also support or constrain the Occupational Performance Process. The goal of organizing occupational therapy services is to maximize the supports and minimize or eliminate the constraints to the process so that clients' needs are met.

The Occupational Performance Process that guides occupational therapists in working with clients, the service environment and the context of society in which service occurs, interact to enable occupation. These three levels are represented by the terms, client, service and society in the model shown in Figure 6, based on the model reported by Stanton (1996).

The process used in working with clients is depicted in the inner circle. Six elements of the service environment are placed in the outer circle. The context of society is identified outside the circles. Definitions of the three levels of this model are:

Client: Represents the client's and occupational therapist's collaboration in the Occupational Performance Process wherever it occurs (e.g. in a home, workplace, a corporation, hospital).

Service: Represents the environment in which the service is organized. Its six elements (Figure 6) interact to support the client and occupational therapist in using the Occupational Performance Process. Examples of service environments such as hospitals, private practices, or consulting groups, are included in Table 14. The service environment may or may not be where service occurs. For example, a consulting service may be organized in an office setting and its services provided where clients live and work.

Society: Represents all people, collectively, in a community of related interdependent individuals who shape the development of public policy, procedures, laws, regulations, and standards for culture, ethics, etc. These features define the societal context for organizing occupational therapy services (see Chapter 2). The societal level is comparable to the institutional element of the environment influencing occupational performance (Table 9, Chapter 3). The societal context may be a resource and support, or a constraint for the client and service levels.

Each level of the Client, Service, Society Model shapes and is shaped by the others. For example, societal decisions about funding determine what kinds of services are organized which, in turn, determine what types of client needs can be met. Conversely, client needs influence the types of services which are organized, and the extent to which occupational therapists and clients seek access to funds, equipment and other resources (from society) to enable occupation. This dynamic interaction among the levels is represented by dotted lines in Figure 6.

Ideally, interactions produce a client-service-society fit so that clients' occupational performance issues are addressed in a service environment and societal context that is organized to support occupational therapists in using the Occupational Performance Process effectively with clients. Services are planned to meet clients' needs, and the plans are implemented so that the marketing, management, education, research and evaluation efforts (Figure 6) support the achievement of client outcomes. For example, occupational therapists who provide services have the necessary education to use the Occupational Performance Process with clients. Societal policies, procedures and resources also support the client, occupational therapist and service in enabling occupation. The example in Figure 7 shows how service elements interacted with the societal context

Table 14: Service Descriptions Focused on Enabling Occupation

- School-based services with children whose physical difficulties limit their participation in school work.

- Community-based services that enable people who have had a stroke and their caregivers to explore opportunities for occupation that can promote their health and well being.

- Home support services that enable adults who have Parkinson's or other debilitating diseases to maintain their participation in valued occupations.

- Hospital-based services that increase skills in self-care and productivity occupations to enable adults and seniors to return home as soon as possible following orthopaedic surgery.

- Boarding home support programmes that promote the mental health of adults through participation in self-care, productivity and leisure occupations.

- Community-based programmes that enable community members to work as partners to raise funds and renovate houses to provide shelter and offer programmes that will enable occupation with and for community members who are homeless.

- Day programmes that address the occupational performance issues of adults who are adapting to life with schizophrenia.

- Occupational performance assessment services designed to evaluate the impact of trauma-related disability on the performance of self care, productivity or leisure occupations.

- Residential rehabilitation programmes that develop skills in self-care, productivity and leisure occupations with adolescents who have had a brain injury.

- Consulting services that enhance the safe performance of work-related occupations by people in industry.

- Services that develop and evaluate programmes that enhance employment adjustment for workers who face employment changes as a result of mental or physical difficulties.

- Consulting services in which occupational therapists enable advocacy groups (people with disabilities, homeless youth, seniors) to develop community employment and housing options that will enhance occupational performance.

Enabling Occupation: An Occupational Therapy Perspective, CAOT 1997

Table 15: Elements in Organizing and Delivering Effective Client-Centred Services

- Plan Services
- Market Services
- Manage Services
- Educate
- Access and Participate in Research
- Evaluate Services

Enabling Occupation: An Occupational Therapy Perspective, CAOT 1997

to support the Occupational Performance Process with Mr Elliott, the individual client introduced in Chapter 4.

When the organization of services or the societal context constrains the Occupational Performance Process with clients, an occupational therapy service is unlikely to enable occupation. For example, a service policy may limit timely access to occupational therapy services, or absent home support services may prevent a client from participating in valued occupations at home. When constraints arise, the occupational therapist can recommend service changes, or advocate for societal changes to enable occupation. An occupational therapy service that is organized to support an Occupational Performance Process with clients, and supports occupational therapists and clients in overcoming service and societal constraints to the delivery of effective and efficient services, is most likely to enable occupation with clients.

SIX ELEMENTS IN ORGANIZING OCCUPATIONAL THERAPY SERVICES

Table 15 lists the six elements of the service environment that are shown in the Client, Service, Society Model (Figure 6). The six elements reflect the organization and marketing, professional accountability, planning, evaluation and management units in the *Profile of Occupational Therapy Practice in Canada* (CAOT, 1996c).

Plan Services is the most important element, and receives the greatest emphasis in this chapter. The service plan directs the implementation of the remaining five elements, and in doing so, provides a template for implementing effective, efficient and accountable services. In addition to the information provided in this chapter, there are many resources to guide occupational therapists in planning new or revised services. Occupational therapy and related literature provide more detailed information on the organization and delivery of services for particular clientele and organizational contexts (e.g. Backman, 1994; Jacobs, 1987; Jaffe & Epstein, 1992; Pagonis, 1987).

Figure 6: The Client, Service Society Model

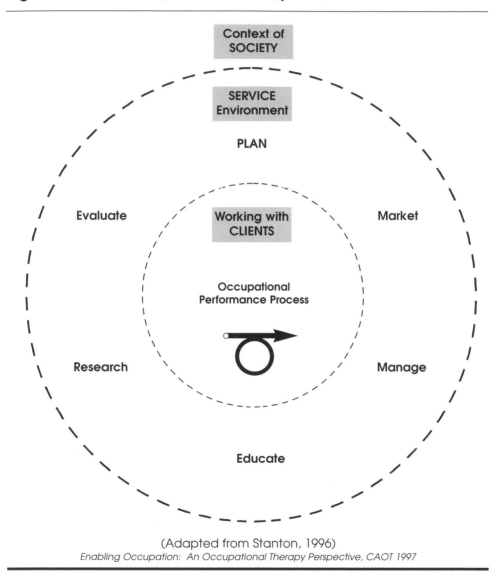

(Adapted from Stanton, 1996)

Enabling Occupation: An Occupational Therapy Perspective, CAOT 1997

Although the planning of services precedes the implementation of the remaining elements, organizing services is not a linear process. Rather, each element is part of an interconnected process for organizing services in everyday practice. For example, while plans are needed to guide the implementation of all elements, planning also occurs on an ongoing basis in response to evaluation results, to service constraints, or other factors such as changes in funding or the reorganization of services.

Likewise, marketing, management, education, research and evaluation activities are each connected to the other elements. Occupational therapy

Figure 7: The Client, Service, Society Model:
Illustrated for Working with an Individual Client

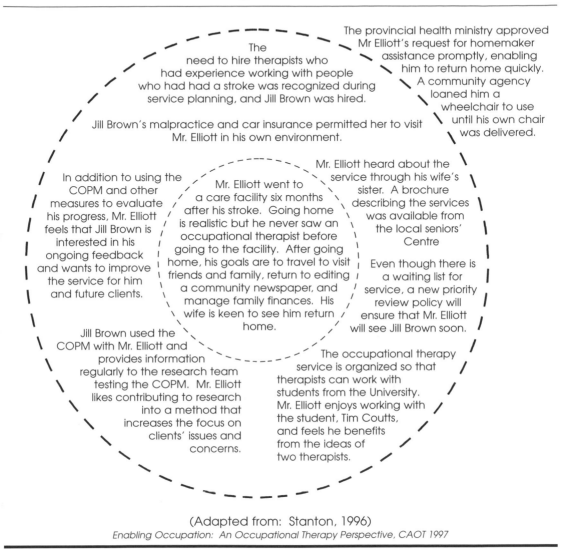

The need to hire therapists who had experience working with people who had had a stroke was recognized during service planning, and Jill Brown was hired.

Jill Brown's malpractice and car insurance permitted her to visit Mr. Elliott in his own environment.

The provincial health ministry approved Mr Elliott's request for homemaker assistance promptly, enabling him to return home quickly. A community agency loaned him a wheelchair to use until his own chair was delivered.

In addition to using the COPM and other measures to evaluate his progress, Mr. Elliott feels that Jill Brown is interested in his ongoing feedback and wants to improve the service for him and future clients.

Mr. Elliott went to a care facility six months after his stroke. Going home is realistic but he never saw an occupational therapist before going home, his goals are to travel to visit friends and family, return to editing a community newspaper, and manage family finances. His wife is keen to see him return home.

Mr. Elliott heard about the service through his wife's sister. A brochure describing the services was available from the local seniors' Centre

Even though there is a waiting list for service, a new priority review policy will ensure that Mr. Elliott will see Jill Brown soon.

Jill Brown used the COPM with Mr. Elliott and provides information regularly to the research team testing the COPM. Mr. Elliott likes contributing to research into a method that increases the focus on clients' issues and concerns.

The occupational therapy service is organized so that therapists can work with students from the University. Mr. Elliott enjoys working with the student, Tim Coutts, and feels he benefits from the ideas of two therapists.

(Adapted from: Stanton, 1996)
Enabling Occupation: An Occupational Therapy Perspective, CAOT 1997

personnel may require education to participate in research, and to plan, market, manage and evaluate services. Evaluation results provide direction for service improvements by identifying the ways in which the other elements support and constrain services, and by revealing needs. Gathering research data and using available research findings can support and enhance each element.

Once a service is established, elements usually occur concurrently. In each element, some activities may occur continuously while others may occur only at designated times. For example, managing is an ongoing activity whereas continuing education may occur only at specific times of the year to coincide with the availability of resources. In contrast, evaluation is ongoing and has components, such as a formal performance appraisal of personnel, that occur only at designated times.

Responsibility for Organizing Occupational Therapy Services

Responsibilities for planning, marketing, and managing occupational therapy services are not limited to those who hold administrative positions. Occupational therapists accept these responsibilities not only when organizing occupational therapy services but also when facilitating the Occupational Performance Process with clients. Education requires increasing attention as occupational therapists strive to keep pace with the rapid changes in practice and practice settings. As well, demands for accountability and evidence-based practice require every occupational therapist to participate in research and evaluation.

When working with clients, occupational therapists may not assume total responsibility for organizing services; however knowledge of organization can help occupational therapists to recognize and remove constraints for enabling occupation. Depending on their work situation and position, some occupational therapists may have greater responsibility for identifying and addressing service and societal constraints to client services.

Role of Theory in Organizing Occupational Therapy Services

When occupational therapists plan, market, manage and evaluate services, participate in research or educate others, they often use additional theoretical approaches that are compatible with the Canadian Model of Occupational Performance and concepts of client-centred practice to guide what they do. For example, when occupational therapists assume management responsibilities, they may draw on management as well as occupational therapy theories. In client education, and in occupational therapy undergraduate, graduate and continuing education, learning theories are integrated with occupational therapy. The combination of occupational therapy and other theoretical approaches provides a new lens for viewing occupational therapy.

Like the Occupational Performance Process that occurs at the Client level (Figure 6), the process and outcomes of the six service elements need to reflect the values, beliefs, and core concepts described in Chapter 3. The Client, Service, Society Model is applied to the six service elements. Examples illustrate how actions at each level can contribute to the organization of effective and efficient occupational therapy services that support the Occupational Performance Process with clients. Reflective questions for the first element, Plan Services guide occupational therapists in developing service plans.

Table 16: Plan Services

- assess occupational performance needs
- state targeted service outcomes
- design service to achieve targeted outcomes
- identify service resources
- develop a marketing plan
- develop a plan to evaluate outcomes

(Stanton (1995), adapted from Backman (1994)
and Fearing (1995) with permission)
Enabling Occupation: An Occupational Therapy Perspective, CAOT 1997

Element #1: Plan Services

Prior to offering new occupational therapy services, a comprehensive planning process is undertaken. Planning is also needed to sustain or revise existing services. Effective planning facilitates the organization of the other service elements. Figure 6 indicates that service planning influences and is influenced by client needs, the service environment, and its societal context.

Besides occupational therapists, there are others who influence the planning of occupational therapy services; architects, engineers, policy and planning personnel, politicians, citizen groups, and many others including occupational therapists define the societal context of occupational therapy practice (see Chapter 2). They also contribute to decisions about which services will be funded, and consequently which client needs can be met. Occupational therapists influence the societal context through community planning boards, government task forces, private initiatives, advocacy coalitions, and other means.

Service planning occurs within the service environment. The first of the six planning steps, Assess Occupational Performance Needs (Table 16) shows how service planning proceeds in response to client needs. The planning steps have been adapted from Backman (1994) and Fearing (1995) to be consistent with the language and concepts of this document (Stanton, 1995).

Occupational therapists, managers, accountants, members of Boards of Directors, potential clients, clients or their representatives (when the service already exists), and others participate in planning. An occupational therapist may plan services as a(n):
- administrator of an agency which includes occupational therapy services;
- coordinator of a interdisciplinary service team;
- manager of an occupational therapy service in an agency;
- member of a consulting group;

- private practitioner working alone or with partners;
- project leader on a specific task;
- staff member who participates on planning committees.

Even though roles and responsibilities for planning may vary from setting to setting, occupational therapists assume primary responsibility for assessing occupational performance needs, and for designing the services that will enable occupation.

The process of planning helps diverse participants (clients, community members, families, managers, professionals) to reach agreement on a common vision for the service and the actions needed to realize that vision. Client participation in the planning assists in developing services that are based on client needs, facilitates client representation in service implementation (e.g. marketing and evaluation), and assures that marketing or communication strategies are congruent with the needs and cultures of potential clients.

Completion of the planning steps leads to a service plan that is not only client-centred and focused on occupation, but also organizes and directs the implementation of the marketing, management, education, research and evaluation service elements. The service plan facilitates the achievement of client and service outcomes and is helpful in obtaining support for the service. A documented plan also provides a basis for evaluation (Fearing, 1995). Reflective questions for each planning step are provided later in this chapter to facilitate service planning.

Assess Occupational Performance Needs

Occupational performance needs are identified when a gap exists between the present performance of (culturally defined) self-care, productivity or leisure occupations and a more desirable future state of performance in these occupations; for example, when members of a community cannot participate in valued leisure occupations but desire to do so.

The assessment of occupational performance needs in service planning is based on a population or community needs assessment. For example, a needs assessment may include:
- elderly people in a province or specific community;
- children with disabilities or only those children within a particular school or school district;
- employees in the forest industry or employees of one softwood mill;
- adults with brain injuries who are seeking employment in a province or those who reside in a particular geographic area.

The people responsible for planning a service decide whether the needs assessment will be defined in terms of a population or a community.

The Purpose of Needs Assessment

The primary objective is to identify clients within a population or community who have occupational performance needs that can be addressed by an occupational therapist. Target clientele for occupational therapy can include individuals, families, groups, agencies, community organizations, businesses and/or governments.

Needs assessment is like market research (Darmon, Laroche & Lee McGown, 1989). If no need for service is identified, a service should not be developed (Backman, 1994). The identification of needs, and the justification and feasibility of meeting them, are necessary prerequisites to seeking funding for services. Fearing (1995) indicates that the needs assessment identifies:

- the target clientele and their occupational performance needs;
- the extent to which these occupational performance needs are being met by current services;
- the number of persons with unmet occupational performance needs, their locations; and
- potential benefits of meeting these needs for the clients and others.

Needs Assessment Methods

A variety of primary and secondary research methods can be used to assess clients' occupational performance needs. Primary research is information gathered by the person who is doing the needs assessment. Methods include conducting interviews, leading focus groups, distributing a survey, or collecting statistics. Secondary research involves reviewing information that has been compiled by others, e.g., published literature, regulations, guidelines, standards, research results, government or community agency statistics (Backman, 1994; Valentino, 1994). Library materials, including technological data bases, are common sources of secondary information available from universities, colleges, agencies, and governments (Valentino, 1994).

Analyzing the Results

The purpose of analysis is to:

- identify the focus of a service;
- assess the potential impact of a service on the target clientele and society;
- determine the best location and setting for the service relative to other service providers;
- determine whether other agencies are providing similar services and if so, assess the potential impact on service funding; and,
- provide a clear rationale for the service.

A needs assessment may identify more occupational performance needs than can be addressed by an occupational therapy service. When this occurs, priorities must be set and justified. Adverse consequences of not providing services to meet identified needs, lack of alternative services and community demand may be some of the considerations in setting priorities.

The analysis of occupational performance needs of a community or population often yields similar information that can guide service planning. For example, results may suggest that occupational performance needs are related to environmental conditions (e.g. poor housing, lack of equipment or community support), and/or occupational performance components (e.g. lack of knowledge and skills).

Needs assessment data also include information that enables the planner to address anticipated objections or criticisms, to predict service demand, estimate resources and provide some suggestions for evaluating the service (Backman, 1994).

State Targeted Service Outcomes

Targeted service outcomes are the best estimates of the future results of services. They describe what the clients will be able to do upon completion of services. These targeted outcomes are derived from assessing the occupational performance needs of a population or community. For example, clients' narratives about the occupational performance outcomes of similar services, research results or statistical predictions may suggest targeted outcomes. While the primary purpose for identifying targeted outcomes is to provide direction for service planning and implementation, they are vital for future service evaluation, and are valuable in communicating the service purpose to funding agencies.

Relationship of Targeted Outcomes to Service Evaluation

Clearly written targeted outcomes provide an essential baseline from which future service outcomes can be evaluated. Even when planning has been thorough, additional outcomes that were not targeted are often identified during evaluation. Whether they are valued or not, such outcomes need to be reflected in the evaluation results.

Service objectives specify what will occur to achieve each targeted outcome. For example, a service may identify the targeted outcomes for a four-part client education programme. The objectives for each educational session reflect what clients will be able to do after each session and should be directly related to the programme outcomes. Targeted outcomes and objectives should be realistic, achievable, understandable and measurable. Both descriptions (e.g. quality of work) and measurements (e.g. changes in test scores) can contribute valuable information to the evaluation of service outcomes.

Planners should consider the relationship between service and societal outcomes when generating the targeted outcomes. When targeted outcomes include benefits for society, they can be classified as targeted

Table 17: Examples of Targeted Service and Societal Outcomes

Service Outcomes
• After receiving occupational therapy service, clients who have had total hip replacements will be able to resume participation in valued self-care, productivity and leisure occupations, at home in a safe manner.

• Following participation in a skill development programme, persons with severe physical limitations who need personal care attendants will be able to hire, educate, supervise, and, if necessary, terminate the employment of personal care attendants, to better meet their needs related to self-care, productivity and leisure occupations.

• Members of a community who cannot make decisions that will enhance access to leisure occupations for all members, will increase its cohesiveness and its members' ability to make decisions through participation in collaborative, meaningful occupations.

Societal Outcomes
• The rate of re-admission to hospitals and residential centres will decrease for people with long-term mental illness who participate in a community-based mental health programme that provides support for productivity and leisure occupations.

• After participating in a work readiness programme, and with assistance from a job coach, clients who have had head injuries will be able to seek and sustain employment.

• The requirements for professional services by clients with long-term disabilities who reside at home will decrease after clients and caregivers participate in a community resources awareness and support programme.

Enabling Occupation: An Occupational Therapy Perspective, CAOT 1997

societal outcomes (of services), such as reducing health service costs. Identifying societal benefits may also increase the likelihood of continued service funding. Examples of targeted service and societal outcomes that benefit clients are shown in Table 17.

It is desirable to include the criteria for evaluating outcomes in the targeted outcomes. Early identification of evaluation criteria enables planners to outline the resources needed for evaluation. For example, a criterion for service evaluation may include changes in scores on a test over time. In this instance, funds for purchasing the test and score sheets, for the education of personnel, and for personnel salaries while administering and interpreting the test, need to be anticipated and obtained for this evaluation criterion to be feasible.

Design Service to Achieve the Targeted Outcomes

Designing a service is a multifaceted process. The primary task of this step is to document the characteristics of the service(s) that will be provided to meet the targeted outcomes. A client-centred service is organized by involving the potential clientele in the design process.

The design process begins by identifying the philosophy and theoretical orientation of a service. When an occupational therapy service includes a philosophy and a theoretical orientation that are based on the occupational therapy values, beliefs, and core concepts described in Chapter 3, the service can be readily differentiated from non-occupational therapy services. Designing a service is simplified when the needs assessment has been thorough and the targeted service outcomes are stated clearly. The rationale for an occupational therapy service is identified in the assessment of occupational performance needs.

Questions related to the Who, What, Where, When and How of the service facilitate the design process. A clear description of what the service will look like and how it will enable occupation will be critical in receiving support for continued planning and funding. It will also be important in marketing the service.

Identify Service Resources

The process of identifying potential service resources often occurs in conjunction with designing the service. The planner's task is to determine what human, material and financial resources will be needed to ensure that the five remaining service elements (Figure 6) can support the client-centred Occupational Performance Process effectively and efficiently. Service resources make it possible to uphold professional standards, and meet legal and other requirements.

The types of resources needed for each service vary considerably. The purpose of a service, the source of funding (i.e. public or private), payment and budgeting methods, organizational structure, size and locations, are some of the variations in services that influence decisions about resources.

Since funding is likely to be limited, planners need to identify which resources are necessary to provide a quality client-centred service that will achieve the targeted outcomes. Attention to details such as defining the type of personnel, and their qualifications, skills and attributes, are important in planning a service environment that makes the provision of effective and efficient services possible. Consultation with potential clients, and others such as architects, non-occupational therapy managers, accountants, engineers, marketing professionals, educators, researchers, fund raisers and volunteers, can also provide valuable assistance in making resource decisions.

Develop a Marketing Plan

"Marketing is an important but often misunderstood activity" (Crain & Rachman, 1991, p. 4). In some situations, marketing may seem unnecessary when funding is part of a large, secure organization. Nevertheless, marketing educates clients and others about the service. It communicates the purpose and scope of the service, its key features and service options, and makes potential service benefits explicit. Today's economic climate makes marketing a necessary part of service provision. Without marketing, a service may not reach its target market and it may not receive the necessary funding support. The Canadian Council on Health Services Acreditation (CCHSA) standards for rehabilitation organizations use the increasingly common terms, *communications plan* or *strategy,* in place of marketing (1995).

What is Marketing? There are numerous definitions of marketing (Beckman, Kurtz & Boone, 1992; Crain & Rachman, 1991; McDougall, Kotler & Armstrong, 1992). The most universally accepted definition appears to be that marketing is "the process of planning and executing the conception, pricing, promotion and distribution of ideas, goods and services to create exchanges that satisfy individual and organizational objectives" (American Marketing Association, 1985, p.1). The purpose of marketing is to exchange ideas, goods or services that will meet the needs of clients, services and society. The promotion of a service to society (government or private agencies) for example, can lead to securing funds for the programme which, when offered, benefits clients.

Marketing and Occupational Therapy

For many people, marketing is associated only with selling products, but this is an old view (Crain & Rachman, 1991). Marketing is recognized as having a market, sales or product orientation (Beckman et al., 1992; Darmon et al., 1989). A market orientation is akin to occupational therapy's client-centred practice. Occupational therapists already recognize the importance of designing services to meet client needs rather than making clients fit existing services. Similarly, occupational therapists ensure that ideas or goods intended to solve problems, actually satisfy the needs of each client. This client fit is central to the market orientation approach (Beckman ct al., 1992).

Exchange is a core concept in marketing (McDougall et al., 1992). For exchange to occur, "there must be at least two parties, and each must have something of value to the other...each party must want to deal with the other party and each must be free to accept or reject the other's offer" (McDougall et al., 1992, p. 7). As Backman (1994) emphasizes, "Marketing involves voluntary exchanges of value between the parties involved" (p. 16). Such exchanges are not only the basis of client-occupational therapist partnerships but also occur when services are provided to benefit society. Numerous exchanges are possible, such as those between:

- occupational therapists and clients in an Occupational Performance Process;
- occupational therapists and potential clients to raise awareness about a service in society;
- occupational therapists in a service and occupational therapists who are being recruited to join the service.

The examples in Table 18 illustrate how marketing can promote occupational therapy services with internal (the service environment) and external partners (society). Marketing with internal partners may be with clients, other professionals and managers who are responsible for organizing financial and other service supports. External partners may be potential clients, persons who might refer clients to an occupational therapist, complementary programmes and services, research and funding bodies, university programmes who assign students for fieldwork, and others.

Developing the Plan

A marketing plan is an essential element in marketing occupational therapy services. Given the specialized knowledge that is required to develop an effective external marketing strategy, marketing professionals are often consulted in the development of a marketing plan.

A client-centred marketing plan focuses on potential clients and is based on market research (Darmon et al., 1989). In occupational therapy, the first planning step, Assess Occupational Performance Needs, provides the market research information that guides the design of the service (the product) that will be marketed to clients and others.

In addition to defining the service, there are three other essentials in a marketing plan: price, place and promotion (Darmon et al., 1989; McDougall et al., 1992). The planner asks: What will the service cost the client or society? Where will the service be offered? and, How will the service be promoted?

While there may be limited options within the price and place components of a marketing plan, there are numerous ways to promote services. The choice of methods is related to the marketing objectives, scope, budget and target market(s). Table 18 shows how marketing methods at client, service, and society levels may be used by occupational therapists to benefit clients.

Develop a Plan to Evaluate Outcomes

Evaluation of outcomes is the process of judging the worth or value of the results of an occupational therapy service. Outcomes may be intended or unintended. A primary purpose for evaluation is to determine the

Table 18: Examples of Marketing in Occupational Therapy

CLIENT level
When ideas, goods or services are exchanged to benefit clients
- The occupational therapist and client discuss the pros and cons of different approaches to resolving an occupational performance issue.
- The occupational therapist shares and discusses information about adaptive devices and equipment with a client.
- The occupational therapist provides a leaflet that describes occupational therapy and includes a short questionnaire about occupational performance to all potential clients, prior to Stage #1 of the Occupational Performance Process.

SERVICE level
When ideas, goods or services are exchanged to benefit future clients, and therefore, the service
- An annual report is submitted to the Board of Directors of a (service) agency describing programme outcomes.
- Information about the service is distributed to other agencies which provide services to the same target population.
- An open house is organized to promote the service to other members of an organization, and to future clients in the community.

SOCIETY level
When ideas, goods or services are exchanged to benefit future clients, the service, and society
- Occupational therapists present a cost-benefit analysis of service outcomes to government or other funders of the service.
- A brochure describing the occupational therapy service is distributed to local associations or societies that serve the target population.
- An occupational therapist speaks about the occupational therapy services to potential clients in the community.
- Occupational therapists present information about their services, educational and research activities at professional meetings and conferences.
- An occupational therapist runs for political office in his/her community.

Enabling Occupation: An Occupational Therapy Perspective, CAOT 1997

effectiveness of services so that decisions can be made about changing, maintaining or discontinuing services (Backman, 1994). Evaluation is closely linked to quality improvement and accountability.

Since the purpose of occupational therapy is to enable occupation, judgements about the value of a service are based on the degree to which they achieve this purpose. In particular, the evaluation of outcomes can provide information about the benefits of occupational therapy for one client, all clients who participate in services, and society. The benefits of occupational therapy are in the achievement of the targeted outcomes that are negotiated with clients in the Occupational Performance Process. Primary benefits may be defined with reference to changes in occupational performance for individuals, organizations and communities. Secondary benefits are changes in occupational performance components and/or environmental conditions. Evaluation findings provide evidence of these benefits.

Key Concepts in Evaluation

Development of an evaluation plan is dependent on understanding the relevance of key evaluation concepts to occupational therapy. These concepts, i.e., outcome versus process evaluation, as well as effectiveness and efficiency, clarify the purposes for evaluation, as indicated in Table 19.

1. Outcome versus Process Evaluation

Briefly stated, outcome evaluation describes the end results of occupational therapy services. It answers the question, "What is the result?" The results are described in terms of occupational performance, i.e., the resolution of occupational performance issues and the achievement of the targeted outcomes that focus on occupational performance. The evaluation of outcomes is of primary importance in client-centred evaluation.

Process evaluations investigate how the actions and context of everyday practice contribute to the results. Information about process assists in explaining outcomes. Process evaluation answers the question, "How were the results achieved, and why?" Also reviewed are service and societal features (e.g., policies) that influence outcomes for clients. If targeted outcomes are not achieved, information on the process can shed light on the changes needed to enhance achievement of outcomes.

2. Effectiveness

The CCHSA (1995) defines effectiveness as "successfully achieving or attaining results (outcomes), goals or objectives. It means working on the right things." (p. 47). When occupational therapists focus on targeted outcomes that have been negotiated with clients, successful outcomes are more likely. When a service can demonstrate that targeted outcomes have been reached successfully, and changes occurred in occupational performance following participation in occupational therapy, the service:
- can be more accountable to clients and funding agencies;
- has evidence that can be used to justify the continuation of services; and
- has information about service effectiveness that can be used in marketing.

The evaluation of outcomes and effectiveness are related concepts. The effectiveness of a service is assessed by evaluating occupational therapy outcomes.

3. Efficiency

Table 19: Three Levels of Evaluation

CLIENT: What are the occupational performance outcomes for the client?

SERVICE: What are the occupational performance outcomes for all clients who participated in occupational therapy services?

SOCIETY: What is the impact of a service on society?

Enabling Occupation: An Occupational Therapy Perspective, CAOT 1997

The CCHSA (1995) indicates that efficiency "refers to how well resources (inputs) are brought together to achieve results (outcomes), with minimal expenditure. It means doing things right." (p. 47). Human, material and financial resources contribute to efficiency. By definition, efficiency is concerned with questions about the processes that contribute to service outcomes, and to cost-effectiveness. Many processes within the service environment or societal context may contribute to the efficiency of the service.

Process evaluation and efficiency are related concepts. The efficiency of a service is assessed by evaluating the processes used to achieve occupational therapy outcomes. Examples include the clarity of educational materials for clients, the timeliness of processing service requests, the degree of organization of the service, the skill and experience of personnel in using the Occupational Performance Process, the extent and quality of team members' collaboration, the transportation used by clients to reach the service location, and the funding for technology and other resources.

When a service or societal process or feature is efficient, it is most likely to support the Occupational Performance Process with clients; when it is inefficient, it can be expected to constrain the process. An inefficient service is unlikely to be cost-effective. When information about service efficiency is available, services can:
- identify the service supports that need to be retained to maintain service to clients;
- modify or discontinue processes that constrain services, with clients;
- make changes that are needed to improve the cost-effectiveness of services;
- negotiate to remove or minimize societal constraints to service to benefit clients.

Theoretical Approaches to Guide Evaluation

The Client, Service, Society Model (Figure 6) provides one model for linking the evaluation of client, service, and societal outcomes. This model assumes a focus on occupational performance and a client-centred approach to practice, and is compatible with the CCHSA requirements (1995). An evaluation plan may also use other theoretical approaches related to evaluation and measurement. Each approach can guide decisions and provide direction in developing an evaluation plan.

The broad question each evaluation level addresses in the Client, Service, Society Model is shown in Table 19. These questions reflect the purposes for evaluation at each level. The evaluation of client outcomes is a prerequisite to the evaluation of outcomes at the service and societal levels. The evaluation of service outcomes may precede the assessment of the impact of service outcomes for society, or occur concurrently. Planning for evaluation at all levels occurs within the service environment. Within each level of the model, the planner needs to select evaluation questions, and decide who will participate, what evaluation methods will be used, where and when the evaluation will occur, and where the evaluation results will be distributed.

Selecting Evaluation Questions

Evaluation of every facet of an occupational therapy service is unlikely to be cost-effective. Deciding what to evaluate and why, is one of the early steps in planning an evaluation (Boyle, 1981). Although the questions in Table 19 clarify the purpose of evaluation at each level, specific questions are required to direct the selection of evaluation methods (McCloy, 1996). The questions are crucial to evaluation. Poorly developed questions are unlikely to provide the answers needed to guide future decisions about changing, maintaining or discontinuing services.

Table 20 shows how sample outcome and process questions are related to the key evaluation concepts described earlier and the Client, Service, Society Model. Planners need to decide what additional questions need to be answered, for example, to facilitate future decision making, demonstrate accountability, and/or support requests for continued funding. Deciding who needs answers to what questions can assist planners in this task. For example, funders of a pilot programme in the community may want to know to what extent the clients who participated were successful in obtaining and sustaining employment after they completed the programme.

Anticipating the questions that will need to be answered before implementing a service enables essential information to be collected during service implementation. Post-hoc or retrospective evaluation is unlikely to produce information that can be used with confidence in decision-making. For this reason, advanced planning for evaluation is critical.

Sources of Evaluation Questions

Table 20: The Interdependence of Outcomes and Processes, Effectiveness and Efficiency, and Client, Service and Society Levels in Evaluation

OUTCOME Related to *Effectiveness* Asks: What was the result?	PROCESS Related to *Efficiency* Asks: How did it occur? and Why?
CLIENT:	**CLIENT:**
To what degree were the client's occupational performance issues resolved through the Occupational Performance Process? To what degree were the client's targeted outcomes achieved?	How did the Occupational Performance Process support or constrain achievement of the outcomes? How did the approaches used to change the occupational performance components and/or environmental conditions change occupational performance?
SERVICE:	**SERVICE:**
To what extent were the occupational performance outcomes of all clients who participated in occupational therapy services achieved?	How did the service environment activities (planning, marketing, management, education, research and evaluation) support or constrain the Occupational Performance Process with clients?
SOCIETY:	**SOCIETY:**
What were the benefits of client participation in occupational therapy for society?	How did the societal context (e.g. public policies, eligibility for services), support or constrain the Occupational Performance Process for clients?

Enabling Occupation: An Occupational Therapy Perspective, CAOT 1997

The Client, Service, Society Model can direct the development of more specific questions, particularly for process evaluation.

In the evaluation of client outcomes, the client-centred Occupational Performance Process described in Chapter 4 guides the selection of outcome and process evaluation questions. The seven stages provide a plan for outcome evaluation. A review of each stage can quickly identify important process evaluation questions.

In the evaluation of service outcomes, the focus moves to evaluating the degree to which the targeted outcomes of the service were met for all individuals, organizations and/or communities who received services. The questions related to service outcomes are readily identifiable when the targeted service outcomes have been defined clearly. That is, for the first example in Table 17, an outcome question could be "To what extent are clients participating safely in valued self-care, productivity and leisure occupations at home three months after total hip replacement?" Likewise, for the last example in Table 17, the question may be, "What is the difference in the use of professional services and community resources by people with long term disabilities who live at home and their caregivers, before and after the occupational therapy programme for clients and caregivers?"

Process evaluation at the service level investigates the extent that the actions of the occupational therapist(s) and others in the service environment, as well as the policies, procedures, equipment, funding, schedules, facilities and service features, have contributed to the results. This involves developing a plan to evaluate the degree to which each of the six service elements support or constrain the achievement of client, and consequently, service outcomes. Since the societal context influences the service elements, service evaluation also identifies societal supports and constraints to services. Focus and restraint are most needed in the selection of evaluation questions. Evaluating every aspect of service in depth is not economic or useful.

Client-centred evaluation focuses on outcomes that are important to clients, potential clients and to society. While the evaluation of workloads, the process for hiring personnel, and management information systems may be important, they are not emphasized in client-centred evaluation. Rather, evaluation of these dimensions is linked to quality management in the element, *Manage Services*. For example, when patrons dine at a restaurant they care most that they have great food and great service. Tasty food, and friendly and timely service are probable evaluation criteria. Patrons are unlikely to be interested in the fact that two chefs rather than six prepared the food, that high-quality stainless steel pots were used and that the restaurant managers had developed a superb inventory system, unless these aspects of organization of this service influenced the outcomes they value. Consequently, the selection of evaluation questions emphasizes outcomes that are relevant to occupational therapy's key role in enabling occupation (CAOT, 1996c), and the processes that make a difference to these outcomes.

The evaluation of societal outcomes focuses on the questions that are important to a community or society. In general, the benefits of occupational therapy to society are the changes in occupational performance that enable occupation. Criteria for evaluating the societal impact of services are defined ideally by occupational therapists in consultation with agencies, community organizations, governments, or business. It is wise to include societal impact in a service evaluation since societal benefits and accountability are questioned by service funders and the public.

The societal impacts of the service outcome examples that were discussed in relation to Table 17, are implicit. However to support continued funding of the service, it is more helpful if the reductions in costs for health and professional services are made explicit. The cost-effectiveness or cost-benefits of occupational therapy services may be evident from changes in health, hospital admission rates, length of institutionalization in long-term facilities, unemployment rates, social assistance requirements, caregiving requirements, and needs for community and other health services.

Questions about the cost-effectiveness or cost-benefits of a service are not the only ones that can be asked in assessing the impact of service on society. The impact of changes in occupational performance on community cohesiveness, participation on community boards and committees, and other dimensions may also be assessed.

Types of Evaluation Methods

Selection of evaluation methods requires an understanding of the types of methods available. The terms, qualitative and quantitative, are used frequently to describe evaluation methods (Law, 1987, Opacich, 1991; Payton, 1988; Spencer, Krefting & Mattingly, 1993). Qualitative methods describe results, whereas quantitative methods measure results. The choice of methods depends on the questions to be answered. Both types of evaluation methods can contribute to the evaluation of client, service and societal outcomes.

Qualitative methods gather information about one or more persons' experiences and perspectives of events or situations which contribute to information about occupational therapy outcomes. Many resources describe qualitative methods (e.g. Glaser, & Strauss, 1967; Hammersley & Atkinson, 1983; Opacich, 1991; Ottenbacher, 1986; Spencer et al., 1993). Examples of qualitative methods include: interviews, narrative stories, diaries, activity logs, audiotapes or videotapes, observation of performance, analysis of the products of occupation and photographs. These methods can be used in client assessment, in evaluating outcomes and in research.

The type of qualitative method used depends on what is to be evaluated. Interviews can use closed or open-ended questions for gathering information about a variety of issues. Narrative stories provide rich detail about people's experiences from their point of view. Documents are helpful in analyzing changes in employment, housing, or other already gathered statistics.

It is common to use a variety of qualitative methods to gather different kinds of information on the same issue (Guba & Lincoln, 1989; Krefting,

1989). For example, interviews with clients may indicate that they required service for a longer period of time because resources were not available in a timely manner. Analysis of satisfaction with service questionnaires completed by family members or work associates may provide similar or different perspectives on the same issue. Information from all sources may prompt a review of the availability of resources to support the Occupational Performance Process with clients.

Quantitative methods are the most common way of demonstrating change over time. They assign numerical values to assessment findings that enable comparisons of between one or more individuals (Law, 1987). There are a multitude of measures for documenting change in performance components (e.g. Asher, 1989; Kielhofner, 1985; Trombly, 1994). However, client-centred measures of occupational performance are still lacking (Pollock, et al., 1990). This lack of measures explains why this document relies heavily on the example of the Canadian Occupational Performance Measure (COPM) as an outcome measure (Law et al., 1994). Concerns about the limited availability of outcome measures in health care and rehabilitation have led to increased efforts to resolve this situation (Canadian Institute for Health Information, 1994a, 1994b; Accreditation Council on Services for People with Disabilities, 1993; Tiens & Wilson, 1995). With increasing emphasis on measuring outcomes, new measures are developing rapidly as this document goes to press.

The absence of formal outcome measures in occupational therapy does not mean that outcomes cannot be measured. Backman (1994) indicated that "systematic counting and recording of target behaviours is also an outcome measure." For example, when a caregiver's ability to socialize is limited by repeated outbursts at friends who visit to provide support, simple counting of the frequency of the outbursts before and after occupational therapy can be useful in demonstrating outcomes. Similarly, a reduction in the incidence of back injuries among workers in a manufacturing plant or the decreased use of home support workers may provide information about the effectiveness of services. This method is useful for evaluating client and service outcomes, and for research (Backman, 1994).

Selecting Evaluation Methods
Strategies for identifying possible outcome measures include consulting references and texts that describe and/or review measures such as the mental measurement yearbooks, test critiques, tests in print, test publishers and conducting a literature search (Law & Sanford, 1994). Asking an expert in the field, asking a colleague, or when no other alternatives are available, developing your own measure, are additional strategies.

Even when a variety of evaluation methods is available, the planner's goal is to select the best method(s) that will provide the needed information (i.e. answer the evaluation questions). The purpose for which the method was developed should be directly related to the outcomes being assessed. For example, the COPM (Law et al., 1994) was not intended for use with groups. Other outcome measures are not suitable for people of all ages, or cannot be used with confidence to compare the performance of all people who receive services. Practical issues such as costs, education needs for administration, and time, space and other resource requirements are additional considerations. Occupational therapists would be wise to use the criteria developed by Law (1987) and others, to assist them in selecting evaluation methods. The key is to select methods that will answer the evaluation questions and produce meaningful results for future decision making.

The choice of evaluation methods and criteria reflect the theoretical orientation(s) and values of those involved in developing the plan. Services that are client-centred use methods that involve clients in the evaluation. Similarly, services that are based on the Canadian Model of Occupational Performance and the Occupational Performance Process use methods that will evaluate the changes in occupational performance, and the processes that produced the changes. Beliefs about the value of qualitative and quantitative methods in evaluating outcomes also influence choice of method. A combination of methods usually provides the most complete results.

Completion of the Evaluation Plan

The plan for evaluation is complete when
- the purposes for evaluation are clear;
- theoretical approaches to evaluation have been determined;
- specific evaluation questions and methods have been justified;
- human, material and financial resources have been identified;
- a realistic time frame for evaluating outcomes at each level has been identified;
- the persons/agencies to whom evaluation results will be communicated are identified.

Identification of human, material and financial resources includes specifying who will be involved in the evaluation (e.g clients, occupational therapists, community agencies). Establishing when evaluation methods will be administered is particularly important if an outcome measure is being used to measure occupational performance over time. If a test is not administered before an occupational therapy plan is implemented it cannot be added later. There should be a commitment among service providers that when service constraints are identified in evaluation, action will be taken to remove or minimize the constraints. In order to reduce potential bias in evaluation, the plan may include contracting an external consultant or agency to assist in implementing the plan. Issues related to the implementation of the plan are discussed in the element, *Evaluate Services.*

Completion of the Service Plan

Service planning is complete when the needs for a service are identified and documented; service outcomes are described; plans for achieving targeted outcomes are outlined; resources for the service are identified; and a plan for marketing and evaluating the service is developed. Once funding for the service is received, implementation can begin. If partial funding is received, the service plan is revised to be congruent with available funding. If funding is denied, the service plan is unlikely to proceed unless other funding sources are found.

Element #2: Market Services

The Market Services element involves implementing the plan that was developed as a step in service planning. The goal is to promote the service to those persons, agencies, or organizations identified in the marketing plan. Implementation of the plan communicates the purpose and scope of the service. It also highlights the key features of the service and the range of service options available. Potential benefits to clients and the types of results clients may anticipate are also promoted.

Student occupational therapists, occupational therapists, clients and others participate in implementing the marketing plan, either directly or indirectly. Their actions raise awareness of the benefits of client-centred partnerships that are focused on occupation. Ongoing marketing increases the visibility of and demand for occupational therapy services.

Developing Marketing Partnerships

Marketing partnerships can expand the effectiveness of the marketing effort. Occupational therapists may form partnerships with personnel in the same or different service environments, with community organizations, client representatives, and others. Partnerships provide opportunities to share marketing costs. When marketing involves direct communication to potential clients and others, choosing partners who can describe occupational therapy is extremely important.

Using Marketing Methods

Examples of possible marketing activities are shown in Table 18. Although marketing methods vary, they have common features. The promotional materials and communication strategies should include the language of occupation in a form that others can understand (CAOT, 1996c). Marketing activities also need to be conducted in an ethical and professional manner that enable clients (and others) to make informed choices (CAOT, 1996c).

Strengthening the Marketing Effort

When a service begins, client outcomes are not known. Until a service is established and has its own success stories, the benefits identified from similar services or through research may assist in the promotional effort. However, when a service has its own success stories, these become a powerful tool and strengthen the marketing strategy.

Regular review and revision of the marketing plan and activities are important in strengthening marketing. Marketing needs to reflect changing market conditions so that it is as effective as possible. The evaluation of marketing is part of the service element, *Evaluate Services.* Results from an evaluation indicate where adjustments are needed.

Element #3: Manage Services

Management activities in occupational therapy have been most associated with the administration of services (Sumsion, 1994). In reality, all occupational therapists use management skills whenever they apply the Occupational Performance Process with clients. They plan, market and evaluate services; and they coordinate educational and research-related activities that will enhance the delivery of services.

Management Functions

Bergeron (1987) describes managerial functions as planning, organizing, directing and controlling. While efficiency is needed to carry out these management functions, Bennis and Nanus (1985) indicate that leadership is essential for effective management. They make the distinction between doing things right (efficiency) and doing the right things (effectiveness). As well, Bennis and Nanus suggest that there is a great need for managers who are visionary, effective, efficient, and able to guide others. Occupational therapists support this view of a leader; as a guide, coach, or facilitator, whether working with clients or organizing services.

Human Resource Management

Occupational therapists function as self-managers and self-leaders, as well as leaders of others. Their self-management and self-leadership activities include evaluating their performance and managing their time when working with clients. As leaders, occupational therapists are proactive in initiating changes to enhance services to clients, and in managing resources to support clients.

Application of the Occupational Performance Process in Management

Occupational therapy management is based on the core values, beliefs and concepts of occupational therapy. There is respect for others and a focus on occupation. The Occupational Performance Process (Chapter 4) can also be adapted for use in marketing, management, education, research and evaluation situations. This process guides the development of collaborative partnerships in the context of issues related to occupation.

Analysis of occupational performance components and the environmental conditions can be helpful in resolving occupational performance issues of student occupational therapists, occupational therapists and other personnel in the service environment. For example, many changes are occurring in

Table 21: Examples of Management Responsibilities of Occupational Therapists at Client, Service and Society Levels

CLIENT
- Coordinate or manage the Occupational Performance Process (as an occupational therapist who is applying the process or as one who supervises others who use the process) to ensure that the process is client-centred and occupation-focused;
- Document the Occupational Performance Process with the client to facilitate evaluation of services and accountability;
- Submit requests for equipment to funding agencies to ensure that resources for occupation are available when needed;
- Provide effective supervision for a student occupational therapist to benefit the client and student.

SERVICE
- Ensure that the planned marketing, education, research and evaluation activities occur, and, in response to evaluation and research results, revise the service to increase effectiveness and efficiency;
- Foster the development of a positive service environment in which all contributions are valued, and personnel, student occupational therapists and volunteers are supported in their work with clients;
- Develop policies and procedures to enhance and support the occupational performance process with clients;
- Manage information systems to support current and future directions for occupational therapy services;
- Ensure that professional codes of ethics, and standards set by regulatory, professional and accreditation bodies are met;
- Organize and promote educational activities for personnel that will increase or maintain the efficiency and effectiveness of services;
- Manage the service budget, and recommend allocation of resources;
- Supervise and evaluate personnel;
- Promote the development of research activities within the service.

SOCIETY
- Liaise with professional and regulatory bodies;
- Coordinate activities with external agencies, groups and consultants (e.g., in research and marketing);
- Liaise with universities to offer fieldwork opportunities;
- Liaise with community agencies to co-ordinate services with clients;
- Provide reports to demonstrate accountability to external funding agencies.

Enabling Occupation: An Occupational Therapy Perspective, CAOT 1997

health services, and change is expected to continue into the future (Baker, 1993; CAOT, 1996c; Gage, 1995). Analysis of findings related to a hypothetical occupational performance issue, "Unable to present assessment findings in a coherent manner in team conferences" may reveal difficulties related to the affective component (e.g. anxiety, poor morale), and the cognitive component (lack of knowledge about the changes and lack of skills required for new roles) that are related to changes in the social, cultural, institutional, or physical environment of the occupational therapy or team service. This information, combined with theoretical perspectives in organizational development (e.g. Senge, 1990), can guide the negotiation of targeted outcomes and the selection of management strategies to resolve this occupational performance issue with personnel. By using the Occupational Performance Process in this way, occupational therapists can be proactive in resolving difficulties associated with service delivery, recommending changes when needed, and coordinating their actions with those of others to provide more effective services to clients.

Materials and Financial Resource Management

All occupational therapists participate in managing materials and equipment, and in ensuring that they are cost-effective and used safely. Similarly, they are involved in financial management. They apply business practices to enhance the cost-effectiveness of services and contribute to the preparation of budgets.

Information Systems Management

All occupational therapists participate in management information systems. Record keeping, development of policies and procedures, writing service reports, and workload measurement are common examples. Occupational therapists have become accustomed to documenting time use in the Canadian Workload Measurement System (Department of National Health and Welfare, 1988b). This system can be used with individuals or groups, and accounts for some types of indirect service time. Indirect time and other time categories are important for occupational therapy since part of enabling occupation involves creating supportive environments, as well as working with individuals. Some indirect time categories record time spent in community committees, changing legislation, working with self-help groups, and other important parts of practice. In response to many of the changes that are occurring in the delivery of health services in Canada, a National Advisory Group was formed in 1996 to develop a "generic actual time workload measurement system" (Topf, 1996, p. 8).

Management Responsibilities at Client, Service and Society Levels

Management responsibilities of occupational therapists can vary a great deal to fit the diverse organizational environments in which occupational therapy services are offered. In each aspect of management, occupational therapists need to demonstrate accountability. Effective quality management demands that occupational therapists take the initiative to ensure that needed resources are available and organized in a manner that benefits services to clients. The CCHSA requirements for 1997 provide helpful guidelines for resource utilization and quality management (1995).

Examples of management responsibilities with clients, in organizing services and in addressing societal issues, are summarized in Table 21. The examples are drawn from the *Profile of Occupational Therapy Practice in Canada* (CAOT, 1996c). They show how management is connected to marketing, education, research and evaluation in service delivery.

Element #4: Educate

Activities in this service element support the Occupational Performance Process and the organization of services by ensuring that occupational therapists have the necessary knowledge and skills to deliver effective and efficient occupational therapy services. Occupational therapists are recipients and facilitators (providers) of education.

Educational activities take many forms, which include formal and informal exchanges of information. Coaching, mentorship, orientation of personnel, staff education, team building activities, participation in self-help groups, demonstration of skills, role modelling competent practice, and the provision of ongoing feedback are additional examples.

In selecting educational methods and activities, occupational therapists use many theoretical approaches. Examples include educational theories, learning theories, adult education theories, communication theories, theories of supervision, curriculum development theories, and theories about interpersonal relationships.

Education occurs at all three levels: with clients, in services, and in society. However, before occupational therapists provide education to others, they must take responsibility for their own learning and ensure that their knowledge and skills can be a resource for others. When occupational therapists organize their own learning, they can view themselves as their own clients. Their actions enable (their own) occupation.

The Occupational Therapist as Client

When occupational therapists see themselves as clients, they take responsibility for their own life-long learning. Life-long learning is the key to maintaining professional competence so that occupational therapy services are effective and accountable (CAOT, 1996c). This requires occupational therapists to evaluate their educational needs continuously, either independently or in consultation with others. When gaps in learning are identified, occupational therapists seek education to advance knowledge and skills, or change attitudes.

Forming journal clubs with peers, joining on-line News Groups on the Internet, reading current professional literature, participating in continuing professional development activities, or enrolling in graduate education are examples of learning activities. Education can prepare occupational therapists for practice in the new organizational contexts that are emerging. Rapid changes in health, social, education, employment and other arenas make continuous professional education a necessity for personal and professional effectiveness.

In order to enhance their skills as educators, occupational therapists may seek opportunities to apply educational and learning theories, and to design educational programmes for clients and others. Similarly, they may take action to increase their skills in service planning, management, research, evaluation, and marketing to support their work with clients.

An important part of education is the requirement that occupational therapists monitor their use of occupational therapy's *Code of Ethics* (CAOT, 1996b), and ensure that they are aware of current professional and ethical practices. They are also required to meet the licensing and/or registration requirements of the regulatory bodies within the communities in which they practice. Although these requirements are less directly related to education, occupational therapists take responsibility for ensuring that they have the knowledge and skills to meet the necessary requirements for professional accountability (CAOT, 1996c).

Occupational Therapists' Education as a Resource for Others
For Clients
With up-to-date and relevant knowledge and skills, occupational therapists can educate clients, student occupational therapists, and others. Conversely, occupational therapists need to be open to being educated by clients, students and others if their practice is client-centred.

For an Occupational Therapy Service
Education at the service level also involves the management of educational activities that are necessary for the provision of effective client services. Activities may include the planning and development of educational sessions for personnel in response to needs, and the ongoing development of educational programmes for student occupational therapists. The modelling of competent professional and ethical practice behaviours to students and peers is a less direct but important form of education at the service level. Occupational therapists often share their knowledge and skills by providing inservice education programmes to peers. Such exchanges can also occur informally.

For Society
Occupational therapists have many educational responsibilities to society. These activities occur outside the service environment. They include

educating the public about links between occupation and health, providing classes for student occupational therapists at a university, offering continuing professional workshops for occupational therapists, and educational programmes for organizations. As occupational therapy's potential for enabling occupation becomes better known, occupational therapists will be invited more frequently to address social issues that impact on occupation, for example, when the occupational performance and health of caregivers is reduced by community service cutbacks, or when productivity and leisure occupations are altered when a single employer leaves town.

Element #5: Access and participate in research

Greater demand for evidence-based practice and accountability has increased the need for occupational therapists to critically appraise research, identify research findings that can enhance service effectiveness, and participate in research. Participation and collaboration in evaluation activities is also linked to research. Research can support approaches with clients, justify new or continuing services, or advance knowledge for use by occupational therapists and others. Examples of ways in which occupational therapists can access and participate in research at the client, service and society levels are shown in Table 22.

The Role of Documentation in Evaluation and Research

Occupational therapists who work with clients regularly report and analyze data as they document their activities. These data are useful for evaluating outcomes for clients, services, or society. Documentation by occupational therapists is viewed as an essential element of competent practice. Accurate documentation is essential for research, and facilitates the evaluation of occupational therapy process and outcomes.

Participation in Research

Some occupational therapists wish to become directly involved in research. For example, research is needed to test theories, develop measurement tools, analyze client experiences, and describe how occupational therapy services enable occupation. Occupational therapists may participate in research by generating ideas for research, recruiting individual subjects for research projects, collaborating with or being principal investigators, collecting and documenting information, and analyzing research results. Research activities are guided by theories about the social organization of knowledge, research methodologies, statistical analysis, and qualitative analysis (Glaser, 1978; Glaser & Strauss, 1967; Hammersley & Atkinson, 1983; Payton, 1988).

Element #6: Evaluate Services

Occupational therapists participate in the evaluation of clients, service and societal outcomes as described in the step, *Develop a Plan to Evaluate*

Table 22: Access and Participate in Research: Examples of Possible Occupational Therapy Actions at Each Level

CLIENT

(within the occupational Performance Process)

- Critique current literature regularly and apply theories and methods that have been validated through research, to enhance practice with clients;
- Develop research projects that can be incorporated into the Occupational Performance Process with clients;
- Record data related to the occupational performance process to enable evaluation, and to study the efficacy of occupational therapy services;
- Document observations and ideas about occupation, and methods of enabling occupation, to trigger ideas for research.

SERVICE

(in a service environment)

- Start a journal club with other occupational therapists to review new literature;
- Establish a research unit within an occupational therapy service;
- Initiate discussions with colleagues about possible research activities related to occupation, and collaborative, client-centred practice;
- Share ideas, experiences and innovations to spark ideas for research;
- Model participation in research (through research partnerships or graduate study) to student occupational therapists and colleagues.

SOCIETY

- Develop/locate funding sources for occupational therapy research.
- Submit proposals for research funding to external agencies;
- Present research results or findings at conferences, to study groups, at workshops, and so on;
- Speak about research results in the broadcast media;
- Publish research results in professional journals and newsletters, and in magazines and newsletters that are more readily available to past and potential clients;
- Develop research partnerships with other service providers, university faculty and other researchers to enable participation in research and share resources;
- Join community, medical, educational, industry, and pharmaceutical teams as researchers.

Enabling Occupation: An Occupational Therapy Perspective, CAOT 1997

Outcomes in the element *Plan Services*. The planning element includes the majority of the evaluation information because it is essential to the development of the evaluation plan.

When occupational therapists evaluate services they implement the plans for evaluating clients (Chapter 4), services and society. In doing so, they gather the required information (e.g. through interviews, tests and other methods), document and analyze the results, communicate the results, and make needed revisions to the evaluation plan. Most importantly, occupational therapists make the changes that are necessary to overcome constraints and enhance services to clients. In addition to the evaluation activities that are planned to occur at specific times, ongoing evaluation takes place as a component of the continuous quality improvement activities for the service.

Evaluation as a Continuous Activity

As soon as service plans are implemented, gaps in one or more of the six elements of service planning may become evident. When this occurs, occupational therapists respond to the issues and problems that arise, determine priorities for making changes, implement the changes as soon as possible, and communicate the changes to others. The need for changes may be recognized because actions at the client, service or societal levels are constraining the Occupational Performance Process with clients. Constraints to the Occupational Performance Process may occur when an occupational therapist lacks the skills to work collaboratively with clients, staff do not receive an orientation before working with clients, or staff lack knowledge of new community health regulations.

Responsibility for making the changes may vary in each setting; however when an occupational therapist's lack of orientation to a new service constrains the Occupational Performance Process, the occupational therapist and the service environment may share responsibility for ensuring the situation is corrected. Self-employed occupational therapists assume full responsibility for ensuring they have the necessary knowledge and skills to provide services. When an occupational therapist lacks the knowledge and skills for a new role, the constraint exists at the service level.

Analyzing Service Outcomes

Not all constraints to the Occupational Performance Process with clients are identified quickly; some may not be identified until the client and service outcomes are analyzed, and the results interpreted. Typically, analysis of the constraints will identify the changes needed to make services more effective. At times, additional information may need to be collected to provide sufficient information for analysis. Evaluation results may reveal intended and unintended outcomes, which may be desirable or undesirable. Examples of service constraints, analysis, and interpretation

Table 23: Analysis of Sample Service Constraints

Constraint	Analysis	Constraint related to:
A community agency representing people with X disability (target population of service) reported that their members did not hear about the service until a year after it commenced.	The agency was not identified during service planning (assessment of occupational performance needs) probably because planning was rushed; as a result, they were not identified as a target market in the development of the marketing plan.	PLAN SERVICE Planning was not client-centred or collaborative, and did not involve those outside the service (in society). The service requires adjustment to meet the needs of the target population. Revision to the planning process would prevent a reoccurrence of this situation.
Clients are discharged from a hospital before essential occupational therapy services are complete. Client safety at risk; 2 clients have been readmitted with fractures during last six months.	Frequent changes in personnel and a lack of team decision-making meant that personnel lacked the information needed to make accountable decisions that supported clients.	MARKET AND MANAGE SERVICE All team members are not aware of role of occupational therapy; team does not work together to enhance service to clients.
Insufficient data are available to justify the value of the service; little research or evaluation data are available to demonstrate changes in occupational performance.	Demands for service and high waiting lists led to little time for planning, research and evaluation. The waiting lists are now shorter, but the future of the service is at risk without evaluation or research data to show the benefits of the service to clients and society.	PLAN SERVICE, PARTICIPATE IN RESEARCH, AND EVALUATE SERVICE Research was not identified as a needed resource; evaluation plan scant. Therefore, occupational therapists did not collect needed data. Problem needs to be rectified to increase likelihood of future service funding.
Evaluation data show some changes in occupational performance components but no changes in occupational performance. Clients' report low levels of satisfaction with services.	Personnel do not focus on resolution of occupational performance issues or occupation in the occupational therapy service. Further questioning with past clients revealed activities used in working with clients were not relevant to clients' needs or occupations (i.e. not client-centred).	MANAGE SERVICE, EDUCATE Although the philosophy was client-centred and occupation focused, new personnel did not have this orientation. No educational programme was developed to assist occupational therapists in offering client-centred, occupation-focused services.

Enabling Occupation: An Occupational Therapy Perspective, CAOT 1997

related to the six service elements are shown in Table 23. The results of the evaluation, together with the actions that will be taken to remove or minimize constraints to service (CCHSA, 1995) should be communicated to the recipients targeted in the service plan.

Funds needed to support the service evaluation process should have been identified in the step, Identify Service Resources, in service planning. Failure to obtain sufficient resources to complete the analysis of evaluation results in a timely manner may limit the effectiveness and efficiency of services. That is, a lack of funds for evaluation may constrain the Occupational Performance Process with clients.

Using the Results to Eliminate or Minimize Service Constraints

When evaluation indicates that change is needed, occupational therapists are responsible for making necessary changes (CAOT, 1996c). Responding quickly to evaluation information is essential in developing effective and efficient services, and it is crucial in securing continued support and funding for a service. Occupational therapists use evaluation results to support the continuation of services and to plan future.

REFLECTIVE QUESTIONS

These questions are designed to assist occupational therapists in reflecting on issues that are important in planning occupational therapy services. They have many potential uses; for example, occupational therapists can use them as a resource for developing the evaluation questions that will guide planning and implementation in service evaluation. They may also guide discussions about the organization, purpose and responsibilities for planning and implementing occupational therapy services.

Element #1: Plan Services

Assess Occupational Performance Needs

- What will be the scope of the occupational performance needs assessment? People in one workplace, community, province, etc. or the entire population?
- How will the potential target clientele participate in the assessment?
- What are the most suitable methods for uncovering the needs? Surveys, interviews, observation, individualized assessments? Analysis of population, community, health, etc., statistics? Reviews of the literature, focus groups, other?
- What information on occupational performance needs is already available from university researchers, government offices, community organizations, libraries, the media, and other sources?
- To what extent are the needs related to occupational therapy's key role (CAOT, 1996c) and issues of health, well being, empowerment, etc.?

- How many people have occupational performance needs that could be addressed through an occupational therapy service?
- How many people have similar needs? (When all types of needs cannot be met through one service, this question may assist in deciding where the greatest service need exists.)
- To what extent are these needs already met elsewhere? Are there obvious service gaps?
- Why are the needs important to address through an occupational therapy service?
- Have the results of the needs assessment been documented?

State Targeted Service Outcomes

- What are the possible impacts of the service for the occupational performance of clients, for the clients' environment, for society, for health service delivery, for length of hospital stay, for admission rates to institutional or community services, for health costs, and so on?
- What are the specific impacts [target outcomes (goals)] of this service?
- Do the targeted outcomes include the key (most significant) impacts of the service?
- How are the occupational therapy service outcomes related to those of linked services that are provided to the same clients by others?
- When services are organized in an interdisciplinary team, what are the specific occupational therapy outcomes?
- Do the targeted outcomes state what clients will be able to do, when services end?
- Are the targeted outcomes written in a way that will meet potential future uses?
- If targeted outcomes are to be included in marketing information about the service, will they be easily understood by clients?
- If targeted outcomes are to be included in the proposal for funding of the service, is there sufficient description or explanation to support the funding request? Will outcomes be perceived as realistic and achievable?
- Are targeted outcomes written in measurable, behavioural terms to facilitate evaluation of outcomes? Are they time limited?
- Do the targeted outcomes reflect occupational therapy values and beliefs, and are they client-centred and occupation-focused, and related to occupational performance?
- Is there consensus about the targeted outcomes from the persons who will be involved in designing the service?
- Are the perspectives of clients reflected in the targeted outcomes?

Design Service to Achieve Targeted Outcomes

- What philosophy, values and beliefs, and theoretical approaches will guide the service design?

- How is the service philosophy consistent with occupational therapy values and beliefs?
- To what extent are the theoretical approaches congruent with the Canadian Model of Occupational Performance and occupational therapy core concepts of occupation and client-centredness?
- What services will be provided to meet the occupational performance needs of the target clientele that are specified in the targeted outcomes?
- How do the proposed services relate to occupation and occupational performance?
- How will the proposed services address issues related to occupational performance components and environmental conditions that limit occupational performance?
- What are the parameters (scope) of the service? If it is not realistic to provide service to all potential clients or address all the occupational performance needs of a community, what will be the focus of the service?
- How will the service be client-centred? How flexible will the service be in meeting client needs?
- When will services be offered? How often and to whom?
- Where will services be offered and located?
- How many clients are projected to receive this service? Each month, year and/or for the duration of a time limited service?
- How will this service complement or compete with other services for the target clientele?
- Is the proposed service related clearly to the needs identified earlier in the planning process?

Identify Service Resources
Human, Material and Financial Resources
- What types and how many personnel will be needed, and why (e.g., managers, non-managers, educators, researchers, direct service personnel [occupational therapists and support staff], volunteers, etc.).
- What qualifications/credentials, licensing and/or experience will be needed for personnel?
- What consulting services will be required to support the service, e.g., accounting, marketing, legal, management, educational, research and evaluation advisors? Are these resources available in the organization or will they need to be obtained elsewhere?
- What type(s) of space (physical environment) will be needed?
- What equipment and supplies (material resources) will be needed?
- What funds are needed to achieve the (targeted) service outcomes and to support the service?
- What are the potential or actual sources of income and funding for the service?

Management, Education and Research Resources

- What organizational structure will facilitate the delivery of the collaborative, client-centred service?
- What institutional environment (climate) will be needed to support personnel and clients in achieving client and service outcomes?
- What additional resources are needed to support the Occupational Performance Process?
- What policies and procedures will guide access to service?
- What policies and procedures will support the Occupational Performance Process with clients?
- What policies and procedures will guide completion of service?
- What policies and procedures will guide documentation of the Occupational Performance Process?
- What educational resources are needed to ensure basic and continuing competency of personnel, e.g., orientation, libraries, access to electronic literature searches and networking, educational programmes, etc.?
- What resources will be needed to support the education of occupational therapy students within the service, e.g., lectures, clinics, fieldwork, etc.?
- What research activities will be needed to support the service?

Standards and Guidelines

- What ethical, legal and moral standards will guide the delivery of the service?
- What professional standards and/or regulatory requirements will guide the service?
- What other guidelines and standards will be used, how and why?
- What types of insurance will be required?

Develop a Marketing Plan

- What will be the potential benefits of the service to the target population?
- How will clients and/or potential clients participate in developing the marketing plan?
- To whom will the service be marketed and for what purpose?
- What aspects (if not all) of the service will be marketed?
- How will the service be marketed? e.g. through personal contact with clients, traditional print, internet, audio, visual, speaking tour, broadcast media, networking, etc.?
- Is the language in the print and audio-visual materials understandable for the intended readers, listeners?
- Will the selected marketing strategy reflect an appropriate image of the service? Will it be accurate? Positive? Professional?
- What public relations resources could be used e.g., community

calendar announcement, open house?

- How will the service's focus on client-centredness and occupation be represented in promotional materials?
- Is the proposed marketing strategy ethical in seeking clients and funding?
- Is the proposed marketing strategy likely to assist potential clients to make informed choices about the service? Does it identify service cost and the location of services?
- How will the promotional materials be developed and tested with the target clientele?
- How often will the various promotional methods be used? Once? Continuously?
- To what extent do the promotional materials differentiate the service from other services?
- Are the marketing approaches suitable for the target populations?
- When will the marketing plan be implemented?
- With what frequency will the plan be reviewed and revised?
- What funds are available to support marketing? Funds from the service budget? Special funds such as demonstration grant funds, etc?

Develop a Plan to Evaluate Outcomes

- Have the purposes for evaluation been decided and documented clearly?
- What theoretical approaches guided the development of the evaluation plan?
- Are the methods and criteria for evaluation congruent with evaluation questions?
- Does the evaluation plan include methods for evaluating client and service outcomes, and for assessing the impact of those outcomes for society?
- Were evaluation questions identified for all levels (client, service and society)?
- Will the evaluation methods (qualitative and quantitative) provide the information needed to answer the evaluation questions (i.e. enable the evaluation of the outcomes being assessed)?
- What methods will be used to assess the degree of client-centredness of the Occupational Performance Process with each client?
- How will service effectiveness, efficiency and cost-effectiveness be assessed?
- Will the methods used to evaluate changes in occupational performance components and environmental conditions provide information about how these changes have led to changes in occupational performance, to guide continuation or enhancement of services?
- Will the methods chosen to measure changes in occupational

performance over time provide reliable and valid evidence of these changes?

- Were the needs of clients reflected in the choice of evaluation methods (e.g. to gather essential information but avoid evaluation overload)?
- How were clients (potential clients) involved in developing the evaluation plan?
- How will clients contribute information about the effectiveness of the Occupational Performance Process? Of the service?
- What measures of client satisfaction with the process and outcomes are included in the plan?
- Are the time frames for evaluation realistic? Are the persons/agencies identified to whom evaluation results will be communicated?
- Does the plan specify what human, material and financial resources will be required to implement the plan? How feasible is the resource plan?

Application

PART III

CHAPTER SIX
Using New Guidelines

PRIMARY AUTHORS
Fern Swedlove
Cary Brown

Purpose

To accent ideas for using this document in enabling occupation.

Objectives

To present ten ideas for:
- Enhancing Quality and Accountability
- Forming Alliances
- Building Knowledge

Summary

Chapter 6 prompts readers to think about ways of using the information in this document. Ten ideas are accented for enhancing quality and accountability, forming alliances, and building knowledge in occupational therapy. While occupational therapists will be the main audience, the document has multiple uses for serving individuals, communities, governments, and others. Readers are encouraged to discover additional ideas to make the document work for them in their particular situations.

$\mathcal{T}$en ideas for using these guidelines are presented (Table 24). They may spark additional ideas that make the document useful in particular situations. The ideas encourage occupational therapists to take a bold stance on practice.

ENHANCING QUALITY AND ACCOUNTABILITY
Educating Occupational Therapists

One of the primary uses of this document will be to educate occupational therapists, since professional education is the cornerstone for enhancing quality and accountability in occupational therapy. In undergraduate, graduate, and continuing professional education, occupational therapists learn to base practice on theory. Continuing professional education, whether formal or informal, has long been recognized as a key element in ensuring competency in occupational therapy practice (Hood, 1976) and has been strongly supported by occupational therapy's provincial and national professional bodies (Gill, 1986). It should be noted that occupational therapy education includes ethics, spirituality and moral reasoning as well as technical skill building (Brockett, 1994). A wide range of texts are used to educate occupational therapists about the profession's history, theoretical approaches and methods. This document can contribute by educating occupational therapists about the broad context, conceptual framework, processes, outcomes, and organization of occupational therapy. Novice and experienced practitioners can use this document as a resource for developing their professional reasoning.

Table 24: Ideas for Using New Guidelines

Enhancing Quality and Accountability

- Educating occupational therapists
- Guiding practice with clients
- Documenting and managing occupational therapy
- Maximizing occupational therapy outcomes
- Guiding programme and policy development

Forming Alliances

- Explaining occupational therapy to others
- Advocating with and for clients
- Marketing benefits of occupational therapy

Building Knowledge

- Focusing occupational therapy research
- Debating issues about occupation, client-centred practice, and occupational therapy

Enabling Occupation: An Occupational Therapy Perspective, CAOT 1997

Students might use this document as a reference for projects, presentations, papers, or other assignments. Academic educators might organize courses to develop ways of enhancing quality and accountability in client-centred practice that focuses on occupation. Fieldwork educators might show students how to incorporate core concepts into practice. Continuing education leaders might organize seminars, discussion groups, or workshops on occupation. Graduate students might conduct indepth studies of occupation, occupational performance, or client-centred practice. This document might also be used to recruit students and stimulate them to think about exciting career opportunities for enabling occupation.

This is a document that educates occupational therapists to make practice consistent with the profession's own values and beliefs. It educates readers to define quality and accountability criteria for enabling occupation.

Guiding Practice With Clients

Quality occupational therapy practice identifies the context and theoretical approaches to be used. This document encourages occupational therapists to identify their client's occupational performance issues and the potential for collaborating in client-centred practice. Ideally, these guidelines will prompt occupational therapists to listen carefully to clients' perspectives and experiences (Picard-Greffe, 1994). The broad interpretation of clients supports occupational therapists' practice with individuals, groups, organizations, agencies, and other clients. Practice with clients is highly variable in occupational therapy. Decisions about assessment, specific approaches, length of contact time, and contact situations are all made through professional reasoning in particular practice conditions. Occupational therapists aim to be flexible and open to change to respond to diverse, changing client needs and assets. This is a document that guides practitioners to be accountable for enabling occupation as the primary role of occupational therapy.

A quality and accountable practice in enabling occupation cannot rely on specific protocols or standards. Therefore flexible guidelines, rather than standards or standardized protocols, are presented. To demonstrate quality or accountability in specific practice situations, occupational therapists can create local guidelines for caseload sizes, working conditions, practice approaches, or outcomes consistent with enabling occupation. Where occupational therapists face constraints in working with clients, they are encouraged to use these guidelines in advocating for change.

Documenting and Managing Occupational Therapy

Every occupational therapist engages in some type of documentation. Quality and accountability are demonstrated primarily through a variety of documentation about client goals, outcomes, time statistics, costs, and more. Careful documentation has long been advocated for many reasons, including the quality management of occupational therapy (Baptiste,1993a;

Gage,1995; Gilewich, 1979; Saunders, 1984). Managers and funders make decisions about occupational therapy based on documentation. Occupational therapists have historically translated their knowledge about people's occupations into medical terms and diagnostic categories. The International Classification of Impairments, Disabilities, and Handicaps (ICIDH) (World Health Organization, 1980) is now being used by occupational therapists since it is quite compatible with the Canadian Model of Occupational Performance. The ICIDH refers to everyday abilities, social roles, and other issues of concern to occupational therapists. The ICIDH recognizes occupational therapy concerns from a perspective outside occupational therapy.

Enabling Occupation encourages occupational therapists to document and manage practice using categories and language that are congruent with this profession's core concepts. These guidelines outline values, beliefs and concepts which can be used in developing ways of classifying and documenting the work of enabling occupation. The principles of client-centred practice might be cited to advocate for collaborative documentation in which professionals and clients each document client needs, strengths and resources from their own perspectives. Occupational therapists and clients might develop documentation and accountability approaches that bring clients' occupational performance needs and issues to the media, funding agencies, or governments.

Maximizing Occupational Therapy Outcomes

Outcome information plays an important part in enhancing the quality and accountability of occupational therapy practice. *Enabling Occupation* advocates that occupational therapy outcomes be defined in terms of occupation, occupational performance, and client-centred practice. Occupational performance outcomes are often described in terms of self-care, productivity, and leisure. In enabling occupation, occupational therapists enable people to choose, develop and engage in occupations that they define as meaningful. In some situations, societal outcomes might be identified to show the broad purpose of occupational therapy. An individualized outcome of enabling occupation might be described as occupational quality of life. A social outcome of enabling occupation might be described in terms of increased opportunities for disadvantaged groups to engage in meaningful occupations. If outcome information is defined in terms of occupation, occupational performance, and client-centred practice, there is a valid information base for demonstrating occupational therapy's effectiveness, efficiency and cost-benefits.

Guiding Programme and Policy Development

Enabling Occupation is an important resource for programme and policy development because all occupational therapists are involved in these areas in some way. Active involvement in an organization's policy and programme development enables occupational therapists to shape the organizational context of practice. This document supports the development of client-centred programmes and policies in and beyond occupational therapy. It also supports the development of programmes and policies that remove institutional and community barriers to meaningful occupation.

The document might be used with individual clients to consider whether programmes and policies are based on the needs and goals identified by these clients. Alternately, one might take an organizational perspective to see how an organization's policies support or limit occupational therapists (and others) who wish to enable occupation. Occupational therapy and other programme developers might use this document to support the inclusion of clients on programme boards of directors and committees. Using this document might also help to support the inclusion of a client-centred, occupational perspective in new or changing programmes. Where service gaps exist, discussion of this document might spark ideas for proposing new projects, particularly in community settings. Questions about the breadth and potential of occupational therapy may be translated into programme and policy decisions that are appropriate for particular communities. Policy developers may be able to use the document to expand client involvement into policies on anything from quality management to professional liability.

Occupational therapists can enhance their accountability by evaluating the effectiveness, efficiency, cost-benefits, resource management, and quality management associated with a focus on occupation and client-centred practice. With this document, occupational therapists have support for programmes and policies that include clients in meeting their needs with respect to occupation. Other disciplines are also encouraged to use this document as a guide in developing policies and programmes for enabling occupation.

FORMING ALLIANCES
Explaining Occupational Therapy to Others

Occupational therapists are continually faced with the challenge of explaining what they are doing and why. Those outside the profession also need to explain why they want occupational therapy. Occupational therapists often work in interdisciplinary practice situations with diverse clients, who may include professionals, business people, government officials, volunteers, families and members of communities associated with clients. This document explains occupational therapy's contribution from an occupational and client-centred perspective. By explaining what is meant by enabling occupation, occupational therapists may discover new allies on professional teams or in the community.

As an example, occupational therapists might use the Canadian Model of Occupational Performance (CMOP) to build alliances with other professionals. Occupational therapists might refer to the Occupational Performance Process for enabling occupation to explain how adaptive technology or skill development contribute to productivity or leisure occupations. The Occupational Performance Process might be used to explain why occupational therapists attend to broad occupational needs even when contact starts with very specific difficulties in performance components. The focus on occupation might be cited in explaining why occupational therapy services are needed in community settings. Reference to client-centred practice would explain why occupational therapists seek client involvement in decisions. The CMOP may help occupational therapists to describe how spirituality resides in persons, is shaped by the environment, and gives meaning to occupation. Reference to features of the context of practice might help to explain why occupational therapists are supporting or not supporting particular social trends.

Alternately, the document might help occupational therapists to form alliances with community or consumer groups which use a client-centred approach. The concepts, process and vignettes can help occupational therapists to articulate why and how occupational therapists involve people as participants in solving problems in everyday occupations. In essence, this is a document that explains the complexity behind occupational therapy and the processes that are consistent with enabling occupation. It supports occupational therapists as they form alliances with clients, professionals, lay persons, and others who work with occupational therapists.

Advocating with and for Clients

Occupational therapists work within a political context. Public policy, generated through the political process, influences the practice of all occupational therapists. Therefore, an important element of occupational therapy practice is advocacy. Advocacy with and for clients has always been part of occupational therapy practice. In advocating for clients, occupational therapists might refer the document to managers, programme developers, economists, and others whose interests are congruent with occupational therapy. In advocating with clients, the document provides a reference for developing advocacy alliances with clients or consumer groups.

Using this document in advocacy may help occupational therapists and others to support consumer-professional partnerships in developing funding, policies, and legislation in many areas, such as making transportation more physically accessible. In addition, the document supports advocacy for the programmes and funding needed to enable meaningful occupation. Occupational therapists who are interested in political activism can use this document as both a conceptual and practical reference. The statement of Occupational Therapy Values and Beliefs

(Table 3) and the Guiding Principles for Enabling Occupation in Client-Centred Practice (Table 10) support activism in favour of equal opportunities for people across Canada. Concepts about persons, the environment, and occupation support activism in favour of expanded options for employment, housing, leisure and community living.

Marketing Benefits of Occupational Therapy

Occupational therapy has not been well known by the general public (Jacobs, 1987; Stan, 1987; Tompson, 1989). People are usually thrilled to discover a profession which can help them through difficult occupational transitions or disruptions. In their search for expertise on coping with or overcoming the challenges of everyday living, they discover occupational therapy. One of the most effective marketing approaches is to form alliances with individuals or organizations that have benefitted from occupational therapy.

Enabling Occupation markets occupational therapy as a profession which is concerned with all the occupations of everyday life, and which strives to be client-centred. Using this document, occupational therapy can be marketed as a profession that involves clients in decisions about occupational therapy and their occupational performance issues. Marketing might then highlight potential individual benefits, such as the quality of life and health that derive from meaningful occupations. Marketing can also highlight the collective benefits of increased occupational performance across a community, such as expanded opportunities for living, and empowerment.

In some situations, occupational therapists may want to market the benefits of including occupational therapy. For example, the document might be used to back up claims that occupational therapy could reduce institutional admissions by creating meaningful home and community environments. Some readers might use the document to gain support for pilot projects. Others might market the benefits of occupational therapy in orientation sessions, open house events, media events, presentations, or policy development. Alliances with anyone, from managers to consumers who have had positive experiences with occupational therapists, are an extremely powerful method for marketing occupational therapy.

BUILDING KNOWLEDGE
Focusing Occupational Therapy Research

Occupational therapy is the profession that most clearly focuses on the broad ranging occupations that comprise everyday life. Moreover, occupational therapy has generated considerable knowledge for enabling people to overcome or cope with problems in everyday occupations. Canadian occupational therapists have also pioneered this profession's adherence to collaborative partnerships in client-centred practice. Knowledge for focusing on occupation and for client-centred practice comes from practice and research. Practice informs research and research informs practice. Occupational therapy research is generating new knowledge while also drawing from other fields, such as anatomy, anthropology, economics, environmental studies, management, medicine, physiology, political science, psychology, and sociology.

This document provides a framework for research, as well as direction for further research avenues. There is much to be learned about enabling occupation, particularly when circumstances like disability, aging, or social crises limit occupation. Those interested in empirical questions might concentrate on developing measures of the various elements of the Canadian Model of Occupational Performance or client-centred practice. Researchers with interests in interpretive methods might gather client stories about their experiences in developing new occupations or transforming their occupations to reduce the effects of a disability. Critical social scientists might concentrate on showing how social organization and structure determine possibilities for client-centred practice or for meaningful occupation. These diverse research approaches are all needed to build knowledge for enabling occupation.

Debating Issues About Occupation, Client-Centred Practice, and Occupational Therapy

Suggestions for using the document are capped by highlighting the importance of debate in building knowledge in occupational therapy. Debates act as springboards for examining occupational therapy contexts, values, concepts, practices, and potential contributions to society. Debates may occur in clinical, administrative, academic or other environments.

The diversity of the profession is reflected in the varied topics that stimulate discussion. These include debates about ethical decision making, continuing professional education, and many other topics. In clinical practice, there are debates around the use of technology, physical treatment modalities, or the fit between occupation and the counselling process. There are ongoing debates concerning the development of standards, given that neither occupational therapy nor clients are standardized. Also of interest are debates about single modality professions that resemble components of occupational therapy but do not operate from occupational therapy's view of occupations and client-centred practice. This document is intended to stimulate debate about occupational therapy's rich and important contributions in enabling occupation.

Debating Occupation: Suggestions

- Why is a broad view of occupation of interest/not of interest to the public? Governments? Corporations?
- What are the consequences for occupational therapists who do/do not focus on occupation?
- Who are/are not occupational therapy's natural allies in taking a broad view of occupation?
- Are some settings more/less conducive for enabling occupation?
- What public/private sources would be most likely to fund the work of enabling occupation?
- What policies and other documents should/should not make occupation explicit?
- What leadership opportunities might emerge/not emerge in health, social, educational, employment, and other arenas of reform if occupation is made more explicit?
- What changes in different models of practice such as education, consultation or clinical, can/cannot be implemented to make occupation more explicit?
- What topics in undergraduate, continuing and graduate occupational therapy education would make occupation explicit/not make occupation explicit?
- Does occupational therapy need/not need to be clearly linked to occupation?
- What will make occupational therapy's focus on occupation thrive/not thrive in generic roles, such as rehabilitation worker, mental health worker, vocational counsellor, case manager?
- How might occupational therapists promote a broad view of occupation with governments, businesses, communities, and others?

Debating Client-Centred Practice: Suggestions

- Why do some occupational therapists use/not use client-centred approaches?
- Why is it important/not important to forge alliances with people in self help or activist groups?
- What makes clinical contact, advocacy, community development, management, consultation, and education client-centred/not client-centred?

- How is spirituality linked/not linked to client-centred practice?
- What is required/not required to form collaborative partnerships in client-centred practice?
- Who will fund/not fund client-centred occupational therapy partnerships with advocacy groups?
- What undergraduate, continuing, and graduate occupational therapy education helps/does not help occupational therapists to learn enablement approaches?
- Should occupational therapists advocate with or for clients?
- How can responsibility and risk be shared/not shared with individual or group clients who have difficulty in decision making?
- Does occupational therapy need/not need to be client-centred?
- What leadership opportunities exist/do not exist for occupational therapists to educate other practitioners about client-centred practice?
- What will determine if occupational therapy becomes publicly known/remains publicly invisible as an advocate for equal opportunities for people with disabilities and other disadvantaged groups?

Debating Occupational Therapy: Suggestions
- Are the core concepts for enabling occupation foundations for all forms of occupational therapy?
- What will help/not help occupational therapists make practice more focused on occupation and more client-centred?
- In programme or regional management, when should occupational therapists be explicit/not explicit about focusing on occupation and being client-centred?
- How important/not important is it that those who assist occupational therapists have occupational therapy in their title?
- What would give the work of enabling occupation a positive/negative reputation in meeting client needs in hospitals? Special Centres? Business? Schools? Correctional programmes? Social programmes for homelessness? Other areas?
- How can a focus on enabling occupation help/not help occupational therapists whose positions are changing because of health reform?
- How might the processes of enabling occupation facilitate/not facilitate greater sensitivity in occupational therapy to culture? Gender? Race? Sexual orientation? Other characteristics?

- What will make occupational therapy more known/less known by the public?
- How should/should not occupational therapy be marketed to convince third party insurers to fund the work of enabling occupation?
- Where does occupational therapy's future lie/not lie in Canada? In other parts of the world?
- What is the worst scenario for occupational therapy's future?
- What is the best scenario for occupational therapy's future?

CHAPTER SEVEN

Vignettes

PRIMARY AUTHORS:
Sharon Brintnell
Jo Clark
Christine Kramer
Tracey Thompson-Franson

Purpose

To offer examples of enabling occupation.

Objectives

To show how occupational therapists enable occupation with diverse clients.

- Vignette #1: Retirement Village
- Vignette #2: Adult with Mental Health Issues
- Vignette #3: Child in the Community
- Vignette #4: Religious Organization
- Vignette #5: Lawyer

Summary

The core concepts of occupational therapy practice are based on values and beliefs about occupation, persons, environment, health, and client-centred practice. Five vignettes are used to show how core concepts can be applied in different situations. These vignettes illustrate the relationship between theory and practice.

*O*ccupational therapy roles and actions vary widely. Diverse forms of occupational therapy are based on a common set of occupational therapy values, beliefs and core concepts, about occupation, persons, the environment, health, and client-centred practice (outlined in Chapter 3). A common Occupational Performance Process can be applied with individual, organizational or other clients (see Chapter 4). While the organization of occupational therapy services differs to respond to the needs and circumstances of each setting, occupational therapists strive to incorporate the values, beliefs, concepts and processes which are characteristic of occupational therapy (see Chapter 5).

An occupational therapy client may be an individual, family, community, social agency, political agency etc. Occupational therapists may work with clients of any age or cultural group in any setting. Chapter 7 presents five vignettes to show how theory and practice are integrated when enabling occupation. The vignette which describes working with a Retirement Village shows how occupational therapists integrate theory and practice for services with an organization (see Chapters 4 and 5). A second vignette describes a positive result when an occupational therapist works with a woman who is hospitalized briefly because of mental health issues. It shows how a focus on occupational performance is integrated with Cognitive-Behavioural approaches to enable occupation and promote mental health. The need to coordinate community and institutional services is evident in the third vignette in which a child and his mother are clients. Another vignette illustrates an occupational therapy consultation with members of a Board of Directors who are mainly volunteers, in this case, in a religious organization concerned about its senior members. Since third party payment is increasing in Canada, the fifth vignette shows an occupational therapist working for payment from one client (a lawyer) while working with a secondary client, the lawyer's client.

The vignettes are based on real situations, with names, locations, and other identifiers changed to protect anonymity. They portray what the occupational therapist is doing because these are guidelines for occupational therapy practice. The underlying assumption is that occupational therapists collaborate in teams with clients, professionals, community workers, families, and others who are working on the same or different goals with clients. In essence, the occupational therapist works with a team which varies depending on the circumstances. The team may be formally organized or it may be brought together to resolve a particular occupational performance issue. An occupational therapist's leadership skills can facilitate the collaboration and coordination required for a team to work effectively and efficiently in the interests of a client. All the vignettes apply the core concepts of the Canadian Model of Occupational Performance and client-centred practice.

VIGNETTE #1: RETIREMENT VILLAGE

Scenario

A community-based occupational therapy consulting group was approached by a nationally operated retirement village to develop and coordinate a rehabilitation service which included occupational therapy.

Stage #1: Name, Validate and Prioritize Occupational Performance Issues

A meeting was arranged with the Service Planning Group which included representatives from the residents of the retirement village, the Village Operations Committee and the retirement village National Office. In the meeting it was evident that changes in the occupational performance of the residents, and their increasing use of acute and rehabilitation services within the community, had led the group to explore the need for and feasibility of providing rehabilitation services on-site. Meeting participants commented: "Many of the residents have lived in the village for 15-20 years and now have health problems that are preventing them from doing things they want to do. In the last 18 months, many of them have had to spend more time away from the village to get the rehabilitation services they need. When they return it takes time to adjust and reconnect with friends. A few of the residents would rather struggle than use the off-site services, but we've seen some of them withdrawing, and being less and less able to do things. Since it seems that more people are needing services, we think it may be better to provide the services here, in the village itself." It was apparent that group members also believed that other residents could increase their participation in occupations, and in doing so, maintain and/or improve their function and health.

The occupational therapist facilitated a discussion in the meeting to name, prioritize and validate the occupational performance issues. In order of importance they were:
- Some residents are unable to participate in valued self-care, productivity and/or leisure occupations
- Other residents are potentially unable to participate in valued self-care, productivity and/or leisure occupations

Members of the planning group perceived that there was an urgent need to provide rehabilitation services in the village so that the first occupational performance issue could be addressed, and where possible resolved. The second occupational performance issue could then be prevented. Group members recognized that before services were developed, it was necessary to assess the occupational performance needs of residents to: (a) identify what was contributing to these occupational performance issues, and (b) determine the number of residents with actual versus potential occupational performance issues. This information would guide the completion of the remaining steps in the planning process. These were to identify targeted service outcomes, establish a service to meet those needs, identify needed service resources, and develop a marketing and evaluation plan (see Plan Services, Chapter 5). Group members' agreed that the initial occupational therapy contract would include completion of the six service planning steps.

The group developed the following principles and parameters for the planning process:

- members of the village community and the planning group would participate in planning and designing the services;
- all services would occur within the retirement village, with the exception of those for residents requiring specialized services who would be referred to community agencies;
- the needs of the residents would direct decisions about required personnel; and
- the services would be cost effective.

Stage #2: Select Theoretical Approach(es)

Along with the planning process described in the Client, Service, Society Model (see Chapter 5), marketing, management, educational, evaluation and organizational development theories guided service planning. Consistent with other vignettes, the Canadian Model of Occupational Performance and the Occupational Performance Process guided the assessment of residents' occupational performance needs.

Stage #3: Identify Occupational Performance Components and Environmental Conditions

A variety of assessment methods were used to identify the occupational performance components and environmental conditions related to the two occupational performance issues, to confirm the nature and extent of residents' occupational performance needs.

Many of the residents were of one ethnic background and religious affiliation, though the village was non-denominational. For most, English was a second language. With a mix of well active elders and elders with specific health issues, it was evident that physical, cognitive and/or affective components of occupational performance were limiting or had the potential to limit participation in occupations. Individual interviews of residents using the Canadian Occupational Performance Measure (COPM) supported this finding. The results indicated that 60% of residents were experiencing reduced participation in valued occupations while the remaining 40% were at risk. Many residents lacked knowledge about how participation in occupations could prevent dysfunction and promote health.

Focus group discussions revealed that residents wanted on-site rehabilitation services that incorporated a holistic approach to lifestyle and health issues. In addition, they wanted programmes that would enable them to be more active and able to participate in valued occupations as long as possible.

For the most part, the social, cultural and physical environment supported rather than constrained occupational performance. Some residents reported that they found meaning in life from participation in family events and helping their neighbours who were frail. Others were gratified and enriched by their role in the adopt-a-grandchild programme with a nearby daycare centre. Here, their life experiences and nurturing skills were welcomed and valued.

The Village Operations Committee and staff of the retirement village were also supportive of the residents' needs for participation in the community; and some assistance, support and resources were available (e.g., tax services, domestic cleaning for apartment residents and a shuttle to downtown shopping area). Consultants were regularly scheduled for educational sessions on legal and social issues.

In contrast, the institutional environment (the community at large/village) was contributing to the occupational performance issues by not providing rehabilitation services and health promotion programmes that met the changing needs of residents. In summary, the occupational performance components and environmental conditions that were contributing to each occupational performance issue were:

Some residents were unable to participate in valued self-care, productivity and/or leisure occupations, due to:
- 60% of residents had physical, cognitive and/or affective occupational performance components that limited their participation in valued occupations;
- lack of client-centred rehabilitation services that address residents' occupational performance needs (issues) and facilitated desired participation in valued occupations.

Other residents were potentially unable to participate in valued self-care, productivity and/or leisure occupations, due to:
- lack of knowledge about the role of occupation in promoting health and preventing dysfunction;
- lack of access to health promotion services and programmes.

Stage #4: Identify Strengths and Resources
Residents were motivated to remain actively engaged in village activities and in publicly offered socio-cultural attractions to the extent that their health made that possible. The village had been chosen by its aging but well occupants because it offered supportive but unobtrusive assistance to individuals committed to an active lifestyle.

The interest, support and availability of funding for rehabilitation services by the Village Operations Committee and staff, and the National office were an asset and enabled residents to continue living in the village community unless emergency, acute care or residential rehabilitation services were required. The past experience of the occupational therapy consulting group led to effective, anticipatory planning.

Given the occupational profile of the residents, their actual and potential occupational performance issues (occupational performance needs) and the number of residents with these needs, it was evident that on-site occupational therapy services were appropriate. In addition to confirming the need for occupational therapy, the findings indicated that other services (e.g., physical therapy) and personnel (e.g., personal attendants) would also be needed.

Stage #5: Negotiate Targeted Outcomes, Develop Action Plan

Following discussion in a second meeting, the planning group agreed that the targeted outcomes for the service, in order of priority, were that:

- Residents who receive rehabilitation services, and timely referral to community specialty services when necessary, will maintain and/or increase their participation in occupations they value, with/without assistance from others and/or environmental adaptations;
- After participating in village health promotion programmes, residents will be able to use knowledge about health and lifestyle issues that are important to them in making choices that will maintain active participation in valued occupations and optimal health;
- Residents who receive rehabilitation services and participate in health promotion programmes that maintain or increase participation in valued occupations will have a lower rate of admission to community health facilities.

In the process of developing the action plans, the last four planning steps were completed. A budget was developed using community service utilization statistics available from the retirement village National Office. Criteria for setting priorities for services were established in collaboration with the village community. The Service Planning Group's plans to meet the targeted outcomes included:

- Set up single entry holistic, client-centred rehabilitation service with an interdisciplinary referral system to on-site service providers and community specialty services;
- Hire qualified personnel and ensure they receive sufficient orientation to provide the needed client-centred services;
- Advise (market) all residents and staff about the new on-site rehabilitation services;

- Develop a rehabilitation services data bank for referral requests, residents' occupational profiles, and records concerning service utilization and occupational performance outcomes;
- Collaborate with community and/or university researchers to ensure that the service evaluation plan will provide information about the effectiveness and efficiency of services, and other data to guide future decision-making;
- Provide individual occupational therapy services (using the seven stage Occupational Performance Process) to residents who request service and have occupational performance issues;
- Develop and offer educational programmes that match the health promotion and lifestyle needs of the residents;
- Conduct monthly resident focus groups for feedback to guide service alterations.

Given the satisfaction of all parties with the service plan, the consulting group contract was extended for six months to implement the plan. Like the planning contract, it included direct, in-direct, non-direct, and travel time. The final contract was approved by the managers in the retirement village National Office. It stated that evaluation of services would be based on the extent to which the targeted outcomes were met prior to the conclusion of the first six-month contract. Contract renewal was contingent on a satisfactory evaluation.

Stage #6: Implement Plans Through Occupation

One of the consulting group members assumed the role of Project Coordinator. Independent occupational therapy practitioners were recruited as sub-contractors. Where possible, new staff with second languages that matched the needs of residents were recruited. With experience in offering educational programmes, the service providers were able to educate personal attendants and other staff efficiently on-site. During orientation, time was spent on strategies to incorporate health promotion ideas during contact with residents.

With an understanding of the retirement village's vision and philosophy, the Project Coordinator facilitated the translation of occupational therapy's holistic approach to service into a language that was compatible with that used by the retirement village operators and the residents.

Implementation was done by sub-contracted occupational therapists who developed relationships with village staff and residents. Concurrently, the development of policies, procedures and a data entry system set the project up for accountability and programme evaluation. Much time was spent on the premises organizing occupational therapy services (e.g., setting up an administrative area in the health centre, arranging a storage area for printed material and frequently used assessments), and visiting with residents.

Notice of the commencement of on-site services was sent to all residents and staff, and an announcement was made using the village communication system. Posters were displayed in common areas highlighting the various occupational therapy services and how to access them. A schedule was posted, for example, for the elders "High Living Programme." This peer-run participatory, health event used a workshop format that focused on food preparation and active occupations that incorporated physical exercise.

The service evolved through ongoing (village) community participation and direction. The retirement village focus groups provided residents and village staff with direct access to the Project Coordinator and opportunity to share perceptions of service development, meaningfulness and benefits. Feedback was immediately incorporated into the delivery and monitoring system to enhance outcomes. Residents' progress was continually re-evaluated and programme goals renegotiated by the occupational therapist and the individuals concerned.

Stage #7: Evaluate Occupational Performance Outcomes

As a small business, the supplier had a goal to maintain the contract. As a consumer, the retirement village and its National Office wanted time to assess the service.

When the service was evaluated towards the end of the first contract some changes in occupational performance were evident. Eighty percent of the residents who had received individual services had maintained or increased their participation in occupations that were important to them. Similarly, 60% of residents who participated in the health promotion programmes were found to be more actively involved in activities in the village and surrounding community. Although the statistics were low, it appeared that the increased participation in programmes may have contributed to the downturn in admission rates to community health facilities. However, it was recognized that the outcomes after one year of service would be more helpful in judging the effectiveness of services.

Outcomes were also measured in terms of village ownership of services and individuals' satisfaction with services. Indicators were referral of new residents by those already receiving services, or residents using the information from the educational sessions to teach others. It was particularly rewarding to have family members ask for information their relatives had told them about. These outcomes could only be achieved through providing and adapting the services to meet client priorities, in this case the retirement village as a unit.

Renewal of the contract and any future expansion of services required the occupational therapy consulting group to report the programme design, evolution of services, outcomes, and financial accountability.

VIGNETTE #2: ADULT WITH MENTAL HEALTH ISSUES

Scenario

Allison Jones is a 28-year-old female. She was admitted to a hospital's mood disorder unit. On admission, her routines and performance in everyday occupations were very disrupted due to her depressed mood and obsessive thoughts.

Stage #1: Name, Validate and Prioritize Occupational Performance Issues

The Canadian Occupational Performance Measure (COPM) was used in the initial interview with Allison. Her initial ratings on performance and satisfaction on three occupational performance issues which she named as being her priorities were:

Performance I	Satisfaction I	Importance	Occupational Performance Issues
1	1	10	Over attention to personal hygiene in self-care occupations. "I feel like I spend half of my day in the bathroom checking myself."
2	2	9	Indecision about career future and possible career change (productivity). "I measure myself in terms of my productivity and my financial status in comparison to others."
2	2	6	Participation in previous physical and social occupations has subsided.

Stage #2: Select Theoretical Approach(es)

The occupational therapist was guided by the concepts of client-centred practice and the Canadian Model of Occupational Performance. Psycho-emotional (primarily Cognitive-Behavioural techniques), socio-adaptive, and environmental approaches were also used as the occupational therapist worked with Allison.

Stage #3: Identify Occupational Performance Components and Environmental Conditions

Self-care: Over-attention to personal hygiene was related to:
*   obsessive thoughts and ruminations regarding appearance

- evaluating self against external variables: "I will only have a relationship if I'm attractive. I'm getting older and all my friends are married. Now my age is working against me."
- absolute thinking on expectations of self and lack of constructive coping strategies.

Productivity: Indecision about career future and possible career change were related to:
- frustration tolerance and problem solving ability clouded by absolute, imbalanced thinking: "I assume the worst, and personalize everything. Therefore, I either avoid things or give up when barriers present themselves."
- lack of clarity regarding vocational interests and capabilities;
- rumination about the fact that she did not pursue post-secondary education and feels she is too old to do so at this time. Her rumination is of particular importance in the climate of a very high achieving family.

Leisure: Participation in previous physical and social occupations has subsided, related to:
- a recent move to a new city;
- external changes in her support network and decreased availability of friends/peers;
- self-deprecating statements and feelings of inadequacy.

In analyzing the identified occupational performance components and environmental conditions, the occupational therapist noted some similarities. It appeared that Allison's style of thinking, particularly her obsessive, absolute and self-deprecating perceptions, as well as her tendency to ruminate about the past and measure herself against external variables, were negatively influencing her self-esteem; in doing so, these behaviours contributed to the three occupational performance issues.

Stage #4: Identify Strengths and Resources
Allison's personal strengths were:
- sincere, fair, kind and honest;
- a good sense of humour;
- musical talent - played a number of instruments and has travelled internationally with music groups;
- articulate, with good sales skills.

Her resources were:
- extensive support from her family;
- financial security.

The occupational therapist's strengths and resources lay in having the knowledge, skills and resources needed to work with Allison.

Stage #5: Negotiate Targeted Outcomes, Develop Action Plans

In the initial stages of negotiating the targeted outcomes and developing action plans, the occupational therapist's analysis of the assessment findings (see Stage 3) was discussed with, and validated by Allison. It was clear that she was eager to begin to work on these items and recognized this was essential for the occupational peformance issues to be resolved. In this, as in other situations, the occupational therapist considered plans that could be directed at the person (i.e. skill building in thinking, feeling and doing), occupation (i.e. the occupations, adaptation and grading) and/or environment (e.g., advocacy, adaptation). Once they had jointly discussed and determined the plans, the occupational therapist and Allison decided who would do what and when to facilitate the achievement of each targeted outcome.

Occupational Performance Issue #1: Over attention to personal hygiene (self-care)

Targeted Outcomes:

By the time of discharge from hospital, Allison will:

- demonstrate knowledge for integrating cognitive therapy techniques into occupation by completing three Thought Records in written format, and implementing use of this technique into occupations that evoke stress or anxiety; [Thought Records (a Cognitive Therapy technique), consists of a seven column record by which clients monitor situations, feelings, and automatic thoughts and gather evidence that supports or does not support a thought with a view to developing more balanced thoughts and feelings.]
- demonstrate two relaxation techniques which she is able to use in at least one occupation in which she has previously experienced anxiety;
- differentiate between internal and external sources of self-esteem;
- brainstorm a list of occupations which she thinks will boost her sclf-csteem internally and participate in at least two of these occupations;
- reduce the amount of time spent in the washroom to check herself;
- participate in re-evaluating her occupational performance issues (all three) at the end of her hospital admission.

Action Plans:

After discussion with the occupational therapist, Allison indicated that she was interested in attending stress management, relaxation, and life styles groups. Since these groups were designed to help participants to develop constructive coping strategies, and also addressed the occupational performance issues that were related to self-esteem, Allison felt they they would be meaningful and valuable to her. It was decided that during individual cognitive therapy sessions with the occupational therapist,

Allison would use techniques to investigate her thought processes with a view to moving towards more balanced thinking. The occupational therapist would encourage Allison to access her sense of humour as an additional tool for maintaining a balanced perspective. As it was Allison's desire to spend less time in front of the mirror checking herself or being worried about her appearance, she decided that she would also monitor and record this on a weekly basis over the course of therapy.

Occupational Performance Issue #2: Indecision about career future and possible career change (productivity)

Targeted Outcomes:

By the time of discharge from hospital, Allison will:

- have direction and information regarding 2-3 different vocational possibilities;
- arrange to investigate career choices through volunteer work, or through contact with academic or vocational training programmes.

Action Plans:

It was agreed that Allison would participate in vocational interest batteries and aptitude tests in the work readiness group. In so doing, she would begin to gather the necessary information to consider in future career planning. Her absolute, unbalanced thinking related to her career decisions would be addressed as she engaged in vocational occupations and used cognitive therapy techniques [as identified under self-care outcomes (see #1 above)].

Occupational Performance Issue #3: Participation in previous physical and social occupations has subsided (leisure)

Targeted Outcomes:

By the time of discharge from hospital, Allison will:

- identify two recreation occupations that she wishes to pursue that incorporate desired physical and social environmental elements;
- observe the two chosen recreational occupations (i.e., meet the team, see the setting, and so on) and if possible, have registered for the upcoming sessions.

Action Plans:

It was decided that Allison would complete the Pie of Life and the Leisure Needs and Interests Survey. After identifying interests in keeping with her personal needs, Allison would explore information regarding community and recreation centres, and other resources. Allison would also use weekends and evenings to call and obtain information about those that might be appropriate from her point of view. As well, Allison planned to make use of the music room daily to practise with the instruments and to participate in an upcoming musical and social event as a means of using her strengths to overcome fears about reconnecting with others.

Stage #6: Implement Plans through Occupation

The plan that was developed in partnership with Allison was carried out. Using role playing to address occupational performance issues related to self esteem; using clearing, thought stopping and creative worrying in occupations that provoked stress; and completing a life script in the Lifestyles Group are some specific examples of the occupations Allison and the occupational therapist utilized to reach the targeted outcomes. Attention to purposeful occupation is of utmost importance in this stage. In Allison's case, choosing meaningful occupations for productivity and leisure was emphasized.

Stage #7: Evaluate Occupational Performance Outcomes

Evaluation with Allison took place approximately four weeks after she set her original goals. A repeat use of the COPM enabled comparison of Performance I and Satisfaction I with Performance II and Satisfaction II scores.

Occupational Performance Issue #1: Over-attention to personal hygiene

Performance I	Performance II
1	6

Satisfaction I	Satisfaction II
1	7

There was a 50% improvement in performance and a 60% improvement in satisfaction.

Allison commented on meeting her goals:

> *"I actually did many more than the three Thought Records that I had set as my goal. They helped me to understand that I was really hard on myself. I was sitting around, doing nothing and talking myself out of trying anything. I felt that the only thing I had left was my appearance and that was deteriorating. The Thought Records gave me the confidence and motivation to try activities that I had been wanting to try. What good feedback it was to be active again."*

Occupational Performance Issue #2: Indecision about career future and possible career change

Performance I	Performance II
2	4

Satisfaction I	Satisfaction II
2	3

There was a 20% improvement in performance and a 10% improvement in satisfaction.

In the client's words:

> *"I feel good about having a lot more clarity and direction now. I feel that sales has always been what I enjoy and what I could be very good at. I'm planning to do some volunteer work with a winery and explore various areas of sales. I've called one of the local colleges about various courses which may be beneficial, and plan to try one or two in the fall. That part still makes me really nervous because every time I think of school I immediately visualize my brothers and sisters and how successful they are. My plan is to use my Thought Records all summer to get me in good shape for doing this."*

Occupational Performance Issue #3: Participation in previous physical and social occupations has subsided

Performance I	Performance II
2	6

Satisfaction I	Satisfaction II
2	8

Physical and social (leisure) occupations showed a 40% improvement in performance and a 60% improvement in satisfaction.

> *"Playing the guitar at the party was the source of lots of anxiety at first. I used my relaxation techniques and came through in flying colours. I felt like I was beginning to be my old self again. I'm so excited I start beach volleyball next week. Playing volleyball here in some of the groups and just being around people has given me the confidence to try it again. I went to watch a game this week and was really pleased. There were a lot of people my age. There was a lot of laughing and joking around and everyone stayed to socialize when it was finished. I feel like I'll get to know the city and develop some friends quickly with this outlet. I've also signed up for a session on ocean kayaking. I figure that I might as well make use of living so close to the water. Once I got going I remembered that one of the old band members from the musical group I used to travel with lived in*

the area. I called her parents and they connected me with her again. We're going to try to get some people together every now and then for a jam session. I don't have the time to worry about my appearance anymore, people will have to take me as I am."

After completing contact with occupational therapy, Allison wrote a note to the occupational therapist:

"I'm really sorry I missed you, my plane leaves at 2:10 so I had to leave by 12:00. I wanted to say thank you for all your help, you showed me some things I really needed to see & I hope that I can put them into practice so that I never feel that way again. It's going to take a lot of pain to get there but - the message is Do, Don't think so much. Anyway, thank-you again! And maybe I'll see you sometime in Life. Take care.
Sincerely, Allison" (actual client message)

VIGNETTE #3: CHILD IN THE COMMUNITY
Scenario

An occupational therapist who worked for a Home Care agency received a request to work with a 9-year-old boy who had acquired a brain injury in a hit and run car accident. The referral came from a local children's rehabilitation facility where the child had received inpatient rehabilitation for 2 months.

Stage #1: Name, Validate and Prioritize Occupational Performance Issues

The occupational therapist contacted the child's mother to set-up an initial appointment. The mother explained that she would be the primary contact since she was responsible for the family's child-care and home management needs. Since the child could not participate actively in the screening assessment, the child's mother was interviewed to name, validate and prioritize the occupational performance issues. The most important occupational performance issues for the child, that were named and validated by the mother were:

Child:
- Difficulty managing dressing and bathing activities, and participating in play activities, in a safe manner;
- Unable to communicate needs re occupations effectively to family members and caregivers;
- Unable to participate successfully in school and organized recreational activities.

While all of these issues were important, the first issue, which placed the child and his siblings at risk, was most urgent to address from the mother's perspective. During the interview it became apparent that the child's mother had occupational performance issues of her own that were relevant to her son's care. She named and validated these as:

Mother:
- "I am unable to help my son in the way I would like to";
- "I have difficulty maintaining organization of family activities";
- "I can't advocate for my son's needs".

The Home Care agency had identified the child as the primary client. Even though the occupational therapist considered the mother as the secondary client, her role in the therapeutic process was recognized as crucial in providing an environment which enabled occupation for the child. The occupational therapist was aware that the mother was not formally recognized, or referred to as a 'client' by the Home Care agency. In this vignette, the agency was identified as the third client because the occupational therapist had entered into a contractual agreement with the agency to provide occupational therapy services to its client, the child.

Stage #2: Select Theoretical Approach(es)

The client-centred Canadian Model of Occupational Performance was used to guide the Occupational Performance Process. Psycho-emotional approaches were identified as valuable in assessing the factors that were contributing to the occupational performance issues of the child and the mother. For the child, neuro-developmental and behavioural approaches were also used. Environmental approaches guided the assessment and planning related to safety issues.

Stage #3: Identify Occupational Performance Components and Environmental Conditions

Observation of behaviour and performance of activities chosen by the child, information from the mother regarding her recent observations as well as her recollection of pre-accident behaviour/performance, and a home assessment were the methods used. Based on these assessment findings it was evident that formal assessment of cognitive and physical function could not occur, given the child's very limited attention span, distractibility, impulsivity, his inability to initiate and complete specific requested tasks, and his difficulty communicating.

Although the child's participation in occupations suggested a satisfactory return of physical strength and fine motor control, some problems were observed in gross motor coordination and balance. He had sufficient fine motor skills to manage self-feeding and toileting, and was spontaneously, but inconsistently, able to manage some components of dressing and bathing. Verbal and physical prompting/direction were often required to initiate and complete self-care tasks such as dressing and bathing. Generally, he was perceived to be "hyperactive" and his behaviour was unpredictable.

Primary care was provided by the mother with relief for 2-4 hour periods, three times a week from extended family and a Home Support Worker. The child's step-father was not seen with the family; he was rarely available to assist at home because of his involvement in the farming activities that were necessary to support the family. The child's two younger female siblings tended to show hesitancy toward their brother as his aggressive behaviour often involved them. The features of the two-storey family home contributed to concerns about the child's safety.

In assessing the child, the occupational therapist was able to observe the mother in caregiving situations. These observations, conversations with the Home Support Worker and the mother's answers to questions contributed to the identification of factors that were limiting the mother's occupational performance.

The occupational therapist's analysis of the assessment findings identified the occupational performance components and environmental conditions that were contributing to (related to) the occupational performance issues for the child and the mother:

Child:
Difficulty managing dressing, bathing, and play, in a safe manner, related to:
- difficulties with gross motor coordination and balance;
- aggressive, impulsive behaviour (a barrier to co-operative play);
- lack of a supportive physical and social environment to facilitate optimal occupational performance;
- difficulty attending to/following instructions.

Unable to communicate his needs effectively to family members and caregivers, related to:
- insufficient concentration to listen and respond to questions;
- inability to organize and express thoughts.

Unable to participate in school and organized recreational activities, related to:
- inability to concentrate for more than 30 seconds;
- distracted in even mildly stimulating environments;
- fears of those interacting with the client, and difficulties managing his aggressive, impulsive outbursts.

Mother:
"I am unable to help my son in the way I would like to," related to:
- "I don't have any information about what I can do at home to best help my son look after himself and play with others";
- lack of time to care for her son in addition to all other home and family responsibilities;
- lack of energy to carry out roles; "I feel completely exhausted,

both physically and emotionally";
- difficulty coping with the changes in her son's status since the injury;
- limited assistance in meeting her numerous responsibilities.

Difficulty maintaining organization of family activities, related to:
- "I feel totally overwhelmed by the ongoing needs of my son and have trouble concentrating on anything else";
- "I have too many things to do and too little time";
- son's unpredictable behaviour.

Difficulty advocating for son's needs, related to:
- lack of knowledge of the health care resources that would assist her son;
- lack of knowledge about how to access available resources;
- lack of knowledge about which services are covered through the family's health insurance plan.

In discussing these findings with the child's mother, the mother reluctantly confirmed the occupational therapist's assessment that addressing the mother's issues first would be essential in creating a supportive home environment for the child.

Stage #4: Identify Strengths and Resources

Other than the child's fine motor skills, physical strength, abounding energy and curiosity, it was difficult to identify his other strengths for enabling occupation. His resources included his mother, who was very supportive and interested in the rehabilitation process, as well as his siblings (despite their worry about their brother's aggressive play). The child's maternal grandmother was also very supportive and able to provide some relief for the mother. The Home Support Worker had excellent rapport with mother and child and was also open to assisting in the rehabilitation process for the child. The Home Care agency was supportive of the client and family, as well as the service providers, and were willing to advocate for additional services and resources.

The family had private extended health care coverage and some money had been awarded to meet the caregiving needs of the child through the insurance and legal proceedings following the hit-and-run accident.

The occupational therapist brought experience from earlier work in childrens' and adult mental health facilities as well as experience in community physical rehabilitation.

Stage #5: Negotiate Target Outcomes, Develop Action Plan

Because the primary client was not able to communicate his concerns in a meaningful, understandable manner, outcomes were negotiated with the child's mother, the Home Support Worker, occupational therapist and the Home Care agency with a view to meeting the best interests of the child and family.

Because the child's behaviour was so unpredictable and impulsive, and the safety of the child and the siblings were considered at risk, the mother's first two occupational performance issues related to coping and managing the family were identified as the priority issues. All parties agreed that these 'family coping' issues as well as the child's behaviour (aggressive, impulsive outbursts) needed to be addressed before the implementation of any plans for other occupational performance issues could be effective.

Targeted Outcomes:

Occupational therapy outcomes are difficult to establish at such a time, when clients are involved in crisis/reactive stages. Therefore, management of the situation through these stages becomes an outcome in itself. Outcomes specific to the identified issues of self-care and leisure occupations of the primary client were discussed among the parties, but given the difficulty gathering accurate and reliable baseline information on the child's occupational performance at the time, it was mutually decided to revisit these issues after the more immediate safety and family coping issues were resolved. Therefore, the first targeted outcome was:
Within one month of referral, adequate community and institutional supports will be accessed and used by the mother (and family) to:
- support the mother and other family members in providing a physical and social home environment that will enable occupation for themselves and the child;
- provide a safe environment for all family members;
- meet the immediate needs of the child for a safe, consistent and structured environment, and daily rehabilitation services;
- identify strategies for the effective management of child's aggressive, impulsive behaviour.

Action Plans:

- Facilitate a short-term readmission of the child to the children's rehabilitation facility to address the immediate needs of the child as outlined; and to provide relief to the family who, despite community-based supports, were unable to cope, and who were unable to provide the supervision, structure, programming and resources needed at this particular stage of recovery;
- Prior to readmission and after discharge home again, request an increase in Home Support Services to assist the family in coping with the current situation, relieve the mother from some of her responsibilities so that she can care for her son and participate in

his rehabilitation, and ensure that the mother obtains sufficient rest to function as an effective parent;

- Initiate a referral to the local hospital-based social work out-patient department to assist the mother in coping;
- Provide information and suggestions to both parents that will enable them to provide a home environment that enables occupation for the child and family, and also manage the child's behaviour.

Stage #6: Implement Plans through Occupation

All referrals and requests for services (and readmission) were made as planned. Documentation was provided to the Home Care agency to advocate for a short-term readmission to the rehabilitation facility which would allow the family supports to be put in place. Documentation was prepared with the mother's input and copies provided for her.

The occupational therapist provided information and suggestions to the mother and the Home Support Worker on ways of enhancing the child's occupational performance. This included: coping strategies; behaviour management; use of support systems; activity choices for the child; environmental changes to improve home safety; provision of a room with few distractions; visual prompts and reinforcement; and methods by which the mother could make her concerns and frustrations known to the appropriate sources. Weekly sessions at the family home took place pending re-admission of the child to the rehabilitation facility. Documentation and communication followed professional and Home Care service provider policies.

Three weeks after the plans were initiated, the child's aggressive behaviour escalated to the point where the rehabilitation facility readmitted the child upon the physician's request. After 1-2 weeks, the decision was made between the family and children's rehabilitation facility to refer the child to a specialized treatment centre elsewhere. Since it was anticipated that the child's length of stay in the centre would likely be long, Home Care services for the child were completed with the documented recommendation for occupational therapy follow-up once the child returned home.

Stage #7: Evaluate Occupational Performance Outcomes

Due to the unexpected early completion of services, all parts of targeted outcomes were not achieved. The occupational therapist made informal contact with the mother to ensure her understanding of the discharge and the recommendation for later follow-up with the family and the child. As the primary caregiver, the mother was satisfied that she had received sufficient information and suggestions that would enable her and other family members to get ready to provide a more supportive physical and social home environment for occupation when the child returned home again.

Postscript:
The client eventually returned to his home approximately one year later with Home Care and occupational therapy follow-up. The Occupational Performance Process resumed. Since the family reported considerable improvement in the child's occupational performance and their own ability to cope, and since the Home Care agency was better able to provide services to fit clients' needs, a decision was made for the occupational therapist to be available on a consulting basis for the child, family and school. The child and mother were much more involved and in control of the total rehabilitation process. Upon conclusion of the consulting contract, the mother was generally satisfied with the Home Care services, but indicated that she was frustrated by the initial lack of coordination between rehabilitation facility and community-based services. It was apparent that the service environment and the societal context (funding) constrained the Occupational Performance Process with the clients (see Chapter 5).

VIGNETTE #4: BOARD OF A RELIGIOUS ORGANIZATION
Scenario

The Board of Directors of a religious organization contacted an occupational therapist with a request to assist the organization with its Barrier Free campaign.

Stage #1: Name, Validate and Prioritize Occupational Performance Issues

The occupational therapist attended the next meeting of the Board where he explained the stages of his potential involvement guided by occupational therapy core concepts and the Occupational Performance Process. The occupational therapist recommended a several-stage contract which the Board approved. At a second meeting with the Board of Directors, the occupational therapist facilitated a round table discussion to identify the occupational performance issue(s). Members of the Board outlined their ideas for implementing their Barrier Free campaign to meet the needs of members with mobility limitations. By the end of the meeting, the occupational therapist had encouraged the Board to look not only at mobility limitations but at all potential barriers. The Board had named one occupational performance issue: actual or potential barriers to members' attendance and participation in the worship, social, and educational programmes at the religious centre.

Stage #2: Select Theoretical Approach(es)

The client-centred Canadian Model of Occupational Performance was used to guide the Occupational Performance Process. In addition, biomechanical and environmental theories, and health promotion approaches guided the identification of occupational performance components and environmental conditions.

Stage #3: Identify Occupational Performance Components and Environmental Conditions

The occupational therapist surveyed members of the religious organization to see who was having difficulty attending or participating in programmes. The purpose was to find out: a) how many members were having difficulty; b) what were the barriers or reasons for not attending or participating; and c) what might the organization do to remove barriers, encourage attendance, or facilitate participation. Analysis of the findings showed that the occupational performance issue, actual or potential barriers to members' attendance and participation in the worship, social, and educational programmes at the religious centre, was related to the following occupational performance components and environmental conditions:

- fear of falling when going in and out of their homes, cars, and the religious centre;
- difficulty negotiating stairs, specifically the 12 stairs to enter the centre and 6 stairs to the worship altar;
- difficulty rising from seats (pews and chairs);
- inadequate space for negotiating walkers and wheelchairs;
- fear of incontinence due to long distances to the accessible washrooms;
- need by persons using walkers and wheelchairs for physical assistance in using washrooms;
- inability to procure transportation to the centre;
- lack of awareness of the Volunteer Driver Programme.

At the same time, Board members and volunteer drivers at the organization were also surveyed. They were asked their perceptions about actual or potential environmental barriers. This survey revealed that:

- volunteer drivers felt that they lacked the knowledge required to assist members with mobility limitations;
- Board members felt they lacked the knowledge to provide leadership in their Barrier Free campaign.

In addition to the identification of these occupational performance components and environmental conditions, the occupational therapist noted that 45% of the membership was over 65 years of age.

Stage #4: Identify Strengths and Resources

The occupational therapist identified numerous strengths and resources which could assist the Board of Directors in resolving the occupational performance issue. These included:

- the membership's and Board of Directors' shared commitment to financing and promoting the Barrier Free campaign;
- adequate space for building ramps;
- worship, common room and washroom areas were all located on the same level;

- wheelchair accessible washrooms;
- a well-established fund raising committee;
- a large pool of drivers who were available in the Volunteer Driver Programme;
- shared spiritual beliefs about assisting members in need.

The occupational therapist summarized and presented his findings from these surveys in a report format that would be understandable to the Board. The Board of Directors discussed the report and developed a contract with the occupational therapist to assist a committee of the Board in formulating targeted outcomes and developing action plans.

Stage #5: Negotiate Targeted Outcomes, Develop Action Plans

The occupational therapist facilitated the development of targeted outcomes and action plans with the committee established by the Board of Directors. In order to respond to the results of the two surveys, one targeted outcome was defined as: all actual and potential members of the religious organization will be able to participate in any programme of choice offered at the centre. Criteria of success were defined in measurable, observable terms, that actual and potential members could:

- achieve physical access to the areas required to allow attendance at their programmes of choice (e.g., attending an educational session might also require physical access to the washrooms);
- based on their own definition of participation, participate in any programme of choice.

Given the survey findings, the targeted outcome, and the three criteria for success, recommended action plans included:

- construction of ramps as an alternate choice to stairs at the entrance to the building and the worship altar;
- modification of worship and common rooms to accommodate raised seating for ease of rising and negotiation of mobility aids such as wheelchairs and walkers;
- expansion of the Volunteer Driver Programme into a Volunteer Assistance Service;
- development of a specialized training programme for the Volunteer Assistance Service;
- publicity to increase awareness of the availability of volunteer drivers;
- inclusion of members who were experiencing barriers to participation on all planning committees.

The occupational therapist also outlined the services he could offer to implement this plan. The Board of Directors discussed the Committee's proposed plan of action and voted to proceed with implementation. Funding was approved for the occupational therapist to:

- consult with the construction company regarding accessibility standards, and issues related to the ramps and raised seating;

- facilitate development of the newly established Volunteer Assistance Service Steering Committee (with the same committee members whom the Board had mandated to develop targeted outcomes and action plans);
- provide information to the Board of Directors and committees on physical accessibility, healthy aging, performance implications of disease processes, and other issues related to the targeted outcome;
- evaluate the level of success in reaching the targeted outcome on completion of the action plans.

Stage #6: Implement Plans through Occupation

The occupational therapist implemented the action plans as specified in the contract with the Board of Directors.

Stage #7: Evaluate Occupational Performance Outcomes

Evaluation of the targeted outcome was done by re-surveying the target population, i.e., the same members who were surveyed initially. The occupational therapist asked questions that focused on the three criteria for success. Evaluation revealed:

- 85% of the target population reported having physical access to the religious centre using the ramp when volunteer drivers were available to take them to the centre;
- 85% of the target population reported having physical access to participate in programmes of their choice;
- of the 85% who attended programs of their choice, 60% indicated that they were satisfied with their participation.

The evaluation report prepared by the occupational therapist outlined the targeted outcome, the criteria for success, and the outcomes achieved following implementation of the action plans. He also recommended that the Board of Directors establish a committee which would provide ongoing monitoring, promotion, and evaluation of the Barrier Free campaign. In anticipation of a rapidly aging membership, another recommendation was that this committee address the specific needs of seniors. The occupational therapist also suggested that the committee explore why 15% of the target population had not utilized the new Barrier Free programme, and how the committee could promote greater participation and satisfaction among members.

VIGNETTE #5: LAWYER
Scenario:

An occupational therapy group practice, operating on a business model, was contacted by a lawyer. The contract was to assess the feasibility for a man who was one of the lawyer's clients to continue his work as a drill hand on an oil rig. The fee schedule was agreed upon.

Stage #1: Name, Validate and Prioritize Occupational Performance Issues

The individual to be assessed was a 35-year-old man with three school-aged children. The man had a grade 7 education and an annual income of $56,000.00. He was intending to quit his job as he was no longer able to tolerate the pain in his right shoulder, lower back, and left leg resulting from a motor vehicle accident (MVA). Without a replacement income of similar worth, he and his family were at risk of losing their newly purchased home and truck. There were also family relationship strains. The occupational performance issue that was named and validated by the lawyer was: potential inability to continue present employment as a drill hand on an oil rig.

The lawyer needed two questions answered about this occupational performance issue: 1) How capable was the man of staying in his present job? and 2) What skills would be useful in seeking other employment if the man's physical, cognitive and affective status and the work environment precluded remaining in his current, physically demanding job?

The occupational therapy contract was drawn up with the lawyer as the primary client. The man to be assessed was a secondary client in that he was the lawyer's client. The contract was to provide a written report to the lawyer. It was expected that the report would detail assessment results that could be defended in a court of law. No action plans beyond the assessment were discussed.

Stage #2: Select Theoretical Approach(es)

The approach was client-centred in meeting the legal information needs of the lawyer, and in respecting the man's needs and situation during the assessment. The Canadian Model of Occupational Performance provided the conceptual framework for the assessment. A biomechanical approach and psycho-emotional approaches guided the assessment of the occupational performance components and environmental conditions that were influencing the man's occupational performance at work.

Stage #3: Identify Occupational Performance Components and Environmental Conditions

With the lawyer as the primary client, a major consideration in assessment was the legal environment. The lawyer provided valuable information by sharing medical records, school and work histories, and other data. The occupational therapist adhered to the Canadian Association of Occupational Therapists' and provincial Codes of Ethics by discussing information only with the man and his lawyer. Permission was sought to contact the man's wife and employer to gain additional information on his occupational performance.

With the secondary client (the man), the focus of assessment was on identifying the performance components and environmental conditions that were affecting the man's ability to continue his present employment. Assessment included affective, cognitive, and physical components, as well as the man's economic, legal, and social environment. Assessment gathered qualitative and quantitative information by using simulated work situations and semi-structured interactions with the man. The man and his wife were also asked to rate family strain, which was high. The employer was asked to clarify options for making job accommodations. Analysis of all findings showed that the occupational performance issue, potential inability to continue present employment as a drill hand on an oil rig, was related to:
- "I am not sleeping well because of pain and anxiety over the family finances, so am barely able to concentrate at work";
- irritability (re his pain) interferred with his ability to work with others on the rigs;
- risk of additional physical injuries. His anxiety over his family's finances drove him to continue working beyond safe productivity levels, placing him at risk physically each time he worked a shift;
- ineffectiveness of pain management strategies in reducing pain during physically demanding work;
- modifying his present job to reduce his pain was not possible.

Since these findings indicated that continuing employment in his present physically demanding job would not be feasible or wise, the man was seen again to explore his career/work interests, and to identify skills, educational opportunities and methods that would be useful in seeking other employment.

Stage #4: Identify Strengths and Resources
The lawyer's case management style indicated that he recognized the man's need to be productive rather than to be merely compensated for employment losses. The man's strengths and resources were his commitment to being a fully contributing member of the rig crew. He was also dedicated to the well-being and financial security of his wife and family.

Stage #5: Negotiate Targeted Outcomes, Develop Action Plans
The lawyer's targeted outcome was to have a defensible opinion on his client's occupational performance in the form of a report that would be acceptable in a legal environment. Action plans related to this outcome were that the occupational therapist would integrate and synthesize the varied assessment findings and recommendations, and write the report.

Stage #6: Implement Plans Through Occupation
Implementation involved completion of the contract with the primary client

who, in this situation, was the lawyer. The occupational therapist prepared an Occupational Profile of the man based on the assessment findings. The report format and content were organized to suit the adversarial nature of civil litigation. The occupational therapist prepared the report, anticipating the need to defend its contents in a court of law. The report highlighted the occupational performance issue for the man, and addressed the two questions posed by the lawyer (could the man go back to work? if not, what else could he do?). The analysis of the occupational performance components and environmental conditions identified in Stage #3 guided the occupational therapist in answering these questions.

A pre-trial meeting was held between the lawyer and the assessment team, which included the occupational therapist and a vocational psychologist. The man's Occupational Profile was submitted to the lawyer. The lawyer used the information to prepare a financial claim.

In this stage, as in earlier stages, the occupational therapist was an advocate for the man's needs, even though the man was actually the lawyer's client. Recommendations were made to the lawyer for future environmental assessment of the man's home, and for exploration of opportunities for educational upgrading and apprenticeship training. No other targeted outcomes or action plans for the occupational therapist to work directly with the secondary client, the injured man, were developed in this contract.

Stage #7: Evaluate Occupational Performance Outcomes

The outcome of occupational therapy services was the writing of an Occupational Profile report for use by the lawyer in preparing a legal opinion. The Occupational Profile was occupation-focused and client-centred in that it documented the occupational performance issue, the occupational performance components and environmental conditions contributing to the prioritized occupational performance issue, i.e., the man's potential inability to continue present employment as a drill hand on an oil rig.

One question about the effectiveness of the Occupational Profile in meeting the lawyer's needs was: What effect did the Occupational Profile have on the lawyer's success in negotiating an out-of-court settlement? At this point, the files on this vignette are still open after three years of involvement.

There was no evaluation of the man's satisfaction with the occupational therapy service. Future contact could only occur in unusual or research situations with written consent from the lawyer and the man. If a settlement is not reached and a trial date set, the occupational therapist could be asked to update the opinion. This new undertaking would provide an opportunity to determine if any of the recommendations were implemented and if they made a difference to the client's occupational performance.

KEY TERMS

Canadian Model of Occupational Performance (CMOP)

A 1997 conceptual framework that describes occupational therapy's view of the dynamic, interwoven relationship between persons, environment and occupation that results in occupational performance over a person's lifespan

Client

Clients may be individuals with occupational problems arising from medical conditions, transitional difficulties, or environmental barriers, or clients may be organizations that influence the occupational performance of particular groups or populations

Client-Centred Practice

Collaborative and partnership approaches used in enabling occupation with clients who may be individuals, groups, agencies, governments, corporations or others; client-centred occupational therapists demonstrate respect for clients, involve clients in decision making, advocate with and for clients' needs, and otherwise recognize clients' experience and knowledge

Components of Performance

Affective, cognitive, or physical performance by individuals

Empowerment

Personal and social processes that transform visible and invisible relationships so that power is shared more equally

Enabling (Enablement)

Processes of facilitating, guiding, coaching, educating, prompting, listening, reflecting, encouraging, or otherwise collaborating with people so that individuals, groups, agencies, or organizations have the means and opportunity to be involved in solving their own problems; enabling is the basis of occupational therapy's client-centred practice and a foundation for client empowerment and justice; enabling is the most appropriate form of helping when the goal is occupational performance

Enabling Occupation

Enabling people to choose, organize, and perform those occupations they find useful and meaningful in their environment
(see definitions for Enabling, and Occupation)

Environment, elements of

Cultural, institutional, physical, and social elements that lie outside individuals, yet are embedded in individual actions

Function

The skill to perform activities in a normal or accepted way (Reed &
Sanderson, 1992) and/or adequately for the required tasks of a specific role
or setting (Christiansen & Baum, 1991)

Health

Having choice, abilities and opportunities for engaging in meaningful
patterns of occupation for looking after the self, enjoying life, and
contributing to the social and economic fabric of a community over the
lifespan; more than the absence of disease

Holism

A view of persons as whole beings, integrated in mind, body, and spirit

Implementation

The process of activating a plan, versus *intervention* which implies doing
to or for people

Intervention, occupational

The process of effecting change in occupational performance using
meaningful occupation. Intervention with individual clients is influenced
by a client's developmental stage, state of mind, and current and expected
health status, as well as time, setting, and the resources available (adapted
from Health Canada & CAOT, 1993, p.81)

Meaningful Occupations

Occupations that are chosen and performed to generate experiences of
personal meaning and satisfaction in individuals, groups, or communities

Occupation

Groups of activities and tasks of everyday life, named, organized, and
given value and meaning by individuals and a culture; occupation is
everything people do to occupy themselves, including looking after
themselves (self-care), enjoying life (leisure), and contributing to the social
and economic fabric of their communities (productivity); the domain of
concern and the therapeutic medium of occupational therapy

Occupational performance

The result of a dynamic, interwoven relationship between persons,
environment, and occupation over a person's lifespan; the ability to choose,
organize, and satisfactorily perform meaningful occupations that are
culturally defined and age appropriate for looking after oneself, enjoying
life, and contributing to the social and economic fabric of a community

Occupational Performance Model

A 1983/1991 view of the interacting elements of individual performance components, areas of occupational performance, and the environment

Occupational Performance Process

A seven stage process for focusing on occupational performance using client-centred approaches with individual, organizational, and other clients

Occupational Therapy

A health profession whose members collaborate with clients, who may be individuals, groups, agencies, or organizations, in enabling occupation; a profession that emerged from 19th century occupational work in asylums and workhouses; occupational therapists' use of occupation as a medium to enable occupation with individuals, organizations and communities

Quality of Life

Choosing and participating in occupations that foster hope, generate motivation, offer meaning and satisfaction, create a driving vision of life, promote health, enable empowerment, and otherwise address the quality of life

Role

A culturally defined pattern of occupation that reflects particular routines and habits; stereotypical role expectations may enhance or limit persons' potential occupational performance

Social Justice

A vision and an everyday practice in which people can choose, organize, and engage in meaningful occupations that enhance health, quality of life, and equity in housing, employment and other aspects of life

Spirituality

A pervasive life force, manifestation of a higher self, source of will and self-determination, and a sense of meaning, purpose and connectedness that people experience in the context of their environment

INDEX

INDEX

INDEX

INDEX

REFERENCES

Abberley, P. (1995). Disabling ideology in health and welfare: The case of occupational therapy. *Disability and Society, 10*, 221-232.

Accreditation Council on Services for People with Disabilities. (1993). *Outcome-based performance measures.* Landover, MD: Author.

Active Living Alliance For Canadians with a Disability. (1995). *Positive images - Guidelines for the appropriate image depiction of Canadians with a disability.* Manitoba, MB: Active Living Alliance Publications.

Alberta Health. (1994). *Decisions about tomorrow: Directives for your health care.* Edmonton, AB: Author.

Alberta Premier's Council on the Status of Persons with Disabilities. (1995). *A new context, a new vision: A paper to stimulate discussion on social and economic policy in the new Alberta context.* Edmonton, AB: Author.

American Marketing Association. (1985). AMA Board approves new marketing definition. *Market Education, 4* (2), 1.

Appel, T. (1991). From quality assurance to quality improvement: The Joint Commission and the new quality paradigm. *Journal of Quality Assurance, 13*, 26-29.

Asher, I.E. (1989). *An annotated index of occupational therapy evaluation tools.* Rockville, MD: American Occupational Therapy Association.

Australian Association of Occupational Therapists. (1994). *Australian competency standards for entry-level occupational therapists: Final report.* Victoria, Australia: Author.

Babiski, L., Sidle, N., & McColl, M.A. (1996). Challenges in achieving health for all in the boarding home sector. *Canadian Journal of Occupational Therapy, 63*, 33-43.

Backman, C. (1994). Programme development. In T. Sumsion (Ed.), *Guidelines for occupational therapy managers: A resource manual* (2nd ed.) (pp. 10-23). Toronto, ON: CAOT Publications ACE.

Baker, F., & Intagliata, J. (1982). Quality of life in the evaluation of community support systems. *Evaluation and Program Planning, 5*, 69-79.

Baker, G.R. (1993). The implications of program management for professional and managerial roles. *Physiotherapy Canada, 45*, 221-224.

Banks, S. (1987). Learning in self-help groups. *Canadian Council on Social Development, 3* (3), 1-4.

Banks, S. (1991). The Canadian model of occupational performance: Its relevance to community practice. *Canadian Journal of Occupational Therapy, 58*, 109-111.

Baptiste, S. (1988). Muriel Driver Memorial Lecture: Chronic pain, activity and culture. *Canadian Journal of Occupational Therapy, 55*, 179-184.

Baptiste, S. (1993a). Clinical programme management: A model of promise? *Canadian Journal of Occupational Therapy, 60*, 200-205.

Baptiste, S. (1993b). Managing diverse occupational therapy resources in a creative, corporate model. *Canadian Journal of Occupational Therapy, 60*, 206-213.

Bassett, J. (1975). Muriel Driver Memorial Lecture. *Canadian Journal of Occupational Therapy, 42*, 91-96.

Bateson, M.C. (1989). *Composing a life.* New York: Plume.

Beck, N. (1992). *Shifting gears: Thriving in the new economy.* Toronto, ON: Harper Collins.

Beckman, M.D., Kurtz, D.L., & Boone, L.E. (1992). *Foundations of marketing.* Toronto, ON: Dryden.

Belenky, M.F., Clinchy, B.M., Goldberger, N.R., & Tarule, J.M. (1986). *Women's ways of knowing: The development of self, voice and mind.* New York: Basic Books.

Bellah, R.N., Madson, R., Sullivan, W.M., Swidler, A., & Tipton, S.M. (1991). *The good society.* New York: Random House.

Bennis, W., & Nanus, B. (1985). *Leaders: The strategies for taking charge.* New York: Harper & Row.

Bergeron, P.G. (1987). *Modern management in Canada: Concepts and practices.* Agincourt, ON: Methuen.

Bernstein, R.J. (1983). *Beyond objectivism and relativism: Science, hermeneutics, and praxis.* Oxford: Blackwell.

Biklen, D. (1988). The myth of clinical judgement. *Journal of Social Issues, 44* (1), 127-140.

Blain, J., Townsend, E., Krefting, L., & Burwash, S. (1992). *Impact study: Occupational therapy guidelines for client-centred practice: Evaluation and recommendations.* Toronto, ON: Canadian Association of Occupational Therapists.

Blain, J., & Townsend, E. (1993). Occupational therapy guidelines for client-centred practice: Impact study findings. *Canadian Journal of Occupational Therapy, 60,* 271-285.

Blazer, D. (1991). Spirituality and aging well. *Generations, 15* (1), 61-65.

Bondar, B.R. (1990). Disease and dysfunction: The value of Axis V. *Hospital and Community Psychiatry, 41,* 959-960, 964.

Bondar, B.R., & Wagner, M. (1994). *Functional performance in older adults.* Philadelphia: FA Davis.

Bowlby, M.C. (1993). *Therapeutic activities with persons disabled by Alzheimer's disease and related disorders.* Gaithersburg, MD: Aspen.

Boyle, P.J. (1981). *Planning better programs.* New York: McGraw-Hill.

Braverman, H. (1974). *Labor and monopoly capital: The degradation of work in the twentieth century.* New York: Monthly Review Press.

Breines, E.B. (1989). Development, change and continuity theories: An analysis. *Canadian Journal of Occupational Therapy, 56,* 109-112.

Brintnell, E.S. (1985). Muriel Driver Memorial Lecture: Career planning in occupational therapy. I want up, not out. *Canadian Journal of Occupational Therapy, 52,* 227-233.

Brisenden, S. (1990). Disability culture. *Adults Learning, 2,* 13-14.

Brockett, M. (1994). Moral reasoning or occupational therapy for sleepless nights. *Canadian Journal of Occupational Therapy, 61,* 240-242.

Brosio, R.A. (1990). Teaching and learning for democratic empowerment: A critical evaluation. *Educational Theory, 40,* 69-81.

Butterill, D., O'Hanlon, J., & Book, H. (1992). When the system is the problem, don't blame the patient: Problems inherent in the interdisciplinary inpatient team. *Canadian Journal of Psychiatry, 37,* 168-172.

Canadian Association of Independent Living Centres. (1992). Research as an empowerment process for the independent living movement. *Abilities, Fall-Winter,* 58-59.

Canadian Association of Occupational Therapists. (1989). Membership Database - 1988. *The National, 6* (3), Centrefold.

Canadian Association of Occupational Therapists. (1991). *Occupational therapy guidelines for client-centred practice.* Toronto, ON: CAOT Publications ACE.

Canadian Association of Occupational Therapists. (1993). *Occupational therapy guidelines for client-centred mental health practice.* Toronto, ON: CAOT Publications ACE.

Canadian Association of Occupational Therapists. (1994a). Position statement on everyday occupations and health. *Canadian Journal of Occupational Therapy, 61,* 294-297.

Canadian Association of Occupational Therapists. (1994b). Position statement on health reform. *Canadian Journal of Occupational Therapy, 61,* 180-181.

Canadian Association of Occupational Therapists. (1996a). *Code of ethics.* Ottawa, ON: CAOT Publications ACE.

Canadian Association of Occupational Therapists. (1996b). Membership Database - 1995. *The National, 13* (4), Centrefold.

Canadian Association of Occupational Therapists. (1996c). Profile of occupational therapy practice in Canada. *Canadian Journal of Occupational Therapy, 63,* 79-113.

Canadian Council on Health Services Accreditation. (1995). *Standards for rehabilitation organizations: A client-centred approach.* Ottawa, ON: Author.

Canadian Hospital Association. (1993). *An open future: A shared vision.* Ottawa, ON: Canadian Hospital Association Press.

Canadian Institute for Health Information. (1994a, July). *Outcome Indicators: A review of the literature and framework.* (Produced by the Community Health Information Systems Working Group). Ottawa, ON: Author.

Canadian Institute for Health Information. (1994b, June). *Outcome Indicators: A user's guide.* (Produced by the Community Health Information Systems Working Group). Ottawa, ON: Author.

Carswell-Opzoomer, A. (1990). Muriel Driver Memorial Lecture: Occupational therapy - our time has come. *Canadian Journal of Occupational Therapy, 57,* 197-203.

Chilton, H. (1990). Reflections on... Manage or be managed: Where do you stand? *Canadian Journal of Occupational Therapy, 57,* 167-169.

Christiansen, C., & Baum, C. (1991). *Occupational therapy: Overcoming human performance deficits.* Thorofare, NJ: Slack.

Clark, F.A. (1993). Eleanor Clark Slagle Lecture: Occupation embedded in a real life: Interweaving occupational science and occupational therapy. *American Journal of Occupational Therapy, 47,* 1067-1078.

Clark, F.A., Parham, D., Carlson, M.E., Frank, G., Jackson, J., Pierce, D., Wolfe, R.J., & Zemke, R. (1991). Occupational science: Academic innovation in the service of occupational therapy's future. *American Journal of Occupational Therapy, 45,* 300-310.

Coady, M.M. (1939). *Masters of our own destiny.* New York: Harper and Row.

Cohen, M. (1994). Impact of poverty on women's health. *Canadian Family Physician, 40,* 949-958.

Cosman, R.W., & Heinz, C.L. (1996). *Professional responsibility of occupational therapists.* Ottawa, ON: CAOT Publications ACE.

Crabtree, J., & Caron-Parker, L. (1991). Long-term care of the aged: Ethical dilemmas and solutions. *American Journal of Occupational Therapy, 45,* 607-612.

Crain, R., & Rachman, D. (1991). *Marketing today.* (1st Canadian ed.). Toronto, ON: Holt, Rinehart and Winston.

Creighton, C. (1992). The origin and evolution of activity analysis. *American Journal of Occupational Therapy, 46,* 45-48.

Crompton, R. (1987). Gender, status and professionalism. *Sociology, 21,* 413-428.

Csikszentmihalyi, M. (1991). *Flow: The psychology of optimal experience.* New York: Harper Perennial.

Cynkin, S. (1979). *Occupational therapy: Toward health through activities.* Boston: Little, Brown.

Cynkin, S., & Robinson, A.M. (1990). *Occupational therapy and activities health: Towards health through activities.* Boston: Little, Brown.

Daniels, A.K. (1987). Invisible work. *Social Problems, 34,* 403-415.

Darmon, R.Y., Laroche, M., & Lee McGown, K. (1989). *Marketing research in Canada.* Toronto, ON: Gage Educational Publishing.

Deegan, M.G., & Brooks, N.A. (1985). *Women and disability: The double handicap.* Oxford: Transaction Books.

De Jong, G. (1979). Independent living: From social movement to analytic paradigm. *Archives of Physical Medicine and Rehabilitation, 60,* 435-446.

De Jong, G. (1993). The John Stanley Coulter Lecture. Health care reform and disability: Affirming our commitment to community. *Archives of Physical Medicine and Rehabilitation, 74,* 1017-1024.

DeMars, P.A. (1992). An occupational therapy life skills curriculum model for a native american tribe: A health promotion program based on ethnographic field research. *American Journal of Occupational Therapy, 46,* 727-736.

Department of National Health and Welfare. (1986). *Achieving health for all: A framework for health promotion* (Cat. 39-102/1988E). Ottawa, ON: Author.

Department of National Health and Welfare. (1988a). *Mental health for Canadians: Striking a balance* (Cat. H39-128/1988E). Ottawa, ON: Author.

Department of National Health and Welfare. (1988b). *National hospital productivity improvement programme: Workload measurement system - Occupational therapy* (Cat. H30-11/3-3E). Ottawa, ON: Author.

Department of National Health and Welfare, & Canadian Association of Occupational Therapists (1983). *Guidelines for the client-centred practice of occupational therapy* (Cat. H39-33/1983E). Ottawa, ON: Author.

Department of National Health and Welfare, & Canadian Association of Occupational Therapists. (1986). *Intervention guidelines for the client-centred practice of occupational therapy* (Cat. H39-100/1986E). Ottawa, ON: Author.

Department of National Health and Welfare, & Canadian Association of Occupational Therapists. (1987). *Toward outcome measures in occupational therapy* (Cat. H39-114/1987E). Ottawa, ON: Author.

Dickson, A. (1993). Rights and limits to risk. National Advisory Council on Aging, *Expression, 9 (2).*

Dillard, M., Andonian, L., Flores, O., Lai, L., MacRae, A., & Shakir, M. (1992). Culturally competent occupational therapy in a diversely populated mental health setting. *American Journal of Occupational Therapy, 46,* 721-726.

Do Rozario, L. (1992). Subjective well-being and health promotion factors: Views from people with disabilities and chronic illness. *Health Promotion Journal of Australia, 2* (1), 28-33.

Do Rozario, L. (1993). *Purpose, place, pride and productivity: The unique personal and societal contribution of occupation and occupational therapy.* Keynote address, Australian Association of Occupational Therapists Annual Conference. Darwin, Australia.

Do Rozario, L. (1994). Ritual, meaning, and transcendence: The role of occupation in modern life. *Journal of Occupational Science, 1* (3), 46-53.

Donovan, J.I.., & Blake, D.R. (1992). Patient non-compliance: Deviance or reasoned decision-making? *Sociology of Science and Medicine, 34,* 507-513.

Driver, M. (1968). A philosophic view of the history of occupational therapy in Canada. *Canadian Journal of Occupational Therapy, 35,* 53-60.

Dunst, C.J., Trivette, C.M., & Deal, A.G. (Eds.). (1994). *Supporting and strengthening families:* Vol. 1. *Methods, strategies and practices.* Cambridge, MA: Brookline Books.

Dunton, W.R. (1919). *Reconstruction therapy.* Philadelphia: Saunders.

Dyck, I. (1989). The immigrant client: Issues in developing culturally sensitive practice. *Canadian Journal of Occupational Therapy, 56,* 248-255.

Dyck, I. (1992). Managing chronic illness: An immigrant woman's acquisition and use of health care knowledge. *American Journal of Occupational Therapy, 46,* 696-705.

Dyck, I. (1993). Health promotion, occupational therapy and multiculturalism: Lessons from research. *Canadian Journal of Occupational Therapy, 60,* 120-129.

Egan, M., & DeLaat, D. (1994). Considering spirituality in occupational therapy practice. *Canadian Journal of Occupational Therapy, 61,* 95-101.

Ellek, D. (1991). Health Policy: The evolution of fairness in mental health policy. *American Journal of Occupational Therapy, 45,* 947-951.

Employment and Immigration Canada Staff. (1993). *National Occupational Classification: Occupational description.* Ottawa, ON: Canada Communications Group.

Fawcett, J., & Down, F.S. (1992). *The relationship of theory and research.* Philadelphia: FA Davis.

Fay, B. (1987). *Critical social science: Liberation and its limits.* New York: Cornell University Press.

Fearing, V.G. (1993). Occupational therapists chart a course through the health record. *Canadian Journal of Occupational Therapy, 60,* 232-240.

Fearing, V.G. (1995). *Program design in occupational therapy.* Presented in RSOT 424: Program design, School of Rehabilitation Sciences, University of British Columbia, Vancouver, BC.

Fearing, V.G., Law, M., & Clark, M. (1997). An occupational performance process model: Fostering client and therapist alliances. *Canadian Journal of Occupational Therapy, 64,* 7-15.

Ferguson, J. (1995). *The effects of added purpose and meaningful occupation on motor learning.* Unpublished master's thesis, University of Boston, Massachusetts.

Finlayson, M., & Edwards, J. (1995). Integrating the concepts of health promotion and community into occupational therapy practice. *Canadian Journal of Occupational Therapy, 62,* 70-75.

Fisher, S., & Todd, A.D. (1986). *Discourse and institutional authority: Medicine, education and law.* Norwood, NJ: Ablex Publishing.

Florin, P., & Wandersman, A. (1990). An introduction to citizen participation, voluntary organizations, and community development: Insights for empowerment through research. *American Journal of Community Psychology, 18,* 41-54.

Forget, A. (1983). Discours commémoratif Muriel Driver: Application d'un paradigme systémique à l'évaluation ergothérapique des personnes âgées. *Canadian Journal of Occupational Therapy, 50,* 107-113.

Fossy, E. (1992). The study of human occupations: Implications for research in occupational therapy. *British Journal of Occupational Therapy, 55* (4), 148-152.

Frank, G. (1992). Opening feminist histories of occupational therapy. *American Journal of Occupational Therapy, 46,* 989-999.

Frankel, N., & Dye, N.S. (1991). *Gender, class, race and reform in the progressive era.* Lexington, KY: University Press of Kentucky.

Frankl, V.E. (1988). *The will to meaning.* London: Penguin Books.

Franklin, U. (1990). *The real world of technology.* Toronto, ON: CBC Enterprises.

Freidson, E. (1986). *Professional powers: A study of the institutionalization of formal knowledge.* Chicago: University of Chicago Press.

Freire, P. (1985). *The politics of education: Culture, power and liberation.* (D. Macedo, Trans.). South Hadley, MA: Bergin & Garvey Publishers.

Gage, M. (1995). The re-engineering of health care: Opportunity or threat for occupational therapists. *Canadian Journal of Occupational Therapy, 62,* 197-207.

Gage, M., & Polatajko, H. (1995). Naming practice: The case for the term client-driven. *Canadian Journal of Occupational Therapy, 62,* 115-118.

George, B. (1990). Consulting unemployed people: Empowerment and the process of research. *Health Promotion, 29* (2), 9-13.

Gilewich, G.B. (1979). Muriel Driver Memorial Lecture: Managers in occupational therapy. *Canadian Journal of Occupational Therapy, 46,* 131-137.

Gill, T. (1986). Muriel Driver Memorial Lecture: You can't take it with you! *Canadian Journal of Occupational Therapy, 53,* 189-196.

Glaser, B. (1978). *Theoretical sensitivity: Advances in the methodology of grounded theory.* Mill Valley, CA: Sociology Press.

Glaser, B., & Strauss, A.L. (1967). *The discovery of grounded theory.* Chicago: Aldine.

Government of Canada. (1982). *Canadian Charter of Rights and Freedoms, Constitution Act, Part I.* Ottawa, ON: Supply and Services Canada.

Grace, V.M. (1991). The marketing of empowerment and the construction of the health consumer: A critique of health promotion. *International Journal of Health Services, 21,* 329-343.

Grady, A.P. (1995). Building inclusive community: A challenge for occupational therapy. *American Journal of Occupational Therapy, 49,* 300-310.

Greenfield, S., Kaplan, S.H., & Ware, J.E. (1985). Expanding patient involvement in care: Effects on patient outcomes. *Annals of Internal Medicine, 102,* 520-528.

Guba, E.A. (1990.) *The paradigm dialogue.* Newbury Park,CA: Sage Publications.

Guba, E.G., & Lincoln, Y.S. (1989). *Fourth generation evaluation.* Newbury Park: Sage Publications.

Guralnik, D.B. (Ed.). (1984). *Webster's new world dictionary* (2nd college ed.). New York: Simon and Schuster.

Gutterman, L. (1990). A day treatment program for persons with AIDS. *American Journal of Occupational Therapy, 44,* 234-237.

Hall, J.A., Roter, D.L., & Katz, N.R. (1988). MATA - Analysis of correlates of provider behaviour in medical outcomes. *Medical Care, 26,* 657-675.

Habermas, J. (1984). *The theory of communicative action: Vol. 1. Reason and the rationalization of society.* Boston: Beacon Press.

Hammersley, M., & Atkinson, P. (1983). *Ethnography: Principles in practice.* London: Tavistock.

Hare-Mustin, R.T., & Marecek, J. (1988). The meaning of difference: Gender theory, postmodernism, and psychology. *American Psychologist, 43,* 455-464.

Health & Welfare Canada. (1993). *Planning for health: Toward informed decision-making. Summary of literature review and a proposed evaluation framework on emerging trends in the organization and delivery of health care services* (HS9-2, 1993). Ottawa, ON: Author.

Hearn, J. (1982). Notes on patriarchy, professionalization and the semi-professions. *Sociology, 16,* 184-202.

Helfrich, C., Kielhofner, G., & Mattingly, C.F. (1994). Volition as narrative: Understanding motivation in chronic illness. *American Journal of Occupational Therapy, 48,* 311-317.

Hobson, S. (1996). Being client-centred when the client is cognitively impaired. *Canadian Journal of Occupational Therapy, 63,* 133-137.

Hood, M.R. (1976). Muriel Driver Memorial Lecture. *Canadian Journal of Occupational Therapy, 43,* 105-111.

Hopkins, H.L., & Smith, H.D. (1988). *Willard and Spackman's occupational therapy.* Philadelphia: J.P. Lippincott.

Hubbard, P., Werner, P., Cohen-Mansfield, J., & Shusterman, R. (1992). Seniors for justice: A political and social action group for nursing home residents. *The Gerontologist, 32,* 856-858.

Human Resources Development. (1994). *Improving social security in Canada: Persons with disabilities: A supplementary paper* (Cat. MP90-2/5-1994). Ottawa, ON: Author.

Illich, I., Zola, I.K., McNight, J., Caplan, J., & Shaiken, H. (1977). *Disabling professions.* London: Marion Boyers.

Jacobs, K. (1987). Marketing occupational therapy. *American Journal of Occupational Therapy, 41,* 315-320.

Jaffe, E.G., & Epstein, C.F. (1992). *Occupational therapy consultation: Theory, principles and practice.* St. Louis, MO: Mosby.

Johnson, J.A. (1986). Wellness and occupational therapy. *American Journal of Occupational Therapy, 40,* 753-758.

Jongbloed, L., & Crichton, A. (1990a). A new definition of disability: Implications for rehabilitation practice and social policy. *Canadian Journal of Occupational Therapy, 57,* 32-38.

Jongbloed, L., & Crichton, A. (1990b). Difficulties in shifting from individualistic to socio-political policy regarding disability in Canada. *Disability, Handicap & Society, 5,* 25-36.

Judd, M. (1982). Muriel Driver Memorial Lecture. *Canadian Journal of Occupational Therapy, 49,* 117-124.

Kaplan, S. (1983). A model of person-environment compatibility. *Environment Behaviour, 15,* 311-332.

Kari, N., & Michels, P. (1991). The Lazarus project: The politics of empowerment. *American Journal of Occupational Therapy, 45,* 719-725.

Katz, A.H., & Bender, I.E. (1987). *Self-help groups in the modern world.* Oakland, CA: Third Party Publishers.

Katz, R. (1984). Empowerment and synergy: Expanding the community's healing resources. *Prevention in Human Services, 3,* 201-226.

Khoo, S.W., & Renwick, R.M. (1989). A model of human occupation perspective on the mental health of immigrant women in Canada. *Occupational Therapy in Mental Health, 9,* 31-49.

Kidd, J.R. (1973). *How adults learn.* New York: Association Press.

Kielhofner, G. (1983). *Health through occupation: Theory and practice in occupational therapy.* Philadelphia: F.A. Davis.

Kielhofner, G. (1985). *A model of human occupation: Theory and application.* Baltimore: Williams and Wilkins.

Kielhofner, G. (1992). *Conceptual foundations of occupational therapy.* Philadelphia: F.A. Davis.

Kielhofner, G. (1995). *A model of human occupation: Theory and application* (2nd ed.). Baltimore: Williams and Wilkins.

Kielhofner, G., & Barris, R. (1986). Organization of knowledge in occupational therapy. *Occupational Therapy Journal of Research, 6,* 67-84.

Kieser, D., & Wilson, D.M. (1995). The Canadian health care system: Trends, issues and challenges. In D.M. Wilson (Ed.), *The Canadian Health Care System* (pp. 87-96). Edmonton, AB: D.M. Wilson.

Kimmel, M.S. (1993, September/October). Invisible masculinity. *Society,* 28-35.

Kirsh, B. (1996). A narrative approach to addressing spirituality in occupational therapy: Exploring personal meaning and purpose. *Canadian Journal of Occupational Therapy, 63,* 55-61.

Knapper, C., Lerner, S., & Bunting, T. (1986). Special groups and the environment: An introduction. *Environment, 18,* 1-5.

Krefting, L.H. (1985). The use of conceptual models in clinical practice. *Canadian Journal of Occupational Therapy, 52,* 173-178.

Krefting, L. (1989). Disability ethnography: A methodological approach to occupational therapy research. *Canadian Journal of Occupational Therapy, 56,* 61-66.

Krupa, T., & Clark, C.C. (1995). Occupational therapists as case managers: Responding to current approaches to community mental health service delivery. *Canadian Journal of Occupational Therapy, 62,* 16-22.

Kuhn, T.S. (1970). *The structure of scientific revolution.* Chicago: University of Chicago Press.

Kuyek, J.N. (1990). *Fighting for hope: Organizing to realize our dreams.* Montreal, QC: Black Rose Books.

Kyserlink, E.W. (1985). Consent to treatment: The principles, the provincial status and the Charter of Rights. *Canada's Mental Health, Sept.,* 7-11.

Labonte, R. (1986). Social inequality and healthy public policy. *Health Promotion, 1,* 341-351.

Labonte, R. (1989a). Community empowerment: The need for political analysis. *Canadian Journal of Public Health, 80,* 87-88.

Labonte, R. (1989b). Community and professional empowerment. *Canadian Nurse, March,* 23-28.

Labonte, R. (1993). Community development and partnerships: The view from here. *Canadian Journal of Public Health, 84,* 237-240.

Labour Participation Advisory Committee. (1993). *Building bridges: A resource manual for the employment of people with disabilities.* Burnaby, BC: United Way of the Lower Mainland.

Laliberte, D.L. (1993). *An exploration of the meaning seniors attach to activity.* Unpublished master's thesis, University of Western Ontario, London, Ontario, Canada.

Law, M. (1987). Measurement in occupational therapy: Scientific criteria for evaluation. *Canadian Journal of Occupational Therapy, 54,* 133-138.

Law, M. (1991). Muriel Driver Memorial Lecture: The environment: A focus for occupational therapy. *Canadian Journal of Occupational Therapy, 58,* 171-180.

Law, M., Baptiste, S., McColl, M.A., Opzoomer, A., Polatajko, H. & Pollock, N. (1990). The Canadian Occupational Performance Measure: An outcome measure for occupational therapy. *Canadian Journal of Occupational Therapy, 57,* 82-87.

Law, M., Baptiste, S., Carswell, A., McColl, M.A., Polatajko, H., & Pollock, N. (1991). *Canadian Occupational Performance Measure.* Toronto, ON: CAOT Publications ACE.

Law, M., Baptiste, S., Carswell, A., McColl, M.A., Polatajko, H., & Pollock, N. (1994). *Canadian Occupational Performance Measure* (2nd ed.). Toronto, ON: CAOT Publications ACE.

Law, M., Baptiste, S., & Mills, J. (1995). Client-centred practice: What does it mean and does it make a difference? *Canadian Journal of Occupational Therapy, 62,* 250-257.

Law, M., Cooper, B.A., Strong, S., Stewart, D., Rigby, P., & Letts, L. (1996). The Person-Environment-Occupation Model: A transactive approach to occupational performance. *Canadian Journal of Occupational Therapy, 63,* 9-23.

Law, M., & Sanford, J. (1994). *Measuring rehabilitation outcomes.* Paper presented at the Algo Club, Sault Saint Marie, Ontario, organized by the Northern Outreach Program, University of Western Ontario, London, Ontario

Leakey, R., & Lewin, R. (1978). *People of the lake. Man: His origins, nature, and future.* (pp. 38-39). Toronto, ON: Penguin Books.

Letts, L., Law, M., Rigby, P., Cooper, B., Stewart, D., & Strong, S. (1994). Person-environment assessments in occupational therapy. *American Journal of Occupational Therapy, 48,* 608-618.

LeVesconte, H.P. (1935). Expanding fields of occupational therapy. *Canadian Journal of Occupational Therapy, 3,* 4-12.

Lincoln, Y.S. (1992). Fourth generation evaluation, the paradigm revolution and health promotion. *Canadian Journal of Public Health, 83, S1,* S6-S10.

Litterst, T.A.E. (1992). Occupational therapy: The role of ideology in the development of a profession for women. *American Journal of Occupational Therapy, 46,* 20-25.

Lloyd, C., & Maas, F. (1993). The helping relationship: The application of Carkhuff's model. *Canadian Journal of Occupational Therapy, 60,* 83-89.

MacGregor, L.J. (1995). *An exploratory study of the personal experience of occupational deprivation.* Unpublished master's thesis, University of Western Ontario, London, Ontario, Canada.

Macpherson, A.S. (1995). Healthy elderly: Coming of age. *Canadian Journal of Public Health, 86,* 221-223.

Madill, H.M., Townsend, E., & Schultz, P. (1989). Implementing a health promotion strategy in occupational therapy education and practice. *Canadian Journal of Occupational Therapy, 56,* 67-72.

Maltais, D., Trickey, F., Robitaille, Y., & Rodriguez, L. (1989). *Maintaining seniors' independence: A guide to home adaptation.* Ottawa, ON: Canada Mortgage and Housing Corporation.

Marjoribanks, S. (1972). Editorial: A tribute to Muriel Driver. *Canadian Journal of Occupational Therapy, 39,* 71-72.

Marx, K. (1943). Economic and philosophical manuscripts. In E. Fischer (1970), *Marx in his own words* (p. 31). London: The Penguin Press.

Mason, R.A., & Boutilier, M.A. (1995). Unemployment as an issue for public health: Preliminary findings from North York. *Canadian Journal of Public Health, 86,* 152-154.

Mattingly, C.F., & Hayes Fleming, M. (1994). *Clinical reasoning: Forms of inquiry in a therapeutic practice.* Philadelphia: F.A. Davis.

Mayers, C.A. (1990). A philosophy unique to occupational therapy. *British Journal of Occupational Therapy, 53,* 379-380.

McCloy, L. (1996, June). *Selecting an outcome measure.* Paper presented at the annual meeting of the British Columbia Society of Occupational Therapists, Vancouver, BC.

McColl, M.A. (1994). Holistic occupational therapy: Historical meaning and contemporary implications. *Canadian Journal of Occupational Therapy, 61,* 72-77.

McColl, M.A., Law, M., & Stewart, D. (1993). *Theoretical basis of occupational therapy: An annotated bibliography of applied theory in the professional literature.* Thorofare, NJ: Slack.

McColl, M.A., & Pranger, T. (1994). Theory and practice in the occupational therapy guidelines for client-centred practice. *Canadian Journal of Occupational Therapy, 61,* 250-259.

McComas, J., & Carswell, A. (1994). A model for action in health promotion: A community experience. *Canadian Journal of Rehabilitation, 7,* 257-265.

McDougall, G.H.G., Kotler, P., & Armstrong, G. (1992). *Marketing* (2nd Canadian ed.). Scarborough, ON: Prentice Hall Canada.

McDowell, I., & Newell, C. (1987). *Measuring health: A guide to rating scales and questionnaires.* Oxford: Oxford University Press.

McKnight, J.L. (1989). Health and empowerment. *Canadian Journal of Public Health, 76, S1,* S37-S38.

Meyer, A. (1922). The philosophy of occupational therapy. *Archives of Occupational Therapy, 1,* 1-10.

Michelson, W. (1976). *From son to son.* Toronto, ON: Rowan & Allanheld.

Moxley-Haegert, L., & Serbin, L.A. (1983). Developmental education for parents of delayed infants: Effects on parental motivation and children's development. *Child Development, 54,* 1324-1331.

Moyers, P.A. (1991). Collaborating for political action. *American Journal of Occupational Therapy, 45,* 566-567.

Navarro, V. (1986). *Crisis, health and medicine: A social critique.* New York: Tavistock Publications.

Navarro, V. (1991). Production and the welfare state: The political context of reforms. *International Journal of Health Services, 21,* 585-614.

Nelson, D.L. (1988). Occupation: Form and performance. *American Journal of Occupational Therapy, 42,* 633-641.

O'Connor, J. (1989). Welfare expenditure and policy orientation in Canada in comparative perspective. *Canadian Review of Sociology and Anthropology, 26,* 128-150.

Opacich, K. (1991). Assessment and informed decision-making. In C. Christiansen & C. Baum (Eds.), *Occupational therapy: Overcoming human performance deficits* (pp. 356-360). Thorofare, NJ: Slack.

O'Shea, B.J. (1977). Muriel Driver Memorial Lecture: Pawn or protagonist: Interactional perspective of professional identity. *Canadian Journal of Occupational Therapy, 44,* 101-108.

Ottenbacher, K.J. (1986). *Evaluating clinical change: Strategies for occupational and physical therapists.* Baltimore: Williams & Wilkins.

Pagonis, J.F. (1987). Successful proposal writing. *American Journal of Occupational Therapy, 41,* 147-151.

Parham, D. (1987). Toward professionalism: The reflective therapist. *American Journal of Occupational Therapy, 41,* 554-561.

Paul, S. (1995). Culture and its influence on occupational therapy evaluation. *Canadian Journal of Occupational Therapy, 62,* 154-161.

Payne, V.G., & Isaacs, L.D. (1991). *Human motor development: A lifespan approach* (2nd ed.). Mountain View, CA: Mayfield Publishing.

Payton, O. (1988). *Research: The validation of clinical practice* (2nd ed.). Philadelphia: F.A. Davis.

Peloquin, S.M. (1991). Time as a commodity: Reflections and implications. *American Journal of Occupational Therapy, 45,* 147-154.

Peloquin, S.M. (1993). The patient-therapist relationship: Beliefs that shape care. *American Journal of Occupational Therapy, 47,* 935-942.

Picard-Greffe, H. (1994). Muriel Driver Memorial Lecture: Back to the future. *Canadian Journal of Occupational Therapy, 61,* 243-259.

Pinderhughes, E. (1983). Empowerment for our clients and ourselves. Social Casework: *The Journal of Contemporary Social Work, 64,* 331-338.

Pinderhughes, E. (1989). *Understanding race, ethnicity, and power: The key to efficacy in clinical practice.* New York: The Free Press.

Pizzi, M. (1992). Women, HIV infection, and AIDS: Tapestries of life, death, and empowerment. *American Journal of Occupational Therapy, 46,* 1021-1027.

Polatajko, H.J. (1992). Muriel Driver Memorial Lecture: Naming and framing occupational therapy: A lecture dedicated to the life of Nancy B. *Canadian Journal of Occupational Therapy, 59,* 189-200.

Polatajko, H.J. (1994). Dreams, dilemmas, and decisions for occupational therapy practice in a new millennium: A Canadian perspective. *American Journal of Occupational Therapy, 48,* 590-594.

Pollock, N., Baptiste, S., Law, M., McColl, M.A., Opzoomer, A., & Polatajko, H. (1990). Occupational performance measures: A review based on the guidelines for the client-centred practice of occupational therapy. *Canadian Journal of Occupational Therapy. 57,* 77-81.

Powell, T. (1987). *Self-help organizations and professional practice.* Silver Springs, MD: National Association of Social Workers.

Primeau, L.A. (1992). A woman's place: Unpaid work in the home. *American Journal of Occupational Therapy, 46,* 981-988.

Primeau, L.A., Clark, F., & Pierce, D. (1989). Occupational therapy alone has looked upon occupation: Future applications of occupational science to paediatric occupational therapy. *Occupational Therapy Health Care, 6* (4), 19-32.

Rachlis, M., & Kushner, C. (1992). *Strong medicine: How to save Canada's health care system.* Toronto, ON: Harper Collins Publishers.

Raphael, D., Cava, M., Brown, I., Renwick, R., Heathcote, K., Weir, N., Wright, K., & Kirwan, L. (1995). Frailty: A public health perspective. *Canadian Journal of Public Health, 86,* 224-227.

Readman, T. (1992). Recruitment of men in occupational therapy: Past, present and future. *Canadian Journal of Occupational Therapy, 59,* 73-77.

Reece, C.C. (1987). The issue is: Gender bias in an occupational therapy text. *American Journal of Occupational Therapy, 41,* 393-396.

Reed, K.L. (1984). *Models of practice in occupational therapy.* Baltimore: Williams & Wilkins.

Reed, K.L., & Sanderson, S.N. (1992). *Concepts of occupational therapy* (3rd ed.). Baltimore: Williams & Wilkins.

Reich, R.B. (1991). *The work of nations preparing ourselves for 21st century capitalism.* Toronto, ON: Random House of Canada.

Reilly, M. (1962). Occupational therapy can be one of the great ideas of 20th century medicine. *American Journal of Occupational Therapy, 16,* 1-9.

Reilly, M. (1984). The Issue Is - The importance of the client versus patient issue for occupational therapy. *American Journal of Occupational Therapy, 38,* 404-406.

Renwick, R, Brown, I., & Nagler, M. (Eds.). (1996). *Quality of Life in Health Promotion and Rehabilitation: Conceptual Approaches, Issues, and Applications* Newbury Park, CA: Sage.

Reutter, L. (1995). Poverty and health: Implications for public health. *Canadian Journal of Public Health, 86,* 149-151.

Robinson, I.M. (1981). Muriel Driver Memorial Lecture: The mists of time. *Canadian Journal of Occupational Therapy, 48,* 145-152.

Rockwood, K., Fox, R., Stobe, P., Robertson, D., & Beattie, L. (1994). Frailty in elderly people: An evolving concept. *Canadian Medical Association Journal, 130,* 489-495.

Rogers, C.R. (1939). *The clinical treatment of the problem child.* Boston: Houghton Mifflin.

Rogers, C.R. (1951). *Client-centred therapy.* Boston: Houghton Mifflin.

Rogers, C.R. (1969). *Freedom to learn.* Columbus, OH: C.E. Merrill.

Rogers, J.C. (1983). Eleanor Clarke Slagle Lecture: Clinical reasoning: The ethics, science, and art. *American Journal of Occupational Therapy, 37,* 601-616.

Rogers, J.C. (1984). The Foundation. Why study human occupation? *American Journal of Occupational Therapy, 38,* 47-49.

Rose, S.M., & Black, B.L. (1985). *Advocacy and empowerment: Mental health care in the community.* Boston: Routledge and Kegan Paul.

Rozovsky, L.E., & Rozovsky, F.A. (1990). *The Canadian law of consent and treatment.* Markham, ON: Butterworths Canada.

Rozovsky, L.E., & Rozovsky, F.A. (1992). *Canadian health information: A legal and risk management guide* (2nd ed.). Markham, ON: Butterworths Canada.

Saunders, B. (1984). Muriel Driver Memorial Lecture: Quality assurance: Reflection on the wave. *Canadian Journal of Occupational Therapy, 51,* 161-170.

Schon, D.A. (1983). *The reflective practitioner: How professionals think in action.* New York: Basic Books.

Schon, D. (1987). *Educating the reflective practitioner: Toward a new design for teaching and learning in the professions.* San Francisco: Jossey Bass.

Schulz, R., & Ewen, R. (1993). *Adult development and aging.* Toronto, ON: MacMillan Publishing.

Schusky, E.L., & Cullbert, T.P. (1987). *Introducing culture.* Englewood Cliffs, NJ: Prentice-Hall.

Schwartz, K.B. (1992). Occupational therapy and education: A shared vision. *American Journal of Occupational Therapy, 46,* 12-18.

Scott, S.M. (1992). Personal change through participation in social action: A case study of ten social activists. *The Canadian Journal for the Study of Adult Education, 6,* 47-64.

Senge, P.M. (1990). *The fifth discipline: The art and practice of the learning organization.* New York: Doubleday.

Shalinsky, W. (1986). Disabled persons and their environments. *Environments, 17,* 1-8.

Sharrott, G.W., & Yerxa, E.J. (1985). The Issue Is - Promises to keep: Implications of the referent "patient" versus "client" for those served by occupational therapy. *American Journal of Occupational Therapy, 39,* 401-405.

Sherr Klein, B. (1993). We are who you are: Feminism & disability. *Abilities, Spring,* 22-26.

Sherr Klein, B. (1995). Reflections on ... An ally as well as a partner in practice. *Canadian Journal of Occupational Therapy, 62,* 283-285.

Shweder, R., & Bourne, J. (1982). Does the concept of the person vary cross culturally? In A. Marsella & G. White (Eds.), *Cultural conceptions of mental health and therapy.* Boston: D. Reidel.

Smith, D.E. (1987). *The everyday world as problematic.* Toronto, ON: University of Toronto Press.

Smith, D.E. (1990a). *Texts, facts, and femininity: Exploring the relations of ruling.* New York: Routledge.

Smith, D.E. (1990b). *The conceptual practices of power: A feminist sociology of knowledge.* Toronto, ON: University of Toronto Press.

Spencer, J., Krefting, L., & Mattingly, C. (1993). Incorporation of ethnographic methods in occupational therapy assessment. *American Journal of Occupational Therapy, 47,* 303-309.

Stan, L.J. (1987). Muriel Driver Memorial Lecture: Making our mark in the marketplace. *Canadian Journal of Occupational Therapy, 54,* 165-171.

Stanton, S.J. (1995). *Occupational therapy program design.* Revisions to Course materials for RSOT 424: Program design. School of Rehabilitation Sciences, University of British Columbia, Vancouver, BC.

Stanton, S.J. (1996). *The client, service, society model: Towards optimal client-centred practice.* Presented in the course RSOT 434: Advanced clinical reasoning at the School of Rehabilitation Sciences, University of British Columbia, Vancouver, BC.

Stanton, S.J., & Jongbloed, L. (1993, June). *Health service delivery and adjustment following stroke.* Paper presented at the Canadian Association of Occupational Therapists Annual Conference, Regina, SK.

Status of Disabled Persons Secretariat. (1991). *A way with words: Guidelines and appropriate terminology for the portrayal of persons with disabilities* (Cat No. S2-216/1991E). Ottawa, ON: Author.

Strauss, A.L., & Corbin, J. (1990). *Basics of qualitative research: Grounded theory procedures and techniques.* Newbury Park, CA: Sage.

Sumsion, T. (1993). Client-centred practice: The true impact. *Canadian Journal of Occupational Therapy, 60,* 6-8.

Sumsion, T. (Ed.). (1994). *Guidelines for occupational therapy managers: A resource manual* (2nd ed.). Toronto, ON: CAOT Publications ACE.

Sutherland, R., & Fulton,␣J. (1994). *Spending smarter and spending less: Policies and partnerships for health care in Canada.* Ottawa, ON: The Health Group.

Tien, G., & Wilson, D. (1995). *A review of rehabilitation outcome measures.* Vancouver, BC: Greater Vancouver Regional Hospital District.

Tompson, M. (1989). Muriel Driver Memorial Lecture: Ripples to tidal waves. *Canadian Journal of Occupational Therapy, 56,* 165-170.

Enabling Occupation: An Occupational Therapy Perspective

Topf, Y. (1996, May). Changes to the workload measurement system. *OT Line* (Official Newsletter of the British Columbia Society of Occupational Therapists), 8.

Toulmin, S.E. (1995). Occupation, employment, and human welfare. *Journal of Occupational Science, 2,* 48-57.

Townsend, E.A. (1993a). Muriel Driver Memorial Lecture: Occupational therapy's social vision. *Canadian Journal of Occupational Therapy, 60,* 174-184.

Townsend, E.A. (1993b). The Regina Conference: Debating client-centred practice beyond the horizon. *The National, 10* (4), 11.

Townsend, E.A. (1996a). Enabling empowerment: Using simulations versus real occupations. *Canadian Journal of Occupational Therapy, 63,* 113-128.

Townsend, E.A. (1996b). Institutional ethnography: A method for analyzing practice. *Occupational Therapy Journal of Research, 16,* 179-199

Townsend, E.A. (1998). *Good intentions overruled: A critique of empowerment in the routine organization of mental health services.* Toronto, ON: University of Toronto Press.

Townsend, E.A., & Banks, S. (1992). Exploring client-centred practice. *The National, 9*(4), 8.

Townsend, E.A., Brintnell, S., & Staisey, N. (1990). Developing guidelines for client-centred occupational therapy practice. *Canadian Journal of Occupational Therapy, 57,* 69-76.

Townsend, E.A., Ryan, B., & Law, M. (1990). Using the World Health Organization's international classification of impairments, disabilities and handicaps in occupational therapy. *Canadian Journal of Occupational Therapy, 57,* 16-25.

Trent, M.E. (1919). Ward Aides. *The Vocational Bulletin, June,* 2-4.

Trombly, C.A. (Ed.). (1994). *Occupational therapy for physical dysfunction* (4th ed.). Baltimore: Williams and Wilkins.

Turgeon, J., & Hay, J.A. (1994). Male occupational therapists in Ontario: A survey of work-related issues. *Canadian Journal of Occupational Therapy, 61,* 277-284.

Urbanowski, R., & Vargo, J. (1994). Spirituality, daily practice, and the occupational performance model. *Canadian Journal of Occupational Therapy, 61,* 88-94.

Valentino, L. (1994). *Handle with care: Communicating in the helping professions.* Scarborough, ON: Nelson.

Walters, T., & Ternette, E. (1994). Discover independent living. *Ability Network, February/March,* 33.

Warner, R., & Polak, P. (1995). The economic advancement of the mentally ill in the community: Part 2. Economic choices and disincentives. *Community Mental Health Journal, 31,* 477-492.

Wasserman, R.C., Inui, T.S., Barriatua, R.D., Carter, W.B., & Lippincott, P. (1984). Pediatric clinician support for parents makes a difference: An outcome-based analysis of clinician-parent interaction. *Pediatrics, 74,* 1047-1053.

Wharton, C.S. (1994). Finding time for the "second shift": The impact of flexible work schedules on women's double days. *Gender & Society, 8,* 189-205.

Whitmore, E., & Kerans, P. (1988). Participation, empowerment and welfare. *Canadian Review of Social Policy, 22,* 51-60.

Wieringa, N., & McColl, M.A. (1987). Implications of the Model of Human Occupation for intervention with native Indians. In F.S.Cromwell (Ed.), *Sociocultural implications in treatment planning in occupational therapy,* (pp. 73-91). New York: Haworth Press.

Wilcock, A. (1993). A theory of human need for occupation. *Journal of Occupational Science, 1,* 17-24.

Woodside, H. (1991). The participation of mental health consumers in health care issues. *Canadian Journal of Occupational Therapy, 58,* 3-5.

Woolfolk, A.E., & Nicolich, L.M. (1980). *Educational psychology for teachers.* Englewood Cliffs, NJ: Prentice Hall.

World Health Organization. (1978). *Declaration of Alma-Ata.* Geneva, Switzerland: Author.

World Health Organization. (1980). *International classification of impairments, disabilities, and handicaps.* Geneva, Switzerland: Author.

World Health Organization. (1984). *Health promotion discussion document on the concept and guiding principles.* Geneva, Switzerland: Author.

World Health Organization. (1986a). *Health promotion, concept and principles in action: Policy framework.* Geneva, Switzerland: Author.

World Health Organization. (1986b). *Ottawa charter for health promotion.* Geneva, Switzerland: Author.

World Health Organization. (1989). *Health promotion: A discussion document on the concept and principles.* Copenhagen, Denmark: WHO Regional Office for Europe.

Yerxa, E.J. (1967). Eleanor Clarke Slagle Lecture: Authentic occupational therapy. *American Journal of Occupational Therapy, 21,* 1-9.

Yerxa, E. (1979). *The philosophical base of occupational therapy: 2000 AD.* Rockville, MD: American Occupational Therapy Association.

Yerxa, E.J. (1991). Seeking a relevant, ethical, and realistic way of knowing for occupational therapy. *American Journal of Occupational Therapy, 45,* 199-204.

Yerxa, E.J. (1994). Dreams, dilemmas, and decisions for occupational therapy practice in a new millennium: An American perspective. *American Journal of Occupational Therapy, 48,* 586-589.

Yerxa, E., Clark, F., Frank, G., Jackson, J., Parham, D., Pierce, D., Stein, C., & Zemke, R. (1990). An introduction to occupational science: A foundation for occupational therapy in the 21st century. In J.A. Johnson & E.J. Yerxa (Eds.), *Occupational science: The foundation for new models of practice.* New York: Haworth Press.

Young, I.M. (1990). *Justice and the politics of difference.* Princeton, NJ: Princeton University Press.

Zimmerman, M.E. (1990). *Heidegger's confrontation with modernity.* Indianapolis, IN: University Press.

ADDITIONAL READINGS

Abramson, J.S. (1990). Enhancing patient participation: Clinical strategies in the discharge planning process. *Social Work in Health Care, 14,* 53-71.

Adam, R. (1990). The role of occupational therapists in community mental health. *American Occupational Therapy Association, Special Interest Newsletter, 33,* 1-2.

Alberta Health. (1994). *Functional plan outline for community rehabilitation program.* Edmonton, AB: Author.

American Occupational Therapy Association. (1989). Uniform Terminology for Occupational Therapy (2nd ed.). *American Journal of Occupational Therapy, 43,* 808-814.

American Occupational Therapy Association. (1991). Special issue on clinical reasoning. *American Journal of Occupational Therapy, 45* (11), 969-1053.

American Occupational Therapy Association. (1991). Statement: The occupational therapist as case manager. *American Journal of Occupational Therapy, 45,* 1065-1066.

Anderson, S.R., & Hopkins, P. (1991). *The feminine face of God.* New York: Bantam Books.

Atkinson, P. (1981). *The clinical experience: The construction and reconstruction of medical reality.* Hampshire, UK: Gower Publishing.

Bair, J., & Gray, M. (1992). *The occupational therapy manager* (Rev. ed.). Rockville, MD: American Occupational Therapy Association.

Banus, B.S. (1979). *The developmental therapist.* Thorofare, NJ: Slack.

Batavia, A.I., De Jong, G., & McKnew, L.B. (1991). Toward a national personal assistance program: The independent living model of long term care for persons with disabilities. *Journal of Health, Politics, Policy and Law, 16,* 523-545.

Bateson, M.C. (1994). *Peripheral visions: Learning along the way.* New York: Harper Collins.

Beckman, P.J., & Beckman Boyes, G. (1993). *Deciphering the system: A guide for families of young children with disabilities.* Cambridge, MA: Brookline Books.

Bell, E.B. (1980). Muriel Driver Memorial Lecture: Directions for the decade. *Canadian Journal of Occupational Therapy, 47,* 147-153.

Borell, L., Gustavsson, A., Sandman, P.O., & Kielhofner, G. (1994). Occupational programming in a day hospital for patients with dementia. *Occupational Therapy Journal of Research, 14,* 219-238.

Bowlby, M.C. (1991). Reality orientation thirty years later: Are we still confused? *Canadian Journal of Occupational Therapy, 58,* 114-122.

Brintnell, E.S. (1989). National perspective: Occupational therapy in mental health: A growth industry. *Canadian Journal of Occupational Therapy, 56,* 7-9.

Brookfield, S.D. (1995). *Becoming a critically reflective teacher.* San Fransisco: Jossey-Bass.

Broyles, A. (1988). *Journaling: A spiritual journey.* Nashville, TN: The Upper Room.

Burke, J.P., & Cassidy, J.C. (1991). Disparity between reimbursement-driven practice and humanistic values of occupational therapy. *American Journal of Occupational Therapy, 45,* 173-176.

Burkhardt, M.A. (1993). Characteristics of spirituality in the lives of women in a rural Appalachian community. *Journal of Transcultural Nursing, 4* (2), 12-18.

Burns, T.J., Batavia, A.I., & De Jong, G. (1991). The health insurance coverage of working-age persons with physical disabilities. *Inquiry, 28,* 187-193.

Canadian Association of Occupational Therapists. (1983). *Report on the Canada Health Act.* Toronto, ON: Author.

Chandler, C.K., Holden, J.M., & Kolander, C.A. (1992). Counselling for spiritual wellness and prevention over the lifespan. Special Issue: Wellness through the lifespan. *Journal of Counselling and Development, 71* (2), 140-148.

Checkoway, B., & Norsman, A. (1986). Empowering citizens with disabilities. *Community Development Journal, 21,* 270-277.

Clark, C., Scott, E., & Krupa, T. (1993). Involving clients in programme evaluation and research: A new methodology for occupational therapy. *Canadian Journal of Occupational Therapy, 60,* 192-199.

Clark, P.N. (1979). Human development through occupation: Theoretical frameworks in contemporary occupational therapy practice, part 2. *American Journal of Occupational Therapy, 33,* 577-585.

Cockerill, R., Scott, E., & Wright, M. (1994). Responding to workload measurement needs. *Canadian Journal of Occupational Therapy, 61,* 219-221.

Condeluci, A. (1995). *Interdependence: The route to community* (2nd ed.). Winter Park, FL: GR Press.

Corcoran, M.A. (1992). Gender differences in dementia management plans of spousal caregivers: Implications for occupational therapy. *American Journal of Occupational Therapy, 46,* 1006-1012.

Csikszentmihalyi, M. (1993). Activity and happiness: Toward a science of occupation. *Journal of Occupational Science, 1,* 38-42.

Davies, L., & Shragge, E. (Eds.). (1990). *Bureaucracy and community.* Montreal, QC: Black Rose Books.

Denzin, N.K., & Lincoln, Y.S. (Eds.). (1994). *Handbook of Qualitative Research.* Thousand Oaks, CA: Sage Publications.

Department of National Health and Welfare. (1984). *Prevention now: A concept and a practice.* Ottawa, ON: Author.

Devereaux, E.B. (1991). Community-based practice. *American Journal of Occupational Therapy, 45,* 944-946.

Doble, S. (1988). Intrinsic motivation and clinical practice: The key to understanding the unmotivated client. *Canadian Journal of Occupational Therapy, 55,* 75-80.

Dossa, P.A. (1992). Ethnography as narrative discourse: Community integration of people with developmental disabilities. *Rehabilitation Research, 15,* 1-14.

Dunn, W., Brown, C., & McGuigan, A. (1994). The ecology of human performance: A framework for considering the effect of context. *American Journal of Occupational Therapy, 48,* 595-607.

Dunn, W., & McGourty, L. (1989). Application of uniform terminology to practice. *American Journal of Occupational Therapy, 43,* 817-831.

Dunning, H.D. (1972). Environmental occupational therapy. *American Journal of Occupational Therapy, 26,* 292-298.

Dunst, C., Trivette, C., Davis, M., & Cornwell, J. (1988). Enabling and empowering families of children with health impairments. *Children's Health Care, 17,* 71-81.

Dunst, C.J., & Trivette, C.M. (1989). An enablement and empowerment perspective of case management. *Topics in Early Childhood Special Education, 8,* 87-102.

Evans, A. (1985). Roles and functions of mental health occupational therapy. *American Journal of Occupational Therapy, 39,* 799-802.

Fidler, G.S., & Fidler, J.W. (1978). Doing and becoming: Purposeful action and self-actualization. *American Journal of Occupational Therapy, 32,* 305-310.

Fleming, M.H. (1991). The therapist with the three-track mind. *American Journal of Occupational Therapy, 45,* 1007-1014.

Folstein, M.F., Folstein, S.E., & McHugh, P.R. (1975). Mini-Mental State: A practical method for grading the cognitive state of patients for the clinician. *Journal of Psychiatric Research, 12,* 189-198.

Foucault, M. (1980). *Power/knowledge: Selected interviews and other writings, 1972-1977* (C. Gordon, Ed.) (C. Gordon, L. Marshall, J. Mepham, K. Soper, Trans.). Brighton, UK: Harvester Press.

Gage, M. (1994). The patient-driven interdisciplinary care plan. *Journal of Nursing Administration, 24* (4), 26-35.

Gage, M., & Polatajko, H. (1994). Enhancing occupational performance through an understanding of perceived self-efficacy. *American Journal of Occupational Therapy, 48,* 452-461.

Gill, T. (1991). A vision for occupational therapy: Tradition meets the future. *Canadian Journal of Occupational Therapy, 58,* 33-35.

Gilligan, C. (1982). *In a different voice: Psychological theory and women's development.* Cambridge, MA: Harvard University Press.

Glenister, D. (1994). Patient participation in psychiatric services: A literature review and proposal for a research strategy. *Journal of Advanced Nursing, 19,* 802-811.

Grady, A.P. (1992). Occupation as vision. *American Journal of Occupational Therapy, 46,* 1062-1065.

Gregory, M.D. (1983). Occupational behavior and life satisfaction among retirees. *American Journal of Occupational Therapy, 37,* 548-553.

Grof, S. (1990). *The Holotropic Mind.* San Francisco: Harper.

Gross, G.D. (1985). The spiritual lifeline: An experiential exercise. *Journal of Religion and Aging, 1* (3), 31-37.

Hagedorn, R. (1992). *Occupational therapy: Foundations for practice.* Edinburgh, UK: Churchill Livingstone.

Hamlin, R.B., Loukas, K.M., Froehlich, J., & MacRae, N. (1992). Feminism: An inclusive perspective. *American Journal of Occupational Therapy, 46,* 967-970.

Heater, S.L. (1992). Specialization or uniformity within the profession. *American Journal of Occupational Therapy, 46,* 172-173.

Hoff, B. (1992). *The Te of Piglet.* New York: Penguin Books.

Irvine, S.R. (1980). Occupational therapy and the need to influence delivery of service. *Canadian Journal of Occupational Therapy, 47,* 59.

Kieffer, C. (1984). Citizen empowerment: A developmental perspective. *Prevention in Human Services, 3,* 9-36.

Kielhofner, G. (1993). Functional assessment: Toward a dialectical view of person-environment relations. *American Journal of Occupational Therapy, 47,* 248-251.

Kilian, A. (1988). Conscientization: An empowering, nonformal education approach for community health workers. *Community Development Journal, 23,* 117-123.

Kinebanian, A., & Stomph, M. (1992). Cross-cultural occupational therapy: A critical reflection. *American Journal of Occupational Therapy, 46,* 751-757.

Kirsh, S. (1983). *Unemployment: Its impact on body and soul.* Ottawa, ON: Canadian Mental Health Association.

Kolb, D.A. (1984). *Experiential learning. Experience as the source of learning and development.* Thorofare, NJ: Prentice-Hall.

Kovacs, J. (1989). Concepts of health and disease. *The Journal of Medicine and Philosophy, 14,* 261-267.

Krefting, L. (1992). Strategies for the development of occupational therapy in the Third World. *American Journal of Occupational Therapy, 46,* 758-761.

Krefting, L., & Krefting, D. (1991). Cultural influences on performance. In C. Christiansen & C. Baum (Eds.), *Occupational therapy: Overcoming human performance deficits.* Thorofare, NJ: Slack.

Krupa, T., Hayashi, C., Murphy, M., & Thornton J. (1985). Occupational therapy issues in the treatment of the long-term mentally ill. *Canadian Journal of Occupational Therapy, 52,* 107-111.

Labonte, R. (1992). Health promotion: Practice problematics and the need for theory. *Institute of Health Promotion Research Bulletin, Spring,* 9-10.

Lalonde, M. (1974). *A new perspective on the health of Canadians.* Ottawa, ON: Government of Canada.

Law, M., Polatajko, H., Pollock, N., Carswell, A., Baptiste, S., & McColl, M. (1994). The Canadian Occupational Performance Measure: Results of pilot testing. *Canadian Journal of Occupational Therapy, 61,* 191-197.

Leighton, A.H. (1982). *Caring for mentally ill people: Psychological and social barriers in historical context.* Cambridge, UK: Cambridge University Press.

Low, J.F. (1992). The reconstruction aides. *American Journal of Occupational Therapy, 46,* 38-44.

Lukes, S. (1986). *Power.* New York: New York University Press.

Lysaght, R., Townsend, E., & Orser, C.L. (1994). The use of work schedule modification to enhance employment outcomes for persons with severe disability. *Journal of Rehabilitation, 60* (4), 26-29.

Madill, H.M., Brintnell, E.S.G., Stewin, L.L., Fitzsimmons, G.W., & Macnab, D. (1985). Career patterns in two groups of Alberta therapists. *Canadian Journal of Occupational Therapy, 52,* 195-201.

Madill, H.M., Cardwell, M.T., Robinson, I.M., & Brintnell, E.S.G. (1986). Old themes, new directions: Occupational therapy in the 21st century. *Canadian Journal of Occupational Therapy, 53,* (Commemorative Issue), 38-44.

Madill, H., Tirrul-Jones, A., & Magill-Evans, J. (1990). The application of the client-centred approach to school-based occupational therapy practice. *Canadian Journal of Occupational Therapy, 57,* 102-108.

Mahoney, F.I., & Barthel, D.W. (1965). Functional evaluation: The Barthel Index. *Maryland State Medical Journal, 14,* 61-65.

Marrone, J., & Gold, M. (1994). Supported employment for people with mental illness: Myths and facts. *Journal of Rehabilitation, 60* (4), 38-46.

Martin, J.R. (1994). *Changing the educational landscape: Philosophy, women and curriculum.* New York: Routledge.

Matheis-Kraft, C., George, S., Olinger, M.J., & York, L. (1990). Patient-driven healthcare works. *Nursing Management, 21,* 124-128.

Mathewson, M. (1975). Female and married. Damaging to the therapy profession? *American Journal of Occupational Therapy, 29,* 601- 605.

Mattingly, C. (1991). What is clinical reasoning? *American Journal of Occupational Therapy, 45,* 979-986.

Mattingly, C.F. (1991). The narrative nature of clinical reasoning. *American Journal of Occupational Therapy, 45,* 998-1005.

Maurer, K.E., & Teske, Y.R. (1989). Barriers to occupational therapy practice in wellness. *Occupational Therapy in Health Care, 5* (4), 57-67.

Maxwell, J.D., & Maxwell, M.P. (1983). Inner fraternity and outer sonority: Social structure and the professionalization of occupational therapy. In A. Wipper (Ed.), *The sociology of work: Papers in honour of Osward Hall* (Carleton Library series #129). Ottawa, ON: Carleton University Press.

McNeil, M. (1987). *Gender and expertise.* London: Free Association Books.

Meyers, C. (1992). Among children and their families: Consideration of cultural influences in assessment. *American Journal of Occupational Therapy, 46,* 737-744.

Mezirow, J. (1978). Perspective transformation. *Adult Education, 27,* 100-110.

Mezirow, J. (1991). *Transformative dimensions of adult learning.* San Francisco: Jossey-Bass.

Miyake, S., & Trostler, R.J. (1987). Introducing the concept of corporate culture to the hospital setting. *American Journal of Occupational Therapy, 41,* 310-314.

Moorehead, L. (1969). The occupational history. *American Journal of Occupational Therapy, 23,* 329-334.

Murgatroyd, L. (1982). Gender and occupational stratification. *Sociological Review, 30,* 574-602.

Murray, H. (1938). *Explorations in personality.* New York: Oxford.

Neistadt, M.E. (1995). Methods of assessing clients' priorities: A survey of adult physical dysfunction settings. *American Journal of Occupational Therapy, 49,* 428-436.

O'Reilly, J.A. (1954). Occupational therapy in the management of traumatic disabilities. *Canadian Journal of Occupational Therapy, 21,* 75-80.

O'Shea, B.J. (1979). Me? Political? *Canadian Journal of Occupational Therapy, 46,* 143-145.

Park, S., Fisher, A.G., & Velozo, C.A. (1993). Using the assessment of motor and process skills to compare performance between home and clinical settings. *American Journal of Occupational Therapy, 49,* 428-436.

Pederson, A.P., Edwards, R.K., Kelner, M., Marshall, V.W., & Allison, K.R. (1988). *Coordinating healthy public policy: An analytic literature review and bibliography.* Ottawa, ON: Health and Welfare Canada.

Pedretti, L.W., & Zoltan, B. (1990). *Occupational therapy practice skills for physical dysfunction* (3rd ed.). St. Louis, MO: C.V. Mosby.

Pollock, N. (1993). Client-centred assessment. *American Journal of Occupational Therapy, 47,* 298-301.

Quinn, B. (1988). The importance of an expanded practice base. *Canadian Journal of Occupational Therapy, 55,* 239-241.

Reaburn, J.M. (1985). Mental health promotion in the community: How to do it. *Community Mental Health, 2,* 22-33.

Rogers, J.C., & Salta, J.E. (1994). Documenting functional outcomes. *American Journal of Occupational Therapy, 48,* 939-945.

Romeder, J.M., Balthazar, H., Farquharson, A., & Lavoie, F. (1990). Self-helpers and professionals. In J.M. Romeder (Ed.), *The self-help way: Mutual aid and health.* (pp. 113-123). Ottawa, ON: Canadian Council on Social Development.

Ryan, B., O'Shea, B., & Townsend, E. (1992). Large field studies of hospital based services: Lessons from occupational therapy. *Canadian Journal of Occupational Therapy, 59,* 214-218.

Sanford, J., Law, M., Swanson, L., & Guyatt, G. (1994). *Assessing clinically important change as an outcome of rehabilitation in older adults.* San Francisco: American Society on Aging Conference.

Serrett, K.D. (1985). Another look at occupational therapy's history: Paradigm or a pair of hands? *Occupational Therapy in Mental Health, 5,* 1-32.

Shackleton, T., & Gage, M. (1995). Strategic planning: Positioning occupational therapy to be proactive in the new health care paradigm. *Canadian Journal of Occupational Therapy, 62,* 188-196.

Shaw, S. (1989). Improving the sensitivity of the Barthel Index for stroke rehabilitation. *Journal of Clinical Epidemiology, 42,* 703-709.

Shogan, D.A. (1993). *A reader in feminist ethics.* Toronto, ON: Canadian Scholars' Press.

Soeken, K.L. (1989). Perspectives on research in the spiritual dimension of nursing care. In V.B. Carson (Ed.), *Spiritual dimensions of nursing practice.* Philadelphia: W.P. Saunders.

Sokoly, M.M., & Dokecki, P.R. (1992). Ethical perspectives on family-centred early intervention. *Infants and Young Children, 4,* 23-32.

Stevenson, G.H. (1932). The healing influence of work and play in a mental hospital. *Archives of Occupational Therapy, 11,* 85-89.

Tate, S.W. (1974). The scope for occupational therapists in the community in the future. *Canadian Journal of Occupational Therapy, 41,* 7-9.

Tobias, M. (1990). Validators: A key role in the empowering of the chronically mentally ill. *Social Work, 35,* 357-359.

Townsend, E.A. (1987). Strategies for community occupational therapy programme development. *Canadian Journal of Occupational Therapy, 54,* 65-70.

Townsend, E.A. (1988). Developing community occupational therapy services in Canada. *Canadian Journal of Occupational Therapy, 55,* 69-74.

Townsend, E.A. (1992). Institutional ethnography: Explicating the social organization of professional health practices intending client empowerment. *Canadian Journal of Public Health, 83,* S1, S58-S61.

Townsend, E.A., Anderson, S., & Jenner, S. (1988). Developing rural health services: An occupational therapy case study. *Canadian Journal of Public Health, 79,* 92-96.

Townsend, E.A., & Ryan, B. (1991). Assessing independence in community living. *Canadian Journal of Public Health, 82,* 52-57.

Trevelyan, G. (1984). *Vision of the aquarian age: The emerging spiritual world view.* Walpole, NH: Stillpoint Publishing.

Trider, M.F. (1972). The future of occupational therapy. *Canadian Journal of Occupational Therapy, 39,* 3-8.

Turner, A. (Ed.) (1987). *The practice of occupational therapy: An introduction to the treatment of physical dysfunction* (2nd ed.). New York: Churchill Livingstone.

United Nations. (1984). *World programme of action concerning disabled persons.* Geneva, Switzerland: Author.

Van Deusen, J. (1990). Can we delimit the discipline of occupational therapy? *American Journal of Occupational Therapy, 44,* 175-176.

Van Deusen, J. (1993). An analytical approach to teaching theory at the post-professional level. *American Journal of Occupational Therapy, 47,* 949-952.

Wallerstein, N., & Bernstein, E. (1988). Empowerment education: Freire's ideas adapted to health education. *Health Education Quarterly, 15,* 379-394.

Watson, D. (1992). Documentation of paediatric assessments using the occupational therapy guidelines for client-centred practice. *Canadian Journal of Occupational Therapy, 59,* 87-94.

Watson, P.G. (1990). The Americans with Disabilities Act: More rights for people with disabilities. *Rehabilitation Nursing, 15,* 325- 328.

Weeder, T.C. (1986). Comparison to temporal patterns and meaningfulness of daily activities of schizophrenic and normal adults. *Occupational Therapy in Mental Health, 6* (4), 27-48.

Weisman, G.D. (1981). Modelling environment-behaviour systems. *Journal of Man-Environment Relations, 1,* 32-41.

Welton, M.R. (1995). *In defense of the lifeworld: Critical perspectives on adult learning.* New York: Suny Press.

West, W.L. (1984). A reaffirmed philosophy and practice of occupational therapy for the 1980's. *American Journal of Occupational Therapy, 38,* 15-23.

Whitehead, M. (1992). The concepts and principles of equity and health. *International Journal of Health Services, 22,* 429-445.

Wilkerson, D.L., Batavia, A.I., & De Jong, G. (1992). Use of functional status measures for payment of medical rehabilitation services. *Archives of Physical Medicine and Rehabilitation, 73,* 111-120.

Williams, D. (1989). Political theory and individualistic health promotion. *Advances in Nursing Science, 12,* 14-25.

Woodward, K.L. (1994, July 18). More than ourselves. *Newsweek.*

World Health Organization. (1988). *WHO Psychiatric Disability Assessment Schedule (WHO/DAS).* Geneva, Switzerland: Author.

Wu, C., Trombly, C.A., & Lin, K. (1994). The relationship between occupational form and occupational performance: A kinematic perspective. *American Journal of Occupational Therapy, 48,* 679-687.

Yerxa, E.J. (1991). Occupational therapy: An endangered species or an academic discipline in the 21st century? *American Journal of Occupational Therapy, 45,* 680-685.

Yerxa, E.J. (1992). Some implications of occupational therapy's history for its epistemology, values, and relation to medicine. *American Journal of Occupational Therapy, 46,* 79-83.

Yerxa, E.J. (1993). Occupational science: A source of power for participants in occupational therapy. *Journal of Occupational Science, 1,* 3-10.